THE SEARCH FOR A NONVIOLENT FUTURE

For Joy,
With best wishes,
Michael Nagler

THE
SEARCH
FOR A
NONVIOLENT
FUTURE

A Promise of Peace for Ourselves,
Our Families, and Our World

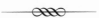

MICHAEL N. NAGLER

INNER OCEAN PUBLISHING
MAUI, HAWAI'I · SAN FRANCISCO, CALIFORNIA

Inner Ocean Publishing, Inc.
P.O. Box 1239
Makawao, Maui, HI 96768-1239

Book design by Lisa Schulz Elliot / Elysium

Publisher Cataloging-in-Publication Data

Nagler, Michael N.

The search for a nonviolent future: a promise of peace for
ourselves, our families, and our world / Michael N. Nagler. —
2nd ed. — Makawao, HI: Inner Ocean, 2004.

p. ; cm.

Originally published: Berkeley, Calif.: Berkeley Hills Books,
c2001, under title: Is there no other way?: the search for a
nonviolent future.

Includes bibliographical references and index.
ISBN: 1-930722-40-0
1. Nonviolence. 2. Violence. 3. Pacifism. 4. Passive resistance.
I. Nagler, Michael N. Is there no other way? II. Title.
HM1281 .N342 2004
303.6/1—dc22 0410

DISTRIBUTED BY PUBLISHERS GROUP WEST

*For information on promotions, bulk purchases, premiums, or educational use,
please contact Special Markets: 866.731.2216 or sales@innerocean.com.*

CONTENTS

To my beloved teacher, Sri Eknath Easwaran
January 2, 1911–October 26, 1999

FOREWORD

IT MAY NOT be the perfect analogy but I can't help feeling that the state of the world today resembles the state of an individual who is terminally ill. Well, you might say, what is new about this? Namely, that the world is terminally ill with violence? We know this too, perhaps. But my imagination has gone wild with the similarities.

The individual is an inveterate smoker. He or she is well aware of the hazards of smoking but he continues nevertheless in the brazen belief that nothing serious is going to happen. He is more or less forced to believe this, because in fact the habit is more than he can control. (I had one friend who became so panicked when a doctor told her she had only a few years to live if she didn't quit that she ran out to have a smoke!) However, when the individual does get lung cancer he rushes to the doctor and pleads for a cure. The doctor suggests a complete recovery might be possible only if drastic changes in lifestyle are sincerely made. Beginning with no more smoking. For the moment the patient swears he will do everything the doctor wants. Just as we recoil right after a war or a particularly heinous act of violence—for a while.

The patient goes home with a new lease on life. Once cured, though, the old habit reasserts itself and he finds himself smoking once more. As we all know, this tragic scenario can end in death.

Do you see the point I am trying to make? The world is terminally ill with violence, and when the disease assumes a virulent form we plead for a remedy; but when we are cured we go back to our old destructive ways. As in the individual, so in societies; cures can only be as effective as one's determination to change bad habits into good.

For centuries the world has been saturated with a Culture of Violence to such an extent that it has seeped down to the very core of our being. Or so it seems. But violence is no more natural than letting your innards be destroyed by constant smoking. If we persist in living, thinking, and being in the Culture of Violence then we will not find the way out of that culture; it is almost as impossible to find a patchwork solution as it would be to stay dry in a swimming pool.

To understand the insidious nature of the Culture of Violence it is important to realize that violence has many facets. There is not only the physical violence of wars, fights, riots, beatings, rapes, murders, etc., but the more destructive "passive" violence, where we hurt people without using physical force. This is more destructive because it is as unseen as cancer. Passive violence manifests in a thousand different ways, like wasting resources, overconsumption, hate, prejudice, name calling, and hundreds of seemingly innocent acts that hurt people even unconsciously. Passive violence fuels the fire of physical violence, which means if we want to put out the fire of physical violence we have to cut off the fuel supply. How? "We must become the change we wish to see in the world," grandfather Gandhi said.

Think again of my analogy, for a moment. You can make someone stop smoking temporarily by scaring him. You can make him stop a bit longer by using a nicotine patch, but that still does not address whatever drove him to smoke in the first place. Finally, you can give him something to live for—some higher purpose—so that he finds the will for a permanent cure.

This book, written by my good friend Dr. Michael Nagler, does all three. It makes us feel how repugnant and how unnecessary violence is in all its forms. It tells us many stories that explain how nonviolence works and reports on many organizations and projects that are coming up with creative, constructive alternatives to violence in many forms—including forms we may have thought were inevitable, or "justified." And it inspires us to find our way to the kind of rewarding life that will permanently protect us and our families and our world from this cancer of violence. I hope this inspiring book will be read and used around the world.

ARUN GANDHI
Founder and President, M. K. Gandhi Institute for Nonviolence

PREFACE

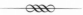

SOME THREE MONTHS before the horrific events of September 11, I attended a panel discussion at the "J School" (School of Journalism) on my campus that the dean, Orville Schell, had arranged in order to open a debate on the new president's resurrection of "star wars," space-based missile defense. The first speaker was a representative from the Lawrence Livermore labs, one of the nation's two nuclear weapons facilities, where, of course, there is stake in promoting such projects. But there is also a strong undercurrent of alarm about them among nuclear scientists, some of whom I had had the pleasure of speaking with during the Cold War when a group of us, professors like myself, along with theologians and weapons scientists, participated in a floating roundtable that went on, at one retreat or another, for several years. It was one of the most intellectually satisfying give-and-takes of my career. But this night I was in for a shock.

The speaker, a well-informed scientist with a flair for public speaking, took complete command of his audience. The first question up for discussion was, Would the technology work? "Of course it would," he sneered. "Technology always works." (Hmm. Has anyone here ever used a computer? I mused.) Then it got worse. "We [the United States] have *so* much money," he went on, "we can do pretty much what we want and nobody can stop us." I will spare you the rest. It was, all in all, the most abrasive and vulgar display of arrogance I could remember seeing before a campus audience. He acted, and even looked, like Mussolini, whom I had seen in newsreels that I had had the misfortune to view over and over again in high school, and now he reached the climax of his talk: "Welcome," he crowed, "to the next American century, and if you don't like it, maybe you should wait another hundred years for the next one."

By this time I was flushed with fear. From somewhere deep in my mind a thought spoke itself in a voice that was almost not my own: *Oh God, we're going to be hit.* Before my inner eye flitted the image of a tackled giant, crumbling to earth.

Three months later I sat gripping the seat in front of me on the commute van as one of my fellow riders, who had a portable radio, stammered out that the towers had fallen. As we left the van and stood in shock on the sidewalk in front of my office, Noel's comment was, "The world will never be the same." He was so right.

But in another way he was exactly wrong. The world is still the same, and it will always be the same. This is what that highly placed scientist did not understand. Violence always begets violence—and the violence that has been begotten by violence begets more violence. Those who enter that cycle do not easily escape. There has to be another way.

I have been, therefore, very gratified by the enthusiastic reception of this book and the chance to write a post-9/11 preface to this new edition. But there was not much that I needed to revise. The search for a nonviolent future is certainly no less urgent now that the violence of the present has broken in on us so cruelly. "In a dark time," wrote the poet Theodore Roethke, "the eye begins to see." Many people were already feeling the gnawing emptiness of modern civilization; now even those who were complacent about that have begun to realize that finding a solution for that emptiness—for the bankruptcy that is materialism—is no longer a luxury. We are being dragged into a maelstrom of violence, and when we realize what's happening to us, one after the other, our will breaks through our lethargy to sound its anguished hope for some way out. Despair is never a successful strategy, but desperation can often force us to find one. That is happening all over America as I write these words on the anniversary of the disaster.

One example appeared in the *New Yorker's* commemorative issue this very week. "This is a week of emotion, but not only emotion," wrote David Remnick and Hendrik Hertzberg. "September 11th has also, from the start, compelled sustained analysis of a series of questions that remain very far from resolved."[1] I entirely agree. But has the analysis happened? Have we asked ourselves, why was our nation so cruelly attacked—and what must we do now to secure ourselves from such violence?

One of the reasons I felt so terrified listening to the lab scientist was that I know that people in his position are close to White House policy and reflect the mood of officialdom; and, as most of us know by now, the word *arrogant* is heard very often when commentators outside the United States—and sometimes within it—seek to characterize the second Bush administration. And anyone who knows any history, or has pondered the dynamics of human relationships in his or her own experience, knows what this clever scientist did not: that no amount of money, no fierce arsenal of weapons, has ever brought security to a person or a nation that waxes arrogant and disregards the rights of others to secure its own happiness. Violence in any form—and arrogance is certainly one of them—begets violence. Choose violence and bid security goodbye.

The events of the past year have made many of us familiar with a bit of technical jargon from the CIA: "blowback." Panama's Manuel Noriega, the Taliban, Osama bin Laden himself, and, yes, Saddam Hussein were all heavily supported and funded by the CIA. The CIA and/or other "security" agencies saw fit to promote these violent men to do things they thought would benefit the United States, of which the vast majority of us were hardly aware—and then these people turned their violence on us. *This* kind of blowback, though, is only one part of a much larger picture, of which the dangerous arrogance of my scientist colleague was another. Blowback is a place where the inexorable logic of violence plays itself out in a way that's open for all to see—for those who will see. The fact is, *all* violence blows back, not just the kind to which governments give covert support. Perhaps the most poignant examples you will find in this book pertain to the first open conflict with Iraq, in 1991.

What is the most common response of people who saw the disaster at the World Trade Center, either live or in its many television replays? If you recall, it was, "I thought I was watching a movie."

Immediately, they connected what they saw in real life with a very common motif of the fiction they have chosen to surround themselves with: disaster, blood, bodies, explosions—what fun. Young Dylan Klebold and Eric Harris left behind a video as they went off to perpetrate the massacre at their high school in Columbine. In that video they told of their dream to hijack a commercial plane and plow it into New York, "killing as many people as we can." What the terrorists did on September 11 was atrocious. But if we are honest, we cannot say it was *unthinkable*. We can't say that because we have created a culture in which we, especially our young people, think of violence all the time—a culture in which, as a colleague of mine said the other day, "we are promoting violence in every way possible."

In some cases we can see a direct connection between violence and the loss of security—as with our government's blind support of Israel today. In others, like the ones just mentioned, it is only a suggestive echo speaking to our intuition. But we must come to realize that every form of violence erodes our security and our happiness. If we want to be free from terrorism, then we have to ask ourselves, systematically, where are we choosing violence and what could we choose instead? That is the agenda of this book.

> I am a veteran, and I oppose violence in all forms. I'm
> not proud to have served [in the Gulf War]. But I've
> learned from my mistakes. Others have too. My hope
> is that we come together on September 11 to remem-
> ber our losses, to *reject a culture of violence and militarism,*
> and to create a lasting movement for justice and peace
> for all.[2] (my emphasis)

As one of her first acts of conversion, Krystal Kyer, who wrote the above recently, "turned off [her] television for the last time."

Unrelated and unnecessary? No, central and indispensable, because human life takes place in a dynamic of kindness and cruelty, empathy and alienation, respect and dehumanization (or, as a scholar

I'll be quoting later puts it, democracy and violence). These two forces, call them what we will, determine the outcome of all human interaction. Have we not often noticed how quarrels, say, ones that we ourselves are having with someone close to us, though they seem to be about substantive issues of one kind or another, are really about bruised feelings and rankled self-esteem? It is when we ignore this simple reality that we find ourselves getting into difficulties of every kind—unable to see why, for example, the more we spend on armaments, the more countries we threaten with them, the more of our own democratic liberties we sacrifice, the less secure we feel. And are. Security is not about bomb-sniffing dogs and spy satellites; it's about learning to live so that others needn't move out of the way to make room for our happiness. More positively, it's about building what Martin Luther King called the "loving community."

9/11 was a wake-up call. This is what *New Yorker* writers Remnick and Hertzberg reminded us. But the waking up is proving to be a lot harder than turning out of bed on a cold morning; a lot harder than going to war. I recall an advertising poster in San Francisco some years ago that had an appealing picture of a candy bar and the message "Go ahead, hit the snooze button one more time." The life of self-indulgence is indeed a kind of sleep. Endless physical gratification is no more fulfilling than a dream, and its pursuit has tied us to an economic system that Gandhi warned nearly a century ago is based on the "multiplication of wants," and was for that reason doomed. Waking up is realizing that we are not pleasure machines, that there is a spiritual meaning in life that alone can make us happy.

The war on Afghanistan, which killed, as far as we can tell, more innocent bystanders than the attacks of 9/11, has had the result, we now know, of scattering the remaining al-Qaida militia all over the world, making them fiendishly difficult to locate—and adding fuel to the fires of hatred that legitimize them. According to today's *New York Times,* "Anger at the United States, embedded in the belief that the Bush administration lends unstinting support to Israel at the expense of the Palestinians, is at an unparalleled high across the Arab world, according to analysts and diplomats in the region. . . . More than in previous bouts of anti-Americanism in the region, the anger permeates all strata of society, especially among the educated, and is tinged, people acknowledge, with disillusionment at their own long-entrenched American-backed leadership."[3] We are dreaming if we think this kind of activity will make us secure. The nightmare of war is no answer to the wake-up call of reason.

In the event, the call functioned as a sharp fork in the road of America's destiny. A slender majority of Americans, and almost all her present leaders, have taken the path of vengeance—of answering cruelty in its own coin. But others, in increasing numbers after the initial shock, have been going quite another way. They have reached out to Arab Americans, they have thought about their own fuel consumption; one colleague of mine said, "Here's my contribution to the war on terrorism: I bought a Prius." And they have redoubled their efforts to create forms of peace, and peace culture, like those discussed in the following pages.

According to studies by Paul Ray and Sherry Anderson, tens of millions of Americans now share the fundamental insight I've just mentioned, that the determining factor in human life is not the econ-omy but the dynamic of kindness or its opposite.[4] More and more of these people have set to work living accordingly. The example of an alternate economy, which I touch on at the very end of this book, is merely a glimpse of the social experiments taking place in that field and in others, as we can now see quarterly in the pages of *Yes!* maga-zine (see Resources and Opportunities).

Yet at the same time, the nation as a whole is moving in the oppo-site direction. We are seeing militarization on an undreamt-of scale in this country; an abridgment of civil liberties that propels us back to the era of McCarthy, if not beyond; a tampering with truth and human rights worthy of a Milosevic (the USA Patriot Act, hurriedly adopted by Congress and signed into law six weeks after the terrorist attacks, tipped laws in the government's favor in 350 subject areas involving forty federal agencies). We may be headed for a showdown.

There are several ways that this tension could end in disaster—and one in which it would not. The forces of reaction, feeding on a hysteria for "security," could overwhelm these hopeful social experiments, leaving the United States an embattled fortress under siege in a hostile world. Or the tension between these communities could tear the country apart more violently than did the Vietnam War.

Or the discovery of nonviolence could save us.

The contribution of this book is to make more visible, more comprehensible, and more accessible the vast unexplored possibilities of that force. We need to understand it, all of us, more than ever. Those of us who maintain that the country is not being well served by violence are still being vilified—absurdly—as unpatriotic; those who point to the tremendous success of nonviolence in the fields of social justice and liberation and try to show how these lessons could be applied to terrorism are still, tragically, misunderstood as naive utopians. I myself have been told by people who apparently don't subscribe to the motto "Our grief is not a cry for vengeance" that I would feel differently if I had lost a family member in the attacks. They are wrong.

I dedicate this preface to my cousin Chick, who suffered a heart attack and died after his wife, Sylvita, staggered home late that night from her job on the first floor of the World Trade Center.

September 11, 2002

ACKNOWLEDGMENTS

IT TOOK MANY years and much help for me to write this book, and I apologize in advance if I fail to acknowledge everyone who lent a hand.

First, thanks go to Sri Eknath Easwaran, who took me under his wing when I was long on passion but dangerously short on wisdom, and who is still and always shall be the guide of my life. I thank him and his wife, Christine, in the same breath, always.

Of the many others I am pleased to recall, first mention goes to my research assistant, Julie Anderson, who, armed only with modest research grants from the university, helped me hunt down many references (often on the obscurest leads) and corrected the irrational punctuation that accompanies the creative process, in my case. Julie was a sensitive reader before she turned tireless researcher. Barbara Gee, who had just the skills I lacked and the free time to put them at my disposal, did everything from the sublime to the mechanical in the last hectic weeks. Veronica Bollow (not even armed with research grants) saved Julie and me from the effects of our computer illiteracy, and finally Christine Nielson and Suraya Breen did the last needfuls.

Glenn Paige was among the first of my peace research colleagues to give this manuscript, or one of its ancestors, a critical read. I wonder how much Glenn will recognize in this published product, or whether he will realize how helpful his comments, negative and positive, have been. The most recent in the same collegial category is Elise Boulding, who has helped everyone in the peace world at one time or other. Where would we be—where would the world be today—without her? Colman McCarthy, the nation's only nonviolence journalist, was always there to mentor me in one pithy phrase that would save me a lot of floundering. ("Don't try to say everything at once, Mike.")

Years ago Candice Fuhrman read this manuscript when it was in dreadful shape, and had the courage to say so. In fact I have been blessed with outspoken readers and editors: Mary Lamprech of University of California Press liberated me from the notion that I was writing another academic book (she called this project "Walden Three"), the sharp-eyed Bernadette Smyth went out of her way to be encouraging even as she was slashing away at typos and idiosyncrasies, and so did Gail Larrick. My editor-publisher John Strohmeier has been intellectual foil, friend, capable businessman, and visionary rolled into one—a joy to work with. This is publishing as it was meant to be: human-scale, personal, responsive, and driven by meaningful values.

To my friends at my nonprofit, METTA, especially Jim Phoenix, Megan McKellogg, and Barb again, and in the nonviolent peace force project—David Hartsough, Mel Duncan, and the whole gang (you know who you are)—through you I have been "plugged in" to the most important social work on the planet and supplied with information and hope for decades.

I thank my two grown children, Jess and Josh, and especially Jess and Rick's nearly grown children, who at times had less of a grand-father than they might have had for the sake of this effort, and of course my spiritual brothers and sisters at our community, the head-quarters of the Blue Mountain Center of Meditation, who have shared their life and struggles with me for over thirty years. Carol, for one, not only challenged me when I was getting intellectually complacent but had to chase me down when I was deep into some subtleties of nonviolence when I should have been deep into some hot, soapy dish-water. I think too, always, of the children of our community, who remind me of all the world's children, who are the reason for every-thing. Without my community, children and adults alike, not only this book but everything I have become would not have been possible.

Lastly, I think back on the innumerable people with whom I have thrashed out these ideas down the years, and first and foremost the students (more than a thousand now) who have taken PACS 164 with me at Berkeley, some of whom are today risking their lives to bring about the kind of world aimed at in this book. I honor them more than I can say.

And special thanks to Lauren and Jason, who put me up in a hotel in Los Angeles so I could finish the references to this book one marathon day before their lovely wedding.

I have likewise had much help in preparing this new edition, and take pleasure in thanking my resourceful agent, Karen Sheehan; the wonderful editor she put me in touch with, Karen Bouris; all the people at Inner Ocean Publishing; and students and friends who pitched in once again: Pieternel de Bie, Sarah Harling, Matthew Taylor, Danielle Brand-LeMonde, and Nalini Ramji. If anyone who should be on this new list has slipped my mind, my sincere thanks nonetheless.

My heartfelt thanks to all who have, in whatever way, poured themselves into the greatest project now confronting humanity, the project of putting an end to violence, to which I hope this book may make a small contribution.

INTRODUCTION

ON AN UNLIKELY, treeless savanna miles from anywhere, Paolo Lugari Castrillón planted his dream. It was 1971. Off in the eastern *llanos* of Colombia, sixteen hours from the nearest city, he and an idealistic band of followers founded what is now Gaviotas, a thriving, self-sufficient, sustainable, and model community in many ways— socially, ecologically, economically—which caused Colombian novelist Gabriel García Márquez to dub Lugari "the inventor of the world."[1] At Gaviotas (named for the nearby river gulls, *las gaviotas*) kids shriek as they pump each other up and down on seesaws, but at Gaviotas there's an extra edge to their satisfaction, for they are also pumping the water for the irrigation system. The music hall's curved stainless-steel roof is also an intensely efficient water heater; in fact, solar collectors of a special Gaviotan design are providing heat for tens of thousands of buildings in Bogotá and throughout Colombia.

By dint of much research, diligence, and insight the Gaviotans discovered that a particular type of Caribbean pine that was doing well in nearby Ecuador would take to the barren *llanos.* Patiently, they planted seedlings, they tended them, and today millions of these pines adorn—and transform—the local ecosystem. For from the soil underneath them, much to everyone's surprise, a richly diverse primordial rain forest has sprung up, evidently from seeds that were hiding in the shallow soil, waiting who knows how many eons for the right conditions to bloom again.[2]

This book will be about a renewal that, if we can make it happen, will resemble the miracle of the pines at Gaviotas, for it also will evoke forces that lie hidden in the thin soil of our impersonal, "bottom-line," violence-prone civilization, where human meaning has faded and human bonds are often scattered like the dust. As with Gaviotas's unexpected forest, the seeds of this renewal do not have to be created; they are waiting there in the soil of our own existence—waiting for us to create the conditions to awaken them. Like those of the new-sprung rain forest of Gaviotas, they are primordial, I will argue: far more native to the human condition than the world of abrasive relationships we have surrounded ourselves with in this industrial era. And, again like the Gaviotans' surprise rain forest, we don't have to know ahead of time what the renewal we hope to achieve will look like. At least not exactly. What we have to be very clear about is how to create the right conditions; then we can let nature—in this case human nature—do the rest.

My own renewal began in the fall of 1966, where a lot of renewing was being attempted in those days: Berkeley, California. That was when I met my spiritual teacher, Sri Eknath Easwaran, who was right on my campus, teaching the form of meditation he himself had developed, on Tuesdays at noon in what was then known as the Meditation Room of the Student Union Building. A friend of mine, Javier Castillo, knowing that I was looking for *something,* some kind of answer to the emptiness left in many of us by the free speech movement, which had started with such hope and ended in such dissatisfaction, suggested we go and "check him out." I needed some renewing. There was an inner emptiness that Javier may have sensed, perhaps more than I did. I had just been "regularized," i.e., advanced from acting assistant professor to the real thing on the completion of my dissertation, invited from the vestibule into the halls of academe; so there I was, teaching Classics and Comparative Literature at Berkeley—the career to die for. I had a family with two angelic kids in a cozy little house across the street from a regional park redolent with eucalyptus trees and laced by twisty paths, one of which took you down to a perfect lake for a before-dinner dip after a hot California day on campus. I thought I was on top of the world, but where was that world taking me?

One day, a few years earlier, I had stood in the living room of my Berkeley apartment looking at my newborn daughter when the news came over the radio that strontium 90 released into the atmosphere by atomic bomb testing was poisoning the spring rain, thus lacing the milk supply with a heretofore unknown, altogether invisible, and cunning poison. At that moment I knew from the depths of my being we were going to have to "stop the machine" (as Mario Savio would later say), but how? Many people my age who felt the same disillusionment were "dropping out" and trekking to India (or at least New Mexico) to find some way out of the oppressive, boring materialism of a culture that was weirdly inimical to life. For some lucky reason all I had to do was walk from my office to the Student Union Building.

Sometime I will write the story of my meeting with Sri Easwaran and all it has meant to me and so many others; for now, what matters is how it turned one particular compartment of my life from anguished frustration to creative action. I had hated violence since long before this fateful meeting, almost as far back as I can recall anything about myself. By the time I came to Berkeley, already a "peacenik" with the rhetoric of the civil rights movement echoing in my ears, I had of course heard of Gandhi—but like most Americans, I knew little enough about him. A few days after my eleventh birthday I saw a picture of the Mahatma's cremation and the wild grief of the mourners on the cover of *Life* magazine, which left a distinct impression of otherness, even weirdness, about the man and his culture, and the little I later heard—about his fasts, his asceticism—did little to dispel this first impression. I admired his achievements, but they seemed almost more than human. I felt that he was probably a great man, and I was not, and that was that.

But when Sri Easwaran began to weave his own reminiscences of Gandhi into his inspiring talks, slowly and from many angles shedding light on who Gandhi really was, an entirely new picture emerged. I began to see that Gandhi was at once much greater and yet more relevant—even to my own little life—than I had imagined.

This was, of course, only one of many changes, and not even the deepest wrought by those early talks. Sri Easwaran was gradually making it clear to me that the emotional anguish I was passing through was not unique to me and, more important, that it had a cure, that my political dissatisfaction—with all its passionate intensity—was really spiritual and could be given a more meaningful direction. With his combination of expertise, patience, and boundless commitment (he sometimes quipped that his initials stood for "Endless Enthusiasm"), he inspired me to make meditation the mainstay of my life. With his values, his compassion, and his vision, along with his personal experience of growing up in Gandhi's India, he enabled me to grasp who the Mahatma was and to sense the practical meaning of his legacy.

So it came about that no sooner had I gotten my foot on "the ladder" (academic jargon for a tenure-track teaching post) than I began trying to set it over to a different perch—something rather difficult to do with a ladder when you're standing on it! I used my faculty credentials to sponsor my new teacher in an experimental course on the "Theory and Practice of Meditation," a magnificent experiment that drew over a thousand students and yet could find no permanent home in the formal structures of the university and was discontinued after two goes. I tried being the chair of Religious Studies for a while, but that was doomed—the academic approach to religion and mine were on different planets. And finally I began teaching my course on nonviolence and Gandhi. That worked. It grew into a spate of articles, the beginnings of peace studies at Berkeley, this book—a career. More important, it grew into many lifelong friendships with the extraordinary young people who have taken the course over nearly a quarter of a century. Only someone who has taught, perhaps, will appreciate how much these students engaged me with their enthusiasm, challenged me with their intelligence, and above all inspired me with their demand for a better world.

That is the background, and this is the conviction that led me to write this book: that after several decades' exploration of nonviolence, I have no doubt whatsoever that we can bring a loving community to birth out of the worldwide crisis we are passing through. Precisely what such a future would look like is difficult to specify just yet, and perhaps we don't need to spell it out completely at this stage, but two things are certain. One is that, like the "miracle" of Gaviotas, it's going to take one heck of a lot of work. Most miracles do. Planting a million trees might end up looking easy by comparison.

Second, the Gaviotans give us a lead that is more than metaphor-ical. Like them, we know that though the results of our efforts may lie beyond the mists of an uncertain future, if it is to be a future that we really want, we will have to make one right choice very similar to the one that brought Gaviotas into existence: the choice for constructive action over (and in the face of) an enormous prevailing negativity. Paolo Lugari chose the godforsaken *llanos* because, he thought, "if we can do this in Colombia . . . people can do it anywhere."[3] In that same spirit we can choose to craft a life of security and vitality even here, perhaps especially here, where a culture of violence seems to dominate. I am not being quixotic. A surprising number of the projects we'll be looking at in the ensuing pages led to results—good results—beyond what the actors had a right to anticipate. Often their best and most enduring successes were not quite what they intended; indeed, sometimes what they intended to do failed. But in every case they did one right thing: they chose persuasion and inclusion over threat power and hatred and domination. They chose nonviolence.

CHAPTER ONE

HARD QUESTIONS, HARD ANSWERS

*All major natural and human systems are in crisis or transition. The signs
of this change range from the crash of fisheries around the world, the
depletion of rainforests, the declining credibility of government, the growing
inequality between rich and poor, and the crisis in meaning and sense of
emptiness that comes with an overemphasis on material consumption.*

—Positive Futures Network Newsletter

*For pain does not spring from the dust
or sorrow sprout from the soil:
man is the father of sorrow,
as surely as sparks fly upward.*

—Job 5:6–7

A FRONT-PAGE photo in the Sunday *New York Times* on August 17,
1997, showed a grieving woman, Linda Reid, putting flowers on the
gravestone of her son, who had hanged himself at the age of seven-
teen. He was the sixth teenager from that community to hang himself
or herself that year. Why? The well-written article describing the suicides in this south Boston area talked about community pride putting
too much pressure on young people, about racial tensions, lack of economic opportunity—all things we are well aware of but that hardly
explain why a young person in a country like ours would take his life.

Or hers. The real explanation must lie much deeper than community pride and economic opportunity. In 1998, the surgeon general reported that children between the ages of ten and fourteen are twice as likely to take their own lives as they were fifteen years earlier. What *is* the explanation? As though sensing that all the talk about community pride and the like was a smoke screen, the writer finally quoted a local priest: "There really aren't any answers."

I refuse to accept this. I refuse to believe in the journalistic cliché "meaningless violence." I refuse to believe that there are no answers to the cheapening of life and the rise of violence against it. Two young men murder their own parents to get their money; a murder-suicide leaves a celebrity and his wife, apparently happy for years, dead in their palatial home; a teenager is shot dead in the street for his running shoes—why? It may be easy to say that there are no answers, but it's not acceptable. If we have no answers to such a basic matter as why we can't live in peace with one another, often can't go on living at all, maybe we're asking the wrong questions.

In one respect, it's only too clear that we are doing just that. It's even clear why: violence is "reported" to us every day by the mass media in a wash of meaningless detail. "Joe X, twenty-six, was shot three times with a 9-millimeter handgun purchased the previous Tuesday for $23." Or, "This month the homicide rate in Dayton was 1.8 percent lower than last month." Frequently, we are solemnly told the trivial "reasons" offered by flustered survivors who hardly understand what is happening to them, and there is no limit to how absurd, how downright insulting to human nature these can be. In what would be called today a frivolous lawsuit, the wife of James Oliver Huberty, who killed twenty-one people in the McDonald's San Ysidro massacre of 1984, said that her husband's murderous rampage was caused by the excessive MSG in McDonald's hamburgers. The way violent events are reported (and this is a large part of what we read and think about today) is virtually always trivializing. It comes to us as a barrage of incidental details, often of cold statistics. Engrossed in one sensational detail or another, one particular violent episode or another, we never think about violence itself.

The right questions, then, are not: Why are very young students turning their schools into battlefields? Why is there an increase in hate crimes right now against gays in Florida or a decrease in sex offenses in New England? They are:

What is violence?

Why is it getting worse? *and*

How do we make it stop?

STIRRINGS OF CHANGE

Despite discouragement by the mass media, there is evidence that people *want* to confront these questions; they are becoming more dissatisfied with the "no answer" school and other forms of dismissal—rightly, for to dismiss something as dangerous as rising violence is treacherous. The tendency to deny violence has been with us for a long time, to be sure, but there are signs that it is weakening. Considering the enormous role played by violence throughout history, Hannah Arendt wrote in her classic study *On Violence* in 1969, "It is . . . rather surprising that violence has been singled out so seldom for special consideration."[1] She was reflecting the fact that a new awareness is dawning, that many feel the time to get past denial and face the issue head-on is right now. It has been half a century since Gandhi observed that the world was "sick unto death with blood-spilling,"[2] and at about that same time, French philosopher Jacques Ellul made the shrewd observation that our era "is not at all the age of violence; it's the age of the *awareness* of violence."[3]

In other words, what really characterizes our time is not so much that there is so much violence—there have been such times before—but that we are challenged, possibly as never before, to deal with it. This being true, the mass media could not have chosen a worse time to make violence appear trivial and incomprehensible. They are doing a singular and untimely disservice to human civilization.

Confronting violence is a little like turning around to face a bright light that's been projecting all kinds of fascinating images and shadows out in front of us (yes, I've been influenced by Plato). It's hard to peer into that glare, but when we succeed, we find ourselves going through a kind of Alice's looking glass. Suddenly we feel like the character from that popular sixties poster, with his head stuck into a whole other universe—or that convict in a cartoon staring wistfully through the bars at a little patch of sky while all along the door to his cell stands wide open behind him.

It is a much wider world out there; the light is harsh at first, but when we face it, problems that seemed impossible to cope with now seem to come teamed with all kinds of solutions—solutions with unexpected good side effects, instead of bad ones.

The prevailing method of dealing with violence has a dreadful tendency to create more problems than it solves. For example, we try to stop young people from bringing guns to school by installing metal detectors. It does cut down on the number of guns they bring in, of course—*and* it demoralizes the students because it implies that they cannot be trusted. It intensifies the excitement of the "game" of sneaking guns into school. And most of all it normalizes the violence. It blunts the shock. How could we have allowed a situation like this to happen, where young people have guns at all, much less carry them in *school?* And without that shock, where do we get the motivation to act? Where's the impetus to confront the real problem, of which guns in school is only one form: the problem of violence?

MOVING TOWARD THE TRUTH

I have been identifying the mass media as a major source of our problem, and I'm going to continue, for one simple reason: that is where it would be most effective to make a change. In all honesty, however, we cannot put all the blame on them. When Hannah Arendt said it is "rather surprising" that violence has not been given special attention before now, she was giving us a scholarly hint that we have a natural inclination to avoid thinking directly about violence, which is understandable: we would be thinking about the most negative side of human nature, which means the most negative side of *ourselves*. I don't like this any more than you do. But although it must be done, it doesn't have to be done destructively. That is, we can peer into the depths of human nature—of ourselves—in a *balanced* way, seeing what is good as well as what is discouraging about us. Today, by emphasizing the shadow side of humanity—and "emphasizing" may be too mild for our obsession with the ugly and violent today—our culture seems to be making us more and more ignorant of our human stature. Let me throw that claim into relief by quoting a brief passage from an era, namely, the fourteenth century, when that was not yet true:

> Beneath you and external to you lies the entire created universe. Yes, even the sun, the moon and the stars. They are fixed above you, splendid in the firmament, yet they cannot compare to your exalted dignity as a human being.[4]

It seems almost fantastic to us that a writer could matter-of-factly describe humanity in these glowing terms; but it would have seemed just as fantastic to him that we matter-of-factly bill ourselves as "natural born killers"—just as fantastic and much more dangerous.

The obsession with negativity that we take for granted paradoxically makes it nearly impossible to understand our negative side; it has blocked us from getting down to the causes of violence, those that lie within us, by creating a sense that *only* causes of violence lie within us. As we shine our light into the murk, therefore, it is essential to be watching for the seeds of change and regeneration that surely lie hidden there along with the drives, the impulses, and blindness that make us violent. Opposites can strangely be the same.

The other day as I was walking across Sproul Plaza, made famous in the sixties as the scene of the free speech movement, I saw a cluster of students handing out leaflets around a hastily knocked-together kiosk. Nothing unusual, for Berkeley. They were clearly agitated (also not too unusual), and I went over to read their large, hand-lettered sign: "Anti-Asian Hate Crimes on the Rise." I was shocked and hurt. At Berkeley, so many of my students and friends and colleagues are Asian that this hit me personally and hard, quite apart from the fact that this kind of thing should not be happening in Berkeley or anywhere in this century. But I've learned something over the years: if I wanted to do something about this, something effective, something that would last, I would have to get my initial reactions under control; I would have to take a step back and try to see the bigger picture.

To be more precise, in this case, I would have to take three steps back. Like letting myself down a chain into murky waters, hand over hand, I would have to back down in my thinking, from:

anti-Asian hate crimes

to hate crimes

to hate.

Hate is the real problem. The more hate there is, the more it will express itself in whatever form. *Some* of those forms will be illegal—crimes, in other words—and some of *those* will be directed against Asians. But the underlying reason anti-Asian hate crimes are on the rise—in Berkeley or anywhere—has nothing to do with Asians or even racism: it is that hate is on the rise. Today it might be Asians; tomorrow it could be Jews, it could be blacks, homeless people, gays and lesbians; yesterday it was Communists—but since these are all only the *targets* of some people's hate, only forms that hatred then takes, trying to cope with each victimized group individually is like trying to fix one leak at a time in a rusted-out plumbing system. Wouldn't it be more effective to shut off the water? Or, to modify that image, hatred is a tide that raises all boats: we won't get far trying to rescue the boats—or even groups of boats—one at a time.

These students were not the only ones trying to deal with one problem of victimization in isolation. We are all doing this, because it has become our culture-wide style. As John Burton, former secretary of Australia's Department of External Affairs and now a well-known scholar of conflict, wrote, "In so far as specific problems are being tackled by authorities as though they were separate problems, there can be no lasting cures for any of them." What civilizations are passing through, he pointed out, is in reality a clash between the systems we've built and the actual human needs they were supposed to address.[5] Not, that is, an isolated clash between group and group.

The trouble with trying to stop one leak at a time is, first of all, that it does nothing about the others. Have a teach-in, raise consciousness, or, if you really want to be unimaginative, provide Asians with more "security" measures. You *may* see some reduction of anti-Asian hate crimes (I will be arguing later that even this isn't guaranteed), but what about anti-black, anti-lesbian, anti-Caucasian hate crimes? What about road rage? What about war?

On the other hand, if you could somehow do something to control hate, *all* the manifestations of hate would subside to that degree. The effect on specific hate crimes might be less obvious at first because it would be indirect, but in the long run it would be much, much more reliable. You simply cannot have anti-Asian hate crimes if you don't have hate. On the whole, this is so obvious that the only reason to repeat it is that as soon as some particular form of violence gets in our face, so to speak—witness my first reaction at the kiosk—it draws all our attention to the details. Emergencies are great motivators, but they create a terrible atmosphere for really solving problems. To solve problems you need to have a little self-control, a little distance, a lot of patience. You need to see, for example, that the problem is not hate against group A or B: it's hate.

Incidentally, as I headed back to my office, whom should I run across but a well-known Berkeley personality haranguing the passersby in a voice I recognized all too well. It's the kind of voice that makes you wince before you even hear what it's saying. I'm not sure what his problem is or why he chooses to bring it on campus, but he's extremely angry and attacks people for hours in a voice raucous with bitterness. He's popularly called the Hate Man. I had the odd feeling that I might be the only one on campus noticing the connection.

Science and Serendipity

It sounds simple, but no sooner have we worked our way down the chain from anti-Asian hate crimes to hate crimes to hate—which is not easy to do when we're caught up in a hateful situation—than we have not only an answer to the question, why this kind of crime?, but the beginnings of a way to solve it. Once we've gotten down to the emotional cause, we start seeing a pragmatic measure that we'll be able to apply, mutatis mutandis, to just about every form of violence: since the underlying cause of the violence is hate, we could fix the problem if we had a way to turn hate into something else. And there is evidence that this trick may not be as impossible as it seems.

In a remarkable experiment first reported in the *Journal of Abnormal Social Psychology* some time ago, schoolchildren of the same age were divided into two groups: one group was encouraged to be aggressive and the other to be cooperative. (In our culture most children are "trained" to be aggressive even before they reach school, but it's fairly easy to overcome that training with a little encouragement of their innate tendency to share, cooperate, think about each others' welfare.) Within a few weeks they were behaving quite differently. Both groups were then brought together and subjected to an acute frustration: They were sat down in a nice big room with a projector that was flanked by several cans of film. For good measure, each child was given a candy bar but told not to start in on it just yet. The room was darkened and the first film started—suddenly, without a word of explanation, the experimenters snapped on the lights, shut off the projector, confiscated the candy bars, and packed the children off to their respective classrooms. Science is rough! But the issue was important—to see if the cooperative training would hold up under such unmerited mistreatment—and the results, duly filmed through the classrooms' one-way glass, were extremely suggestive. The children with pro-aggression training were of course hell on wheels; their frustration boiled over in fights, arguments, and general mayhem more than ever. That was not very surprising. But the rest was: the children who had been systematically encouraged to cooperate with each other were *more cooperative than ever.* Apparently their cooperation training not only protected them from frustration, it allowed them to thrive on it. They were able, that is, to divert the negativity it released within them into constructive channels. Psychic tension, it seems, is neither good nor bad in itself; it can be thought of as raw energy that becomes destructive *or* helpful when it is made to flow through aggressive or cooperative channels. Peace could be a simple matter of training.

As you have guessed from the cans of film and the projector, this study by Joel Davitz was published over fifty years ago, at the height of the Cold War.[6] Many political commentators were saying back then that if we made it through that year, 1952, we could survive anything. It might be thought that at such a time the question of what human beings can and cannot be trained to do with their aggressive drives would be of first importance. But Davitz's study was by and large ignored. This was the heyday of the "innate aggression" theory; at that time the idea that human aggression is biologically programmed and there is nothing anyone can do about it, an idea now largely discredited (but still uncritically believed by the mass media and the general public), was about to break over the public in a series of pseudoscientific publications by Robert Ardrey *(The Territorial Imperative* would come out in 1966), Raymond Dart, and several others. The heyday of that sensationalistic "science" is now behind us, however, and we are free to imagine that there may indeed be ways to turn hate and other negative energies into something else; that, as this experiment suggests, human nature may contain the cure as well as the cause of the violent trend that's engulfing us.

Science has not stood still since 1952, and we know a good bit more about cooperation. Mediation training in schools has become a growth industry, for example, but the implications of the Davitz study are still far from fully realized. The study itself is known among peace-oriented psychologists, but its implications have not been systematically explored despite their potential importance. With or without popularizers like Robert Ardrey and their "swashbuckling" theory of innate aggression (I borrow that adjective from philosopher Mary Midgley), pessimism about human nature is the norm in public opinion and, I'm afraid, in mainstream science. People study, talk about, and explore the shadow side. We have to look hard to find the side we need.

IN SEARCH OF PREVENTION

Berkeley students, among whom I've studied and taught for more than thirty years and who will always have a special place in my heart, are, as I say, far from alone in showing us the need to let ourselves down the chain of causality. If you really want justice for your own group, or any group you identify with, you have to step back in your vision and your emotions, not for the purpose of caring less, but to give yourself the space for a better-aimed passion. This is what all of us have to do if we are ever to see a life secure from violence, even if we're nonminorities living in a comfortable community—like south Boston. Whether we are activists angered by some form of injustice or we just want to get from our car to our house without being mugged, we are going to have to change our way of thinking. We have to slow down our initial reactions—not by any means the same thing as losing the intensity of our feelings about the problem, but on the contrary, in order to convert those valuable feelings from fear, panic, or resentment into determination. The more clearly we can see the underlying causes, the better we'll be able to identify the long-lasting, and only real, solution.

But there's an important point I only just began to mention: why wait until we're being mugged, or people with ugly attitudes have started insulting our communities? Obviously, it's tons more effective not only to be working at the root of the problem instead of the leaves, but to be working *steadily* instead of being caught by surprise every time there's a violent incident. How can we? We've already had one clue: we start doing this the minute we stop being taken in by the details that the media think is in their best interest to deluge us with, and do some reflecting about what is going wrong; the minute we step back from the hurt and anger about what's happening to us personally and start to think about inhumanity itself.

In the summer of 1998, a dedicated teacher and school principal in South Africa, Sister Theodelind Schreck, was shot and killed in an apparent robbery while driving to pick up her niece. Although KwaZuluNatal province has a long history of political violence, this slaying was a shock. "Sister Theodelind Schreck was dedicated to her teaching and religious duties," said Ben Ngubane, premier of the province. Then he made an observation that rose above the fuss about why *her*, about *this* murder being unacceptable, and provided useful insight for all of us. "Violence remains violence, irrespective of motivation."[7]

This shows exactly how we have to think about violence in order to cure it. There is a hopeful side to this view: since violence is violence, anything we do to reduce violence anywhere will do something toward reducing violence everywhere.

Premier Ngubane's insight is borne out by scientific research. One of the papers read before the British Psychological Society in 1994 was about the negative impact of TV news bulletins. By then it was well known to social scientists that the parade of bad news that we see on the media depresses us. What was surprising, however (but perfectly logical, when you think about it), is that the anxious and depressed states we get into from watching this news—or various forms of "entertainment," which paint the same dismal picture of human nature—have a very general impact: we start seeing *everything* more negatively. Evidently, the negativity we take in—and other studies show that it doesn't much matter whether we think we're seeing news or fiction—"tend[s] to promote a negative frame of mind in which negative events, thoughts and memories *are likely to be dwelled on and positive ones filtered out and ignored.*"[8] (my emphasis)

Clearly, that could lead to a vicious circle—and clearly, in fact, it has. There is a lot of bad stuff in the world; by seeing it up close, out of proportion, we come to expect things to be that way, and when we have negative expectations, life obligingly fulfills them. That part of the circle is easy to understand: negative expectations mask from view our positive potentials, which are the very ones we need if we're going to avoid and resolve problems like violence.

Note that the London psychologists compared the effects of bad news to what they called "neutral" news—not to actual good news. Maybe there wasn't enough good news out there to build a sample. But this is the main point: the principle that they were dealing with, the principle that negativity generalizes in the viewer's mind, is one of the most important things to know about violence. Think how differently we would form policies and regulate our own viewing habits if we became aware of what it's doing to our outlook on life, what it's costing us emotionally and spiritually, to take in so many violent, depressing images and stories.

In practical terms, though, the real importance of the London study comes out when we turn it around. To take in uplifting images and stories must have exactly the opposite effect. Logically, that would make things better as surely as seeing violence makes them worse. But somehow we never think to explore the bright side of the principle. A recent news story on "emotional literacy" (a current term for the kind of cooperative training Davitz was talking about fifty years ago) for example, had the title "Today's Lesson: Curbing Kids' Violent Emotions."[9] You could put it that way. But what if, just for the argument, we were to title that article "Today's Lesson: Unleashing Kids' Compassionate Emotions"? Unthinkable; but actually more correct. It is a better description, I believe, of what is really happening in young people when they are trained to be compassionate. Their natural drive to cooperate, when keyed to positive emotions like compassion, takes up some of the energy that would otherwise be fueling their aggressions. The results of this simple process took the Davitz experimenters quite by surprise—like the Gaviotans when they created the conditions for a rain forest they didn't know was there.

Recently, at my daughter's house, I watched a PBS documentary on the aftermath of colonialism in the second half of the twentieth century. The film brought out extremely well the contrast between the aftermath in India and the aftermath in other colonial areas, primarily Africa. It pointed out with unusual sensitivity, I thought, how despite India's many problems she remains the most populous democracy on the planet, with robust institutions to keep her that way, and enjoys rewarding relationships with the former colonial power—all this in contrast to names that make us wince today, such as Somalia, Rwanda, Liberia, the Congo, Ghana, Algeria. The film, as I say, brought this out very well. What it didn't think to mention was *why*. It is as though the filmmakers did not dare to say that nonviolence (which was, with a few lapses, the liberation method chosen in India) led to one result while violence (which predominated in Africa with a few exceptions) led to quite another. By the end of this book you will see why I dare to say exactly that.

Let me emphasize the simple but important step we've already taken in this direction. As journalist Daniel Schorr wrote recently, "Television, celebrating violence, promotes violence. . . . By trivializing great issues, it buries great issues. By blurring the line between fantasy and reality, it crowds out reality."[10] But if television and other media celebrate, promote, and trivialize violence, that doesn't mean we need to. My hope is that after reading this book you'll never hear a news report or see a violence-packed film in quite the same way again. While the details of that crime report are being reeled off— what caliber was the gun, where was the wound, what was the motive, if any —something in you will cry out, "This is violence. Forget every- thing else and figure out what's going wrong!" Let that reminder come on over the cultural messages of negativity or meaningless detail.

That step taken, we can take the next: to see through events to an underlying story that contains scintillae of hope, and a few examples of that follow.

Strength Is Strength

As part of wrapping up the second Christian millennium, *Time* magazine ran profiles of one hundred key people who, in the editors' opinions, had left their marks on that embattled century. It was not inspiring. What they did with Gandhi was shockingly bad, but they did manage to relate an eye-opening story about Nelson Mandela.[11] When the young Mandela stepped onto the quay with a boatload of other prisoners at the infamous Robben Island, where he was to spend so many years of his life, guards shouting "Huck! Huck!" tried to herd the new arrivals like cattle, to force them to trot up to the prison, and to submit them to other humiliations; but Mandela and a friend refused and kept on walking calmly though the guards threatened, "Do you want me to kill you?" Once inside, the head warder, Captain Gericke, went a little too far, calling Mandela "boy." "Look here," Mandela calmly told the startled Gericke, "I must warn you, I'll take you to the highest authority and you will be poor as a dormouse by the time I finish with you."[12]

"Incredibly," *Time* reported, Gericke backed off.

But is this so incredible? Don't bullies frequently cave in when they meet with unexpected resistance? We've all seen examples of this, and in the next chapters we'll not only see a few more but will start working out their scientific explanation.

Let's follow the lead the *Time* writers missed. First connection: intuition leads us to a famous event a quarter of a century later, when Mandela was in a position of strength, in fact the first president of a free South Africa. As most of us remember, during his inauguration speech he paused, turned to his arch enemy, F. W. de Klerk, *took his hand,* and said, "I am proud to hold your hand—for us to go forward together. . . . Let us work together to end division."[13]

What is the connection between these two events? In the ordinary way of seeing things, nothing. In the ordinary way of thinking, every conflict, if not every interaction, has to have a "winner" and a "loser." Did de Klerk win or did he lose when Mandela made his gesture of reconciliation? Absurd question. What about Mandela? As an individual,

Nelson Mandela may not have liked F. W. de Klerk, but he used his strength of character to overcome his personal dislike; and we can clearly trace, through his change of roles, the thread from his strength as a prisoner on Robben Island to his strength as president in Johannesburg. This intriguing connection does not appear in the ordinary way most of us think about conflict and human relationships, but in the emerging new way of thinking about conflict and relationships it's clear enough: the capacity to stand up to a bully and the capacity to forgive one—the strength of character to rise above anger, even if that anger is perfectly justified—are closely connected. These qualities not only can coexist, they explain each other: strength is strength.

We miss this whole fascinating connection if we think "strength" means the ability to prevail, to dominate, and only that. Mandela's great role model, Gandhi, would, by contrast, often confess his blunders in public; he seemed to enjoy it, much to the consternation of his coworkers. Once, his sister was alarmed at what seemed to her a particularly damaging confession, and he said, "Tell sister there is no defeat in the confession of one's error. The confession itself is a victory."[14]

That real strength is so much more than "power over" another explains the strange conversions of angry, violent people that keep cropping up in the annals of peace. When segregationist George Wallace became governor of Alabama, he kept his campaign promise and literally "stood in the schoolhouse door" to block black students from entering the University of Alabama in June of 1963, making himself a national symbol of defiance in the cause of segregation. But in the course of time, something apparently happened to lift the fog of hatred from his mind, and on March 11, 1995, he came in his wheelchair to the celebration of the Selma-to-Montgomery civil rights march to apologize to the marchers, black and white, whom his state troopers had clubbed and fire-hosed thirty years before. That took guts—but then, so did the way he defied the whole country back when he saw things differently. From an icon of segregation he became, on the front cover of *Life,* an icon of reconciliation. No wonder Gandhi often said that there's hope for a violent man to become nonviolent, but not for a coward. In nonviolent logic, this makes perfect sense: what we're seeing is the same courage and strength, put to better use.

Second connection: Now link both these events in Mandela's life, the defiance and the generosity, with his impressive leadership—his ability to pilot a brand new state that had just emerged from horrendous conditions with still-unresolved tensions of frightening magnitude. This is a little subtler than the courage to defy and/or forgive: is someone who forgives his or her enemies, in public, a good leader? Of course. He or she will tend to have access to creative resources for order, which we'll have a chance to explore later (especially in chapters 5 and 6). For now, let's consider one more nonviolent event that was misunderstood—and this time not just by the press.

In August 1991 a counterrevolutionary coup that would have pushed Russia back to Stalinism was thwarted by a popular uprising. This is how one important liberal magazine characterized the event: "The coup failed. The regime collapsed. For once, *the world was lucky*."[15] (my emphasis) But the successful popular resistance to the August coup was not "lucky"; it was the result of deliberate acts carried out by courageous nonviolent resisters who had been systematically studying nonviolent tactics for months, in part through workshops run by experienced American trainers (one friend of mine had done an average of two such workshops a day all over Russia throughout that summer). All of this was totally unknown to the press. "The August coup was not a surprising event," wrote conscientious objector Alexander Pronozin shortly after it occurred. "The real surprise was how quickly the coup was brought down and that the 'weapon' that won the day was nonviolent social-based defence."[16]

I will say more later about this remarkable form of defense (chapters 4 and 8), and when I do, I hope to clarify what it could mean for the majority of us, who are not likely to participate in a "people power" resistance. What I want to emphasize now is that the rapid success of the resistance to the coup, which seemed so inexplicable, so "lucky" to the news media and general public—and, I have little doubt, to the political leadership of the time—was neither. It was the result of hard work and sacrifice; it followed the rules of the game with perfect predictability. You do not have to glean news about non-violence on special Listservs, as I do, to be more aware of these rules; if you have a hunch that life is not so haphazard as it appears, that everyone responds to love or hatred when it's offered to them, you will know what I'm talking about.

My colleague and friend Sergei Plekhanov, then deputy director of the Soviet Institute for U.S. and Canadian Studies, was not in Moscow on the critical day the coup was thwarted. A year later I heard him describe what he had gone through when he saw the starkly juxta-posed television images of the Kremlin, ringed by grim walls and armored vehicles, and the Russian parliament building, in white mar-ble and glass, guarded only by unarmed people, almost a mythic image of civil authority under attack by violence. I still remember the quiet passion in his voice that so gripped the international scholars gathered around him: "And what do you have against them?" he said. What can you wield against those tanks and armored personnel carriers? "Nothing. Nothing but spirit, a sense of legitimacy, and the willingness of some people to risk their lives." I hope the delicate irony was not lost on my colleagues, for this "nothing" is the classic recipe for suc-cessful nonviolence: spirit, a sense of legitimacy (that one's cause is just), and the willingness to sacrifice—if necessary, to lay down one's life. Those are precisely the three things that make resistance to an unjust regime successful. Basic Nonviolence 101. To miss this is to be unable to explain what forces were at work in the confrontation of August 1991—and why the people won.

THE PURLOINED ANSWER

This side of the Iron Curtain there was a land called Yugoslavia, where people of different cultures and ethnicities lived side by side. They worked together, despite their tensions. They went to schools together. They quarreled; they intermarried. This went on for centuries. Then one day, when the lid of centralized state-socialist control came off, the three major cultural groups (they are not ethnic groups) blew apart. The result was the most appalling violence seen in Europe, and possibly anywhere, since World War II. Many asked, "Why? How could they be putting people in cattle cars all over again?"

As usual, there were those who said there was "no answer." Others cited "history," as though memories of the famous battle of 1389 had to be avenged even though the people who fought it had been dead for 500 years.

> But in all this, one banal factor has been overlooked: the poisonous power of propaganda. The Slav populations of the other formerly Communist East European countries just to the north, in Hungary and Romania, developed a hearty skepticism about what they saw on state television or read in government-run newspapers. For some reason, that kind of doubt died in Yugoslavia if it ever existed. People here have always believed, and still believe, what they see and hear on television.[17]

In a way, this is nothing new; we all know about the "yellow journalism" that put the United States into conflict with Spain in 1898. Then it was mainly newsprint; now it's television (or, in the case of Rwanda, radio). But the difference between then and now is not just technological, or for that matter political: it's the difference of half a century's "background" message of alienation and violence, the cumulative mental poison that makes all of us more edgy, dispirited, and prone to react with violence along whatever fault lines present themselves, be it between races, between cultural subgroups in a formerly viable community, or between two cars on a crowded freeway. The London study I quoted earlier points to this effect; so do the wise words of Daniel Schorr; so do these from a twelve-year-old schoolchild in Santa Rosa, California.

If there was no violence on the television less people would make violence on the streets. Also I think less people would be shot, murdered, kidnapped and other things.[18]

They sure would. It's as simple as "violence in, violence out," a result that is obvious to science, common sense, and our own personal experience, and that we nonetheless like to regard in some circles as controversial. It isn't. If we play up violence, we'll have more violence; if we play up money and greed, there will be more robberies; and in the words of another wise twelve-year-old: "People get a lot of ideas from sex [on television] and think it's okay and then they rape people." Several writers have recently pointed out that the same video games the military uses, off the shelf, to prepare soldiers for combat are being played by our young people, for example the young people who have left us one of the most painful memories in America—Columbine.[19]

It seems so—well—stupid to do this to ourselves that one can understand the bitterness behind these hard words of Wendell Berry:

Always the assumption is that we can first set demons at large, and then, somehow, become smart enough to control them. This is not childishness. It is not even "human weakness." It is a kind of idiocy, but perhaps we will not cope with it and save ourselves until we regain the sense to call it evil.[20]

If it helps, call it evil. But be careful: there is a world of difference between calling something evil and calling some*one* evil. The first strategy mobilizes resources against the problem; the second only recycles the ultimate cause of the problem, which is ill will, resentment, lack of empathy, and eventually hatred.

When the members of a European contact group sutured together a "peace" for the remains of Yugoslavia in 1998, they made no provision for reeducation; incredibly, *no one paid any attention* to the govern-ment-run television stations that kept right on whipping up the same hatreds that had started the violence, particularly in Serbia. As one of my colleagues on the scene ruefully told me, "Most people continue to be fed a steady diet of nationalism and propaganda, hatred, half-truths, and prejudice." The war over Kosovo soon followed.

When we see someone deliberately fanning hatreds in this way, we have to feel the hurt of it so deeply that we cannot rest without doing something about it—but calling it "evil" is a tricky way to go. Where there's evil, there has to be an evildoer—someone other than us. Very "other." But in fact, the media are *our* media; we patronize and support them. There is a reciprocity to this process, to be sure: they feed us violence and vulgarity, and we then get a taste for it and demand more, which they obligingly supply—a truly vicious cycle, but where shall the spinning finger of blame land?

On the whole, I prefer to think that we are unleashing these demons through a kind of tragically blinkered vision (what Berry calls "idiocy"). Still not very complimentary, but it's a more practical approach, as we will see in chapter 2.

The Why of Living

The media have purposes of their own; helping us grasp the significance of violent events does not seem to be one of them—much less helping us find our role in eliminating such events. That is why when they run out of superficial answers for one act of violence or another, they have taken to saying that there isn't any answer. But there is. We have seen part of it already. It's that we, collectively, have created such a climate of violence and negativity that life doesn't seem terribly worth hanging onto—ours or anyone else's. At the same time, violence begins to seem an intriguing, pseudomeaningful, "exciting," and normal alternative. Suicide fits into this picture as a kind of inverted violence directed against oneself—or have some of our young people become so alienated that their own self is "other" to them? In any case, it is the phenomenon of teenage suicides that forces us to step *way* back and look at the whole picture. Let me put it as simply as possible.

Life has a purpose. Animals can live without discovering this, but people can't. In the course of historical time, civilizations can get off on a tangent, get fascinated by some sidetrack, and lose sight of why they are alive. When this happens—and it seems to happen periodically—a whole culture can no longer see where it's going. That's when life loses its purpose (or seems to), and individuals, in the grip of a gnawing despair they may not be able to articulate, start to give up on life itself. Then we see teenagers committing suicide as though it were a fad, we see doctors who help people die instead of helping them live, we see the return of the death penalty—all symptoms of what the pope has called a "death-oriented" civilization. It's not really death-oriented *per se;* it's death-oriented *by default.* When life doesn't seem to offer us a goal to live for, then, by default, repellent things can actually look attractive, because they're the only things that are at least "exciting." Death and violence take on a lurid appeal. Yet, as an ancient Indian classic puts it, "Those who get drawn to the shadow side of life go to blinding darkness."[21] To play with the dark side of human nature is to end up in a crisis of violence and not understand why.

So the violence we're seeing today is intimately linked to the "crisis of meaning" cited by the Positive Futures Network in the epigraph heading this chapter. The network listed it as a symptom; I would argue that the crisis of meaning belongs center stage. If people don't know where the journey of life is leading them, why should they be enthusiastic about continuing? Teenagers can be very direct, and here is what one of them said when President Clinton advocated an educational campaign on the dangers of smoking to dissuade teens from doing it:

> In my opinion, many young people who smoke and
> say they don't know why are subconsciously choosing

death. So telling them over and over that smoking will kill them is not the answer. . . . If the president is serious . . . he's got to find ways to help them imagine a future.[22]

When a young person ends his or her life in south Boston or kills someone along a California freeway, when a father turns on his own family or a nation sets off nuclear explosions, it is not about money or jealousy or traffic. Ultimately, it's because life has lost its meaning for them—they cannot "imagine a future" with any hope or purpose. Money and all those other factors can *precipitate* violence, but only among people for whom, consciously or otherwise, life has lost its meaning—or more accurately, who have lost sight of life's priceless value and what a Greek philosopher called its "inexhaustible meaning."[23]

Because the media so effectively obscure the meaning of life today, they are, again, potentially a most effective way to shut off the rising tide of violence, but only one way among others. My young friend Sean is taking intensive German to help him with his senior thesis project on the poet Rilke, at Johns Hopkins. After I helped him out a bit with that awhile back, we found ourselves talking about his friends who were studying science at places like Berkeley and MIT. "I can't understand," Sean said. "It's as though there were no controversy about it, as though everyone agrees that there's only the physical body and laws and molecules—haven't they heard of something called the mind?"

I found myself thinking of an article I had read the day before in a newsletter from my own campus, about a truly remarkable breakthrough in molecular genetics. My colleagues had been able to "photograph" the very site on the cell where genes are "switched on" or off, where DNA is told to go ahead and produce messenger RNA to begin making part of an organism. While I was reading along, marveling how far we have come since my brief stint in medical school (never mind how long ago *that* was), my literary senses were setting off a little alarm. I stopped and counted something: in this brief article, about 600 words, the word *machine* occurred *thirteen times*. This is what's called in literary circles a "subtext": even while the writer was telling us about a great human achievement, he was also telling us, in that powerful stream of suggestion that runs underneath the literal meaning of our words, "You're a machine, you're a machine, you're a machine . . ."[24]

"For our culture as a whole," Huston Smith recently pointed out, "nothing major is going to happen until we figure out who we are. The truth of the matter is, that today we haven't a clue as to who we are. There is no consistent view of human nature in the West today."[25]

"Who we are" is a question that will be hovering in the background of every argument in this book. Are we separate, material creatures—in which case it's hard to see how we could *not* be doomed to competition and conflict—or are we invisibly connected through what Mahatma Gandhi called "heart unity" underneath all those real-as-far-as-they-go differences of body, culture, likes and dislikes, ideologies, and fashions? In the latter case, life may have a profound hidden meaning after all; and in that case, we've got a lot of learning ahead of us.

The dark side of modern science—and unfortunately it has one—does not arise from science itself, still less from any of the facts of nature. It arises from the impression we allow science to give us: the impression that we are merely biological machines in a meaningless material universe, which reinforces the already disquieting sense many moderns have that life is devoid of purpose. Science has every right to confine its attention to the physical, i.e., the outside world; it has no right to say, when it has done so, that it has given us the whole story.

When scientists, some of them, talk about "the biological basis of violence," they are out of their depth. Science, at least as they practice it, can study the infinitely vast reaches of outer space, but it cannot very well study the inner dimensions of the human being. As a result, in course of time, those who turn to science for their answers to life come to feel they do not have such dimensions. They feel empty. Human will, nobility, beauty, and life's overriding purpose are all in the category of things scientists do not study and that some eventually come to believe, quite without justification, do not exist.

This drive toward reductionism within science becomes exaggerated in the minds of nonscientists, especially when it is greatly amplified by the mass media. The media report new "discoveries" in material determinism at the rate of about a gene a day: obesity, sexual preference, intelligence, sex appeal, and whether you like peanut butter—they've just found the gene or the hormone or the what-have-you that "causes" it. No responsible scientist would actually claim that we can trace something as complex and subtle as anger or cravings or attitudes to a gene or a hormone, but we in the general public are spared such subtlety. We come to feel we do not have a will, that there is no redemptive drama going on in the human being, that we are without meaning or direction, and so, as Dostoevsky said in *The Possessed,* we die of despair.

> The one essential condition of human existence is that man should always be able to bow down before something infinitely great. If men are deprived of the infinitely great they will not go on living and will die of despair.[26]

The six south Boston teenagers were examples of that, and today there are many, many others.

When a family becomes "dysfunctional" (a remote euphemism for the tragedy), the children grow up deficient in security and self-esteem, easy prey to what the Positive Futures Network called "the crisis in meaning and sense of emptiness that comes with an overemphasis on material consumption" through which our civilization is passing. They find it most difficult to discern the meaning of life, or believe that there is one, and begin to "die of despair," in a thousand ways—even if they never see a television set.

When I think about the new world of mass media, I'm reminded of something a social worker recently pointed out about child care:

"We have no idea how destructive a situation we have created. It is a social experiment on a grand scale with virtually no controls."[27]

But this book is about solutions, not just problems. Some of the stories I told and more that I will tell are really about ordinary people doing in their way what Dostoevsky described in his grand register—people rising toward the "infinitely great" through response to the reasonably good. For we have arrived at not one, but two answers to the question, what can be done to keep young people from despairing of their lives? What almost all people can do to create a nonviolent culture is to reduce violence and to find a new sense of purpose. And as we've begun to see, these two grand projects are closely related.

CHAPTER TWO

HOPE IN DARK TIMES

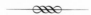

I do admit that the destructive energy is there, but it is evanescent,
always futile before the creative, which is permanent. If the destructive one
had the upper hand all sacred ties—love between parents and child, brother
and sister, master and disciple, ruler and ruled—would be snapped.

—M. K. Gandhi

If public opinion would but frown upon violence, it would lose all its power.

—Lev N. Tolstoy

AS OF THIS writing, hundreds of young people from North America, Europe, and elsewhere have gone to Central America and other places to protect threatened human rights workers with their presence. Their work is still largely unknown to the American public —the news media shroud this fascinating experiment in profound silence. Nonetheless, they are there.

Karen Ridd was one of them. In 1989 Karen and four other international volunteers were working with a group called Peace Brigades International (PBI) when they were suddenly arrested by the Salvadoran National Guard. Three of the five were Spanish nationals, and they were promptly deported, leaving Karen, who was Canadian, and her friend Marcela Rodriguez, who was from Colombia, to face whatever was coming. Fortunately, Karen had had time to call the Canadian consul and alert another PBI volunteer who happened to call in at the right moment. This was some comfort, as was the civility—

at first—of the soldiers, but no one from the team had had to face arrest before (to date, no international volunteer has been killed in Central America despite the enormous violence all around them) and from another room Marcela heard the soldiers describing them as "terrorists from the Episcopal church."[1] Their spirits did not improve when the two women, along with other detainees, were loaded onto a truck, taken to an army barracks, blindfolded, and subjected to five hours' interrogation about their alleged connection with the guerilla FMLN, while sounds of torture and the sobbing of victims came from nearby rooms. Karen knew that PBI would quickly alert their world-wide network about the arrests, but she also knew that time was short—there was no telling what would happen in that barracks if someone didn't get them out before nightfall.

PBI had in fact activated its worldwide network, and before long hundreds of people were sending faxes to the Canadian and Colombian embassies, calling and sending e-mail messages to their representatives to urge Karen and Marcela's immediate release. All this got no response at all from the Colombian embassy, but Canada brought official pressure on the Salvadoran government, no doubt hinting that its extensive trade relations with El Salvador could be compromised if Karen were not released immediately. Whatever it was that got through to whoever was in charge, Karen found herself walking across the barrack grounds toward a waiting embassy official a few hours later, a free woman. But when the soldiers had removed her blindfold inside the barracks she had caught a glimpse of Marcela, face to the wall, a "perfect image of dehumanization."[2] Glad as Karen was to be alive, something tugged at her. Feeling terrible, she made some excuses to the exasperated Canadian official who had come all the way from San Salvador to get her, turned, and *walked back into the barracks,* not knowing what would happen to her in there, but know-ing it could not be worse than walking out on a friend.

The soldiers were startled, and almost as exasperated. They handcuffed her again. In the next room, a soldier banged Marcela's head into the wall and said that some "white bitch" was stupid enough to walk back in there, and "Now you're going to see the treatment a terrorist deserves!" No more mister nice guy. But Karen's gesture was having a strange effect on the men. They talked to Karen, despite themselves, and she tried to explain why she had returned: "You know what it's like to be separated from a *compañero*." That got to them. Shortly after, they released Karen and Marcela. The two women walked out together under the stars, hand in hand.

This story speaks for itself, but it will do no harm to spell out what it says. Karen did something that changed the minds of some unsympathetic, indeed pretty dehumanized, soldiers. What was it? Is it something *we* could learn to do? It's as though her very vulnerability put in her hands some kind of force that worked a minor miracle, even though Karen had not counted on it. She had not thought through how the soldiers would react when she walked back into that hellish place—she only knew she could not walk out on a friend.

Events like this (and they're not all that rare) are virtually never reported in the mainstream media—nor are, for that matter, what international volunteers have been doing in Central America, Hebron, Haiti, Sri Lanka, Northern Ireland, etc. The fact is, our usual way of thinking about conflict offers no ready explanation for such an occurrence. When and if we turn against violence we have bumper stickers that encourage us to "practice random acts of kindness and senseless acts of beauty"; but something is going on here that *isn't* random and senseless. There is a kind of logic to events like this with which we simply haven't reckoned.

In the slowly emerging field of peace research, however, people have begun to piece together the dynamic of such events. One of the foremost peace scholars of the twentieth century, Kenneth Boulding, developed a model toward the end of his long, polymathic career that seems to explain the situation very well. Boulding, a Quaker, distinguished economist, poet, and once president of the prestigious American Academy of Arts and Science, who had already made enormous contributions to peace research, wrote a book toward the end of his life called *The Three Faces of Power*.[3] We don't get one another to do things with only a carrot or a stick, he argued: we get things done by three different kinds of suasion we can exert on those around us. He called them *threat power* ("Do something I want or I'll do something you don't want"), *exchange power* ("Give me something I want and I'll give you something you want"), and *integrative power* (which I would paraphrase as "I'm going to do what I believe is right, something authentic, and we will end up closer").

All three kinds play their respective roles in the episode we're considering—and such a mixture, Boulding was quick to add, is how real life usually works. That the Salvadoran soldiers were using threat power is only too obvious. The Canadian government also relied on threat power of a kind, but they relied more on exchange power since they hinted they would pull out of trade agreements unless they got what they wanted (in addition to economic trade, a subtler medium of exchange, respect, and legitimacy was no doubt also involved). But Karen used the third, unfamiliar form called integrative power. We need not be too surprised if we are relatively at a loss to explain how this power works. As Boulding pointed out, "Threat power is particularly the concern of political scientists; economic power, of economists . . . [but] the study of integrative power seems to belong to no particular discipline."[4]

Let's start our own discipline, then. We can start with this reasoning: wherever there is a human need, there is a kind of power, insofar as others can be in a position to supply or withhold that need. One of the strongest needs of the human animal is for integration, for acceptance, community, fellowship. In her book *Human Nature—Revised,* my friend and colleague, biologist Mary Clark, pointed out that all human beings strive for three things above and beyond food, clothing, and shelter: (1) *bonding* (unconditional acceptance by other human beings), (2) *autonomy* (freedom of individual behavior), and (3) *meaning* (a sense of purpose in life). I think Clark did well to put bonding first. William Blake put it beautifully in *The Marriage of Heaven and Hell:* "The bird a nest, the spider a web, man, friendship."[5] Everyone has this need; even "lower" forms of life exhibit a powerful tendency to form communities, as life scientists are well aware. In fact, long before scientists of the modern kind documented this drive, Saint Augustine made it the basis of the peace theory he developed in his monumental classic *The City of God*. In the following passage, which to my knowledge is the first time in Western civilization that peace has been the subject of more than a passing mention, Augustine observed that even animals form families and societies of a kind:

> It is even more so with man. *By the very laws of his nature* he seems, so to speak, forced into fellowship and, as far as in him lies, into peace with every man.[6] (my emphasis)

It is by this law of nature that an act like Karen's has power, because she both opened the soldiers' eyes to Marcela's humanity and offered them an escape from their own hostility. It is because of this law that we are always moved by stories of reconciliation, more so when they come after bitter alienation. Think of former governor George Wallace coming to the reenactment of the Selma-to-Montgomery civil rights march to apologize for his former racism or, a bit earlier, the *Time* cover photo of Pope John Paul holding the hand of Mehmet Ali Agca, the man who had tried to assassinate him two years earlier. Who doesn't thrill to scenes like these? Even though Homo sapiens do an impressive job of hating and demonizing one another, apparently there is still some primal need within us for community, for integration, which we can smother but cannot utterly destroy. Nonviolence is the science of appealing to that need.

The human being is, as Aristotle named us, a "community animal" who craves fellowship despite himself or herself. That is why solitary confinement is the worst form of punishment for even the most unsociable of people. And why, conversely, anyone who plucks up the courage to offer opponents a way out of their conflict can find herself or himself wielding an unexpected power.

What Is Violence?

The "three faces" model can be resolved into a still simpler one of two opposed forces. We can call them, conventionally, violence and nonviolence—but to do so is to invoke words that are less than crystal clear.

The word *violence* comes from *violare* in classical Latin. That is useful, for etymologies often allow us to peer into a time when some things were more innately understood than they are now. *Violare* means "to bear in on with force" and in the classical period it came to mean "injure, dishonor, outrage, violate."[7] Like all important words, *violence* has extended, metaphorical meanings. We speak about "a violent storm" or say, "I got a violent shock when my car hit the pothole," but that's not the kind of violence we're concerned with in this book. Even the predatory behavior of animals isn't really that kind of violence; a lion may be very hard on a lamb, but that's how nature works (or one way nature works). The lion does not "dishonor, outrage, or violate" the lamb that instinct drives it to kill; it just kills that lamb. Another way of looking at it is, there is no bond between the lion and the lamb that is torn asunder when the predator strikes. Animals have a wide range of emotions, but righteous indignation isn't one of them, so far as we can tell.

Violence, as I mean the term, is a human phenomenon. We are violent when we injure one another, or any part of the subtly interconnected biosphere—of life. Elevate to the highest degree that sense of sacred connectedness that violence harms and you can say, with French resistance fighter Jacques Lusseyran, "God is life, and everything that does violence to life is against God."[8] Animals compete with and prey on each other, but they do so in a mysteriously balanced, harmonious, and ordered way that could go on indefinitely—that is, in a word, sustainable. Not so humans. When we prey on each other, something goes shockingly wrong, and it has led to the devastation of whole societies. In that sense of violating the order of things, only humans can, properly speaking, be violent—or nonviolent.

Now, the concept of violence as injury also has to be limited, in two ways. First, even in the case of human beings, it is not violence when a person injures someone or something by accident. The law recognizes that. One person can injure another accidentally and they can remain friends—happens all the time. But if one person injures another *purposely,* one or both of them is going to have to do some work to erase that injury. And that work, incidentally, is a part of the nonviolent process.

Second, once we understand that violence tears the fabric of life, it follows that the real violence lies not in the act but in the very *intention* to injure, and this is exactly the meaning of the Sanskrit word for violence, *himsa.* Here we have to dip into the science of language for one brief, but crucial point. *Himsa* (the "m" indicates a nasal sound as in the French *dans)* comes from the root *han,* "to strike, slay"; but *himsa* is thought to be a special form of that root. It may well be what linguists call a *desiderative:* it means not the act but the *desire* or intention to do the act, in this case injure. The mind is very real to these ancients: "You have heard how it was said to our ancestors: You must not kill. . . . But I say this to you, that anyone who is angry with his brother will answer for it." [9] In fact, we at least pay lip service to this mind reality: does not the UNESCO Charter state, "War begins in the minds of men"? The point, though, is learning to *use* that perdurable wisdom, so it becomes not just a truism gracing some high-sounding documents but a practiced reality.

All violence arises, then, within the mind. By the same token, the hurt caused by violence can be psychological or spiritual as well as material and physical, which brings us close again to the meaning of the Latin word, "violate, dishonor." This is both good and bad. Bad because it is disquieting to realize that we can be violent when we're just sitting there, harboring bad thoughts but not hurting anyone physically. This is not particularly comforting—but after all, it is better to be aware of it if it's true. Almost all the approaches to violence we are currently taking are failures. Most of them, even if they manage to contain the problem over here, make it worse over there. Our approach to crime has put more and more people in prison (while barely denting the crime rate out on the streets); our approach to world peace seems to be leading to an endless series of wars; the "war on drugs" and the "war on terrorism" are costly, violent failures. So it's a great relief to get our finger, finally, on the pulse of the problem, even if it turns out that we're holding our own wrist.

In recent years, we have all become aware of one further clarification. To say that violence arises in the mind is not to say that all violence is done with our conscious will. There is a kind of violence we commit without being quite aware of it; in fact, a lot of what we'd have to call violence today arises not from any felt hostility but through passive or even unconscious willingness to take advantage of others. Does the nice shirt I'm wearing come from a comfortable factory in Wisconsin, or a sweatshop in Thailand? Is that homeless man the price of my company's success? Or my country's defense spending? Was a rain forest razed somewhere to bring the food I'm looking at right now onto my plate? Exploitation built into a social system is called *structural violence,* a term we owe to another great peace scholar, Johan Galtung. Although structural violence is very widespread today because of the way modern economic systems operate, it probably existed as soon as human beings got organized into complex societies. When the Buddha defined a nonviolent person centuries ago he used the telling phrase *Na hante, na hanyate,* "He or she does not kill *nor cause to kill.*" He or she does not consciously cooperate in any system that hurts life.

Even in the case of violence of which we are not quite aware, however, the key issue is intention. There is a saying in Latin, *Quod ultimum est in executione, primum est in intentione,* "What finally comes out as action was first in intention." Children growing up in a world that's partly built on structural violence may take a long time to become aware of its presence, and until they do they may unwittingly benefit at the expense of others: no one would call them violent for doing so. Only when they go on cheerfully benefitting *after* becoming aware of this can they be called in some degree violent—which may be one reason people resist being educated about violence. It would be misleading to call unwitting participation in a wrong system violence; in other words, suppressed awareness is different from awareness that has not yet dawned.

All these considerations lie within the very useful definition of violence arrived at by Galtung: violence is an *avoidable insult to human needs*.[10] This definition keeps in view the hidden, or "structural," violence that I have just been describing, a violence that makes its way into the institutions of virtually all known societies. But it also suggests something extremely important about that or any kind of violence: the word *avoidable* suggests that life could be lived without such insults, that in an ideal world all violence could be avoided. This is an important article of faith shared by all who have believed in the possibility of widespread nonviolence down the ages, not excluding our own time. Accidents happen, conflict is inevitable, disputes will normally arise. But none of these necessarily cause *violence.* Conflicts and disputes can be creatively resolved without violence. Violence is an unnecessary evil.

Here again the model of integrative power can be helpful. At a deep level, whoever commits real violence, i.e., nurses an intention to harm someone, suffers from the very intention—never mind the consequences of any resultant action. We have all heard by now of Post-Traumatic Stress Disorder (PTSD). But there is a new concept psychologists are studying called Perpetration-Induced Traumatic Stress (PITS) that documents exactly this kind of trauma.[11] Violence cuts both ways. If the web between two parties is torn, both parties feel the tear (in fact, in a more remote sense, everyone in the web feels it). Thus violence is a question for psychologists before it becomes a question for lawmakers or criminologists, and Saint Augustine, once again, who knew the mind as perhaps few others in the Western world do, put it beautifully: "Imagine someone thinking that his *enemy* could do him as much harm as his own *enmity* that he harbors against him."[12]

In our modern culture, perhaps the best way we can appreciate this principle is in the extensive medical evidence on what it does to our health to hate, to be unable to forgive.[13] Violence, by any meaning-ful definition, is a phenomenon that cries out to be repaired, something that in an ideal world human beings would not do to one another—or to the environment or any of its living inhabitants. More important, it is something they'd be very likely to *stop* doing if we could somehow make them aware that they're hurting themselves along with their vic-tims. Keep this thought in the back of your mind, because it's the key to an entirely new way to deal with violence. It's the key to the new world we're looking for.

THREE LENSES

Some years ago, the city of Walnut Creek, California, ran into an intractable problem that is still coming up in many American commu-nities. A gay teacher was under attack by parents who had a somewhat fundamentalist outlook. They did not want their children influenced by such a "sinful" person. Unfortunately for that community, the peo-ple who wanted to defend this man's right to teach and the people who wanted him out of the classroom could not communicate with each other, and the reason was that they were using incompatible models to characterize him and to think about what was at issue. The defenders saw it as a question of his civil rights, while the irate parents saw it as the religious well-being of their kids. In other words, the for-mer were using a *political model* and the latter, a *religious,* or a *moral, model.* This is a very common kind of dilemma today, and it can cause bitter confusion.

It's clear that the way we think about violence is extremely imprac-tical, because violence goes on increasing; and if you think about it, the main reason for this is that we use the logic of violence itself in our attempts to control violence: the "war on drugs," the "war on crime," the "war on terrorism"—one researcher even referred to modern medicine as a "war on bugs." All this has led to virtually no useful meas-ures for making violence a progressively smaller part of our life.

What we need is a completely different logic, or, as the Walnut Creek example shows, a different window or frame of reference with which to think about the problem. I'm going to outline three such windows, or "lenses" (to use a term from Howard Zehr's important 1990 book, *Changing Lenses*): one that's most commonly in use; a better one that's coming into use; and one that I, at least, think we should use.

The Moral Model

The way we think about violence today is closely akin to the moral model invoked by the distraught parents in the Walnut Creek school; we tend to think of violence as a sin (something that violates the laws of God) or a crime (something that violates the laws of society, of humankind). Unfortunately, we no longer have a generally agreed-upon concept of what "sin" or even "crime" means: how do we define what's "moral"—those of us who still invoke the term?

In modern culture, human relationships seem to be sliding more and more into a state of raw competition; more and more of the interactions between us are thought of in a win/lose framework. As the definition of what is legal becomes increasingly a matter of negotiation by lawyers, our agreed-upon concept of natural law, that which formal legislation is supposed to represent, is steadily weakening. The mass media are a bad influence in this unfortunate process. As far as the media are concerned, a legal process, like the political process itself, is construed as a power struggle between the participants—and, secondarily, entertainment for the general public. "Mafia Murder Trial Provides Colorful Theater for New Yorkers," ran a recent headline of the *San Francisco Chronicle*.[14]

Looking on violence as a crime or sin, when both crime and sin have become so vague, has had an extremely unfortunate effect on our thinking. Recall Jacques Ellul's characterization of our age, the age when we began to become conscious of violence in a new way. We have now an unparalleled opportunity to take a great step forward in human culture, by taking advantage of this new awareness to *deal* with violence at last. Instead, almost the opposite has happened: "violence" has become something we *want:* "The new action thriller which crash-lands at Bay Area theaters has all the modern virtues," said a *Chronicle* review on June 6, 1997. And what were those virtues? "*Violence,* volume, stupidity"—all those good things. While this review may have been partly tongue-in-cheek, check any video store or mass-market bookshelf: you'll find that "violent" now means "thrilling"—the sense of right and wrong is gone. What is the use of calling violence an unnecessary evil, which it is, when no one can relate to the term *evil* except as a technical term in some people's religious vocabulary?

Using the moral model as a window on violence can also intensify rather than mask the nature of violence—and here the problems involved are, if anything, more serious. Since we still do have a strong emotional response to violence (which in itself is a good thing), to label a person or group as "violent" can bring down on them the strongest feelings of hatred and righteous indignation. The next step is to slap polarizing labels on them, like "impure" or "guilty," which make us quickly forget that those people are, after all, human beings. This is called scapegoating, and though it can arise as a knee-jerk reaction to violence, it is, ironically, itself a dangerous form of violence. It is no coincidence that the architects of the Holocaust deliberately used images of dirt and impurity to put their intended victims beyond reach of human sympathy, and they have had many imitators.

When my book *America Without Violence* appeared in 1982, I was interviewed on a major radio station late at night in New York. I was shocked at the reaction of the listeners. It seemed that every caller was blaming the violence (all of it) on his or her own favorite enemy: "You know perfectly well it's the Puerto Ricans." "Have you read the statistics on blacks under twenty-five?" "It's white men that are causing all the violence," and so forth. This is the same mistake the Berkeley students were making when they focused on hate crimes against Asians, only here it was the victimizers instead of the victims who were being singled out in groups, as though groups, not violence, were the issue. Since that time, we've remained far from taking the necessary steps in

our thought from the manifestation to the cause (and no one's deny-
ing that some groups of people commit more violence than others, for
whatever reason), and a more tragic category has been singled out for
blame: "It's the teenagers." Racism is bad enough, but if we've reached
the point of scapegoating our own children, then our approach to
violence is going to cost us more than the malady. It could cost us our
civilization.

The failures of the moral window are particularly obvious in the
area of criminal justice, and we'll be revisiting this area in chapter 5.
What I propose to do now is just close the moral window altogether.
We don't need to find out who is to blame for all the violence; we just
need to find out how to make it stop.

The Medical Model

A newer model that has been much more effective is the medical
model. In this way of thinking, violence is not unlike a disease, and
peace is a kind of health. This is probably a much more accurate way
to think about violence than to construe it as a sin or crime. Note how
readily medical people are able to cut to the chase and not be caught
up in the particulars about violence in the following from the first
issue of *Medical Abstracts Newsletter*:

> It is the leading cause of lost life in the U.S. today. It
> kills more people than AIDS or cancer. It has shown
> no signs of cure. It is *violence* . . .[15] (their emphasis)

Violence as disease is not a new idea, of course. Augustine made
good use of it in developing his famous definition of peace as
"the harmony that comes from the ordered relationship of all parts"
of, for example, the body. But most of us will remember how,
during the antinuclear era, the peace movement was carried to
unprecedented heights by doctors, and in particular one very elo-
quent and caring doctor, Helen Caldicott. What made Physicians for

Social Responsibility and its European counterparts so effective was not just the fact that doctors have a deserved authority for most people, or even that the extension of their role from preserving people's health one by one to keeping them alive by the millions is only natural; it was the vivid image of the war system as dysfunctional—sick, if you will. That made it much easier for millions of people to work against this system, including many who had uncritically thought of war as highly patriotic and a form of "defense." That new lens made antiwar activists who had been stridently protesting war preparations quite a bit more effective, since it gave people something sensible rather than recriminatory to do about it. Politicians are people, this model reminded. If you reason with them you *can* get them to understand you; while as long as you're pointing fingers of blame at them, they will only shrink away and harden their stance, if not their hearts.[16]

The power of the medical window became very real one summer day in 1993 in the emergency room of a Los Angeles hospital. A distraught woman entered the hospital intending to gun down a nurse she believed was having an affair with her estranged husband. She found the woman she was looking for and shot but did not kill her. The wounded nurse lurched down to the emergency room with her assailant in pursuit. ER nurse Joan Black was on duty. She had heard the code signal that a person with a gun was loose in the hospital moments before her wounded fellow nurse and then the woman, .38 in hand, burst through the door. Black, sixty-two, reacted with the instincts of an experienced medical person: "I put my arm around her and started talking to her. She kept saying that she didn't have anything to live for, that this woman had stolen her family. I kept saying, 'You're in pain. I'm sorry, but everybody has pain in their life. . . . I understand and we can work it out.'"[17] (The story about the shooting was front-page news; Nurse Black's heroic saving of the situation appeared only in a later section. What can you do?) Talking steadily like this, and in the meantime pushing down the gun every time the woman tried to kill herself with it, Black finally calmed her down.

The classicist in me has to point out something here before we go on. Nurse Black instinctively followed, point for point, the pattern laid down by the ancients for calming distraught or inconsolable people. First of all you identify with, rather than blame, them ("You're in pain. I'm sorry . . ."). Then you give them some detachment by reminding them of the first thing we all lose sight of when we're in such a state— that what they're going through is a universal human experience ("Everybody has pain in their life"). Remember Hamlet's uncle: "You must know your father lost a father / That father lost, lost his . . ." You can also remind them that the unbearable moment they are experiencing has got to pass, then finally exhort them to snap out of it ("We can work it out"). The fact that Nurse Black was inspired to deliver this perfect imitation of a classical *consolatio* at such a moment illustrates something about the universality of human dynamics that we'll make use of later.

Joan Black must be a great ER nurse. Certainly in this case she succeeded in quelling an extremely violent situation partly because she *was* a nurse, and on duty in an emergency room. All this allowed her to see the situation quite differently than if she had, say, been confronted with a gunman in a dark alley. She did not "see" a criminal coming through the door, but a patient. She literally said: "I saw a sick person and had to take care of her." The newspapers almost entirely missed the point; always wedded to a wrong model of violence, they seized on a remark of hers that is completely misleading: "That was probably the stupidest thing I've done in my life." But that's the newspapers' problem, and not ours, as long as we don't believe in them. Joan Black was a hero and she was able to do an extraordinary thing in the face of violence. Why? Because she saw the perpetrator as a patient, a person in trouble, not a criminal.

Three thousand miles away in another emergency room, a medical student named Deborah Prothrow-Stith had a rather different epiphany. Fortunately, she was able to grasp and hold onto it—in fact, to turn it into an institution. It happened one night after she stitched up a young man who had just been wounded in a knife fight. While she was getting him ready for release he turned to her and said, "Don't go to bed . . . the guy who did this to me is going to be in here in about an hour." It was partly meant in jest, partly male bravado, but Prothrow-Stith, a medical person and the mother of a teenage son, pondered what he had said. The futility, the absurdity of patching up the victims of violence *after* it has happened, without doing anything about the causes, was made clear to her. It was against everything she was learning in medicine: an ounce of prevention is worth a pound of cure, for the disease of violence as for any other. Later, when Prothrow-Stith went on to become the Massachusetts commissioner of public health, she founded an educational and mediation program to prevent teen violence with a curriculum that has been followed in 325 cities in forty-five states. She put it well:

> The mission in the criminal justice system is to estab-
> lish blame when there has been a violent episode and
> to institute the punishment. That's an appropriate
> mission but it's not a preventive mission. So what we
> advocate in [my book] *Deadly Consequences*—and in
> this movement to look at violence as a health problem
> —is that we start talking about prevention.[18]

Interestingly, Prothrow-Stith also gave a superb definition of structural violence in a widely aired interview:

> Quite honestly, if you define violence very narrowly
> as physical injury, then you limit your understanding
> . . . a lack of opportunity, an education system that
> doesn't work, even a family that doesn't work—those
> are very violent experiences.[19]

Health and illness are very good analogies for peace and violence; to use them is far more practical than trying to use the concept of crime and punishment, however appropriate that may sometimes feel. Thinking of violence as disease takes blame out of the picture: unless you're George Bernard Shaw, you don't blame people for getting sick. For another, it puts your focus where it belongs, where efficiency and compassion want it to go—on prevention. When you can do something creative that addresses the root causes of violence Prothrow-Stith just cited, deep in the societal and family systems, you are doing something vastly more effective than putting more police on the streets or stronger deadbolts on your front door; something that some health professionals, borrowing a term from peace scholar John Burton, have called *provention*.

The Educational Model

Despite the utility of the medical window, I am going to open still a third one. If violence is not a sin but more like a disease, it is even more like a kind of ignorance. I believe that a beloved mystic of modern India, Swami Ramdas, meant it perfectly literally when he said:

> Ignorance is the cause of all quarrel and strife in the
> world. Ignorance is not a crime. It does not deserve
> to be condemned, but it has to be removed. And by
> the power of your love, you can remove ignorance.[20]

This seems to me to sum up the nature of violence in a nutshell—and direct us toward its "provention." To look at violence as a kind of ignorance helps immediately to see wisdom and love as the solution.

Once I was in a heated discussion at an impromptu seminar with a group of journalists in San Francisco. A Berkeley colleague turned to me and said, "OK, what is violence?" and I shot back, "A failure of imagination." While I'm still not entirely sure what I meant, I think I was groping in my own dim way toward Swami Ramdas's insight. If I don't have the imagination to realize that you and I are one, despite our physical separateness and the differences in our outlooks on life, what's to prevent me from using violence if I think you're getting in my way? You might almost say that there's a kind of violence already being done in that very failure to see that we're one—violence to the truth.

Ignorance, as Swami Ramdas implies, can be cured. Failures of imagination can be reversed. Love plays some kind of role in both these processes.

OK, What Is Nonviolence?

My good friend Alain Richard and I were commiserating in an out-of-the-way restaurant in San Francisco just before he went back to his native France after many years' work as a leading nonviolent activist. The topic of our commiseration was how unhelpful the word *nonviolence* often is, and how no one has come up with a good substitute. But Alain had found a brilliant way to describe nonviolence without calling it that when he was giving workshops in rural Africa some time back. Forget nonviolence, he told me: "I started off by asking them, have any of you (they were mostly village women) ever used inner, moral power against physical force?" Sure enough, he told me, hands shot up. One woman offered this story: Her husband used to beat her a lot. Once, though, something snapped inside her, and instead of trying to protect herself she stood up and looked him right in the eye and said, "Why don't you just kill me and get it over with?" He never struck her again.

Everything I've said about the "shadow side," about violence, was a good preparation, but only that, for the real job that we can tackle now, which is understanding the power that so dramatically changed this woman's husband. Violence is disintegrative, while nonviolence is integrative power; it is, like the intention to harm, first of all a question of mind, and only then an expression of a state of mind in action. And it can be *learned*. It is the implications of that learning process that mainly concern us.

As the Davitz experiment showed, it can be surprisingly easy for people to learn positive, cooperative, and even self-sacrificing behavior. This is because, upholders of nonviolence argue, what they're really doing is *un*learning aggressive, competitive, and other-sacrificing behavior, which has been superimposed on the former. When I say that nonviolence can be learned, I do not mean that it wasn't there already. It actually was, but a lot of the conditioning that makes us social humans today seems to obscure it. The conditioning is secondary, and can therefore be dislodged relatively easily: last in, first out. The biggest problem with civilization as we know it is that it has somehow taken the shadow for the light.

Let me call on etymology, as I did with violence.

The term *nonviolence* (or *non-violence*, as it is still sometimes spelled) is barely a century old (unlike the term *violence!*), having first appeared, to be exact, in 1923.[21] *Nonviolence* serves as a literal—but, as it turns out, misleading—translation of the Sanskrit word *ahimsa*, the negation of *himsa*, "(desire, intent to) harm." In accordance with what we've already seen, *ahimsa* would mean "the absence of the desire, or intention, to harm." But this negative (the *a-* prefix in Sanskrit is basically like the same prefix in Greek, which we take up in English, cf. *amoral*) needs a little explanation. Unlike the situation in English, the *non* word in Sanskrit is as old as its opposite: *ahimsa* appears in texts even older than Gandhi's venerable "reference book," the Bhagavad Gita (written down roughly from 200 B.C.E. to 200 C.E.). And again unlike the English situation, in Sanskrit abstract nouns often name a fundamental positive quality indirectly, by negating its opposite. Thus *courage* is conveyed by *abhaya*, which literally means "non-fear"; or we encounter *akrodha*, "non-anger," for "kindness," and the Buddha's *avera*, "non-hatred," meaning "love."[22] The reason ancient India's great thinkers expressed themselves in this apparently oblique way is that phenomena like love, absolute courage, and compassion are primordial things that cannot be fully expressed in fallible, conditioned human language. As many texts remind us, whatever we think or say about God falls short of the truth. English does not do that (though "infinite" might invite comparison), with the result that *nonviolence* in English does not really convey the meaning of *ahimsa* in Sanskrit.

Ahimsa is not really a negative term, as to our ears *nonviolence* decidedly is. *Ahimsa* suggests something profoundly positive, which would not be possible to name directly. *Ahimsa,* a kind of double negative, actually stands for something so original that we cannot quite capture it with our weak words.

I have put you through all this linguistics because—well, for several reasons. Because it is humbling that modern languages are still struggling for a word to express everything that was enshrined millennia ago in the word *ahimsa*. Because that ancient term was so far ahead of us in prioritizing the mental dimension of violence/nonviolence; because, finally, in that misleading translation of *ahimsa* into an English negative we see the most important misunderstanding of violence, the mental block that has been preventing us from having the realization that, as Ellul suggested, our age needs to fulfill its promise: the realization that nonviolence, by whatever name, is a positive force that holds the solution to most of our major personal, social, and global problems.

Gandhi faced this obstruction from the outset of his career in South Africa. When they first met with his disconcerting new form of resistance, Westerners and Western-educated Indians looked for something at least partly familiar that they could compare it to; it must be like the tax refusal of "nonconformist" (i.e., non-Anglican) denominations back in England, they mused, and particularly like the women's suffrage movement that was raising eyebrows at that time.[23] There, too, a minority was fighting for its rights without using physical violence—but there, alas, the resemblance ended. The superficial similarity was "apt to give rise to a terrible misunderstanding," Gandhi feared, and it was, ironically, a staunch European friend of the movement whose fate it was to fall into the "terrible misunderstanding" in such a way that Gandhi had no choice but to pull him up short, in public.[23] In the pivotal year 1906, when the Indians' resistance had shown its mettle and the white settlers were thoroughly alarmed, this friend, William Hoskens, arranged a meeting of prominent Europeans to hear what the Indians were up to, and at that meeting he introduced

Gandhi with the following well-intentioned remarks:

> The Transvaal Indians have had recourse to passive
> resistance when all other means of securing redress
> proved to be of no avail. . . . Numerically, they are
> only a few. They are weak and have no arms.
> Therefore they have taken to passive resistance which
> is the weapon of the weak.[25]

A modern nonviolence scholar would wince at this classic mistake.
When he heard it, Gandhi dropped the nice speech he had prepared
and contradicted his well-meaning friend point for point. He wanted
to make it as clear as possible that the Indians' movement was different
in kind from that of the suffragists, even though both causes were just
and neither relied on physical violence. First of all, Gandhi explained,

> the suffragist movement did not eschew the use of
> physical force. But brute force had absolutely no
> place in the Indian movement in any circumstance,
> and . . . no matter how badly they suffered, the
> Satyagrahis never used physical force, and that too
> although there were occasions when they were in a
> position to use it effectively. Again, though the Indians
> had no franchise and were weak, these considerations
> had nothing to do with the organization of
> Satyagraha.[26]

As we can see, Gandhi had already invented a new word for what
he was doing—so misleading are both *nonviolence* and *passive resistance*.
Satyagraha, or "soul force," as he often paraphrased it, is no double
negative. It literally means "clinging to truth." It is not the "weapon of
the weak," as Hoskens thought, but the weapon of the strong—for
there is a kind of strength that does not come from numbers or from
weapons. It is in favor of this strength, which the nonviolent believe is

even greater, that the *satyagrahi* (a practitioner of Satyagraha) renounces the use of physical force, voluntarily and on principle. Later, back in India, instead of being a minority of 13,000, the resistors would be almost 300 million people, opposed by a mere 150,000 British colonials. The Indians still used Satyagraha, by choice.

Yet to this day, almost a century after Hoskens's gaffe, we go on repeating it—with no Gandhi around to correct us. A well-known journalist declared recently that Israeli settlers in Hebron, fully one-quarter of whom are heavily armed and fanatically ideological, are using "Gandhian tactics: i.e., passive resistance"[27] He did not know, and most of his readers would not know, that nonviolence and passive resistance can actually be as different as nonviolence and violence. Satyagraha is not passive and you are not being "Gandhian" when you are full of hatred but happen—for the moment—to be keeping your finger off the trigger. One could go on and on quoting examples of this confusion. They would be laughable if they were not so damaging.

It's often easier to see this confusion on a larger scale. It's fairly common knowledge now that peace is more than the absence of war (though what it *is* remains unclear to decision makers and most of us). I've mentioned that the Dayton accords were supposed to bring peace to ex-Yugoslavia but failed to address what was causing its wars— ethnic hatreds stirred up on state television by nationalistic politicians. This absence-of-war state today is rightly called "negative peace." One of the most egregious examples was greeted by well-deserved derision by antinuclear organizations when it was put forward, in all seriousness, by the Department of the Navy. They proposed to define peace as "perpetual prehostility." This is peace? (Can you imagine Jesus, his hand upraised in blessing, saying, "My perpetual prehostility I give unto you?")

But it's just as absurd to think that nonviolence is only the absence of (physical) violence as it is to think that peace is only some kind of interlude between wars. In both cases we would be trying to understand a light by studying its shadow. It is time to turn around and see what's casting it.

When I wrote *America Without Violence* back in 1982, the idea of "nature red in tooth and claw" had a firm grip on popular imagination, and I had an uphill battle trying to show that the picture painted by certain popularizers of ethology (the science of animal behavior) was wrong. Only a few scientists and philosophers, like Ashley Montagu and Mary Midgley, were trying to correct what Midgley called the "swashbuckling" view that nature is a violent place and the human being is a puppet pulled by nature's strings. That has begun to change. Soon after my book appeared, UNESCO convened a seminar of some of the world's most distinguished behavioral scientists to make a public statement on this theory of innate aggression. Unheralded, but crucial, the resulting Declaration of Seville, released in 1986, pilloried the popular view that a complex behavior like human aggression could be programmed by our genes, that we were therefore stuck with it.

This is not to say that the general run of behavioral scientists—not to mention the general public—would easily give up the "swashbuckling" image. The riptide of cynicism within our present culture pulls many of us back into the sea of hopelessness just when we have a chance to get up onto dry land, but here and there some scientists are starting to turn that tide.

One day in 1975, about a decade before Seville would appear, the Dutch primatologist Frans de Waal had a career-changing breakthrough in the Arnhem zoo. He suddenly realized that his chimpanzees had an extensive system of reconciliation behaviors—and scientists had never studied it.

> Fires start, but fires also go out. Obvious as this is, scientists concerned with aggression, a sort of social fire, have totally ignored the means by which the flames of aggression are extinguished. We know a great deal about the causes of hostile behavior in both animals and humans, ranging from hormones and brain activity to cultural influences. Yet we know little of the way

conflicts are avoided—or how, when they do occur, relationships are afterward repaired and normalized. As a result, people tend to believe that violence is more integral to human nature than peace.[28]

This revelation sounds familiar to anyone working on human violence. The first time I read this passage it occurred to me that at a time when five million teenagers were signed up for volunteer service jobs in their communities, and two teenage boys committed a particularly repellant murder, guess who got the coverage?[29]

The important thing to remember is, whatever model we use to think about human potential, whatever we believe we are, will tend very strongly to be self-fulfilling. Not to know that nonviolence is possible, or to think that it's only the province of a few hard-pressed activists on some ragged social fringe, is to be resigned to the everincreasing violence in our culture, and therefore condemned to endure it without remission. To know that nonviolence *is* possible, to know that it's not a non-something but a force grounded in nature and exampled in history, is to begin getting our culture back on course.

To say that nonviolence is possible means two things, and both are important. The first is that we have it in us to be nonviolent, to "offer Satyagraha," as Gandhians put it, even under tough circumstances. The second is that when we are, it "works." It will become clear why I put "works" in quotation marks later, but let me make some preliminary observations about how nonviolence helpfully affects those around us—or ranged against us.

A remarkable statement was made the first time Satyagraha was offered full blown in the modern era, during the Indians' struggle to recover their stolen dignity in South Africa, by a secretary to General Jan Christiaan Smuts, head of the South African government in the Transvaal, and Gandhi's chief adversary in this struggle. It gives us a glimpse of what it feels like to be offered high-quality Satyagraha by committed, well-trained activists:

I do not like your people, and do not care to assist them at all. But what am I to do? You help us in our days of need. How can we lay hands upon you? I often wish that you took to violence like the English strikers, and then we would know at once how to dispose of you. But you will not injure even the enemy. You desire victory by self-suffering alone . . . and that is what reduces us to sheer helplessness.[30]

As Midgley says, nature has to be green a long time before she is red. If we read between the lines of this testimonial (and there are similar things on record from the Franco-Belgian invasion of the Rhineland, some twenty years later, and from other events), we can sense something quite compelling at work that we might readily call an appeal to something deep and perhaps not normally visible in human nature. Gandhi's own explanation for the power of such an appeal constitutes, I think, one of the most insightful descriptions of nonviolence ever made:

What Satyagraha does in such cases is not to suppress reason but to free it from inertia and to establish its sovereignty over prejudice, hatred, and other baser passions. In other words, if one may paradoxically put it, it does not enslave, it compels reason to be free.[31]

Talk about an educational model! Any teacher will tell you that this is the kind of education we dream of, where the student doesn't just learn some facts, doesn't just learn how to put facts together, but awakens to a new realization. It is more a growth experience than just acquiring knowledge, and after *this* kind of learning one does not go back to sleep.

I once had a friend who smoked three packs a day. Bill knew—with his head—all about the effects of smoking on his health, but he somehow went right on smoking. Several times he tried to stop, without success. Then one night he had a dream that he was walking through a churchyard. As his dream eye moved over the tombstones, one epitaph caught his attention and he found himself zooming in on it:

HERE LIES BILL.
QUIT SMOKING AT LAST.

He never lit up again.

I submit that a successful nonviolent episode also works at this preconscious level. The Salvadoran soldiers suddenly and—as Gandhi implies, and Smuts's secretary confesses—almost in spite of themselves were allowed to "see" Marcela not as a thing tied to a chair, a "victim," but as a person because of Karen's act of extreme caring for her, and the brilliant connection she made between that concern of hers and their own comradely feelings for one another—their *compañeros*. Her courage, her love, and her assumption that they, too, were human beings capable of such feelings were the ingredients of her transformative effect on the men, her magic waking potion.

This kind of awakening, this rehumanization, is the highest kind of education, and it is the kind at which the nonviolent actor aims. As we'll see from many following examples, nonviolence is a whole-being experience, which has much more long-lasting effects than those obtained—or sometimes obtained—by threat power. When the German ranks broke in July of 1918, French infantrymen were heard to mutter at the fleeing enemy, "*Ils reviendront.*" They'll be back. How right the seasoned soldiers were, much more right, as we know to our devastating cost, than the giddy celebrations of the triumphant world, which only sobered up when, twenty years later, in a hail of shredded treaties, they came back, all right, with a vengeance.

Any act of coercion must produce an equal and opposite reaction. In his cell on death row in the Georgia State Prison, Brandon Astor Jones saw the following message, literally a handwriting on the wall, left by a previous inmate of that cell: "I will act the way I am treated, so help me God." Jones recalled, "Suddenly a chilling fear of—and for—society engulfs me as I remember the poignant pencil message scrawled on the wall" in Cell 38.[32]

As Hannah Arendt observed, "The practice of violence, like all action, changes the world, but the most probable change is to a more violent world."[33]

Real nonviolence, by contrast, rarely has a backlash, because if it's real nonviolence it does not operate by coercion. It operates by persuasion, often a kind of deep persuasion that moves people below the conscious level. "Compelling reason to be free," or as Gandhi put it elsewhere, "moving the heart," is qualitatively different from merely forcing others to do something by punishment or sanction. Since the opponents have changed willingly, they are not looking for an opportunity to get back at us. When Satyagraha works, it doesn't just change one party's position, it changes the *relationship* between parties. Once they have "seen" the situation from our point of view, those who once were our opponents move closer to us in spirit. This is integrative power. It is apparently no mean force, for Karen's courage did something that the entire government of Colombia was unable or unwilling to do. That's a lot of power! Something wakes up in a Karen Ridd or a Gandhi—or you and me—and that something is going to change people. It is not something learned with our intellect (though the intellect can later help us understand it) but heart knowledge. And one of its characteristics is that it communicates itself on the same "gut level" to onlookers.

> [Martin Luther] King started from the essentially religious persuasion that in each human being, black or white, whether deputy sheriff or manual laborer or governor, there exists, however tenuously, a certain natural identification with every other human being; that, in the overarching design of the universe which ultimately connects us all together, we tend to feel that what happens to our fellow human beings in some

way also happens to us, so that no man can continue to debase or abuse another human being without eventually feeling in himself at least some dull answering hurt and stir of shame. Therefore, in the catharsis of a live confrontation with wrong, when an oppressor's violence is met with a forgiving love, he can be vitally touched, and even, at least momentarily, reborn as a human being, while the society witnessing such a confrontation will be quickened in conscience toward compassion and justice.[34]

RECONSIDERING HISTORY AND SCIENCE

We have now begun to see some of the deeper implications of the educational model as the approach of choice for reducing—who knows, perhaps someday eliminating—violence. It is through this model that we most easily grasp the key fact that nonviolence is fundamentally a kind of *force*. Gandhi, at least, used that kind of language in his earliest period:

> Power is of two kinds. One is obtained by fear of punishment, and the other by acts of love. Power based on love is a thousand times more effective and permanent than the one derived from fear of punishment.[35]

Or again:

> Sanctions are of two kinds: one, physical force, and two, soul force—Satyagraha. Physical force is nothing compared to the power of truth.[36]

Today, science itself is learning to speak another language. The mind-boggling discoveries of "new physics" are widely felt to hold deeper significance for what we think the world is than any conceptual breakthrough in recorded history, and the implications for areas beyond the physical world (one of the major breakthroughs has been precisely to breach that barrier between the material and other worlds) are intriguing but far from understood. As this new language has slowly made its way from the minds of physicists to the world at large, it has given us a new and promising vocabulary to describe the nature and the effectiveness of nonviolence, which was rather difficult to account for in the "hard" language of Newtonian objects.[37] The noted criminologist Harold Pepinsky is one person who has taken advantage of the new, more powerful vocabulary (where he has said "responsiveness," I would say "nonviolence"):

> Violence and responsiveness operate by the same principles at all levels, from the interpersonal to the international. Every human being . . . is at once the subject and the object of both violent and responsive energy. Crosscurrents of violence and responsiveness run constantly in all of us, and help to account for perversity and unanticipated behavior at any given level.[38]

However we name these forces, we human beings experience them as a deep choice which is extremely simple—and here Pepinsky uses more conventional language: "From moment to moment, it is a profoundly religious choice whether to commit to violence or to democracy."[39]

Whether we use a scientific or a religious vocabulary, Pepinsky's insight brings out something quite odd: why is it that we are usually so unaware of nonviolence? If it is a moment-to-moment reality, should we not be talking about it cogently and often? Should it not be common fare in history and science, among other venues?

Sometimes, it seems, we are better at perceiving what are *not* moment-to-moment realities, just as it is hard to "see" the Milky Way because we're part of it, hard to see things that are in the woodwork instead of sitting out there on the table. The ancient Greeks, that most inquisitive people, discussed how to wage war and manage slaves at great length, but they never discussed war or slavery as such, or for that matter economics, or the position of women. So the history of nonviolence is just beginning to be written and there's as yet no account of it in standard behavioral science. This was a galling frustration for Gandhi. By the time he wrote his classic 1909 manifesto, *Hind Swaraj,* or "Indian Home Rule," he knew that he was up against more than an empire; it was nothing less than what we would call today an outworn, inadequate paradigm. "History" as we knew it in this paradigm was constitutionally unable to help.

> The fact that there are so many men still alive in the world shows that it is based not on the force of arms but on the force of truth or love. . . . Little quarrels of millions of families in their daily lives disappear before the exercise of this force. Hundreds of nations live in peace. History does not and cannot take note of this fact. History is really a record of the interruption of the even working of the force of love or the soul. . . . History, then, is a record of the interruptions of the course of nature. Soul-force, being natural, is not noted in history.[40]

Those are sobering words, which anyone who has tried to get the press to cover a nonviolent event can verify. The case of the unreported teenagers doing volunteer service to their communities I mentioned is only one example of millions. During the sixties a daylong student demonstration at Columbia University was disrupted for exactly one minute by a fracas of some sort, very possibly caused by outsiders and even provocateurs. That evening, on the network news, exactly one minute was dedicated to reporting on the students' demonstration. Guess which one? 1909 to 1969—nothing changed. The press was still doing this, albeit with a slight budge of difference, in Seattle in 1999. How many people died, I wonder, while the learning curve lay there, flat as a Kansas prairie?

Yes, the news media sometimes suppress stories of corruption in high places; that is political bias. But there is a cultural bias that runs even deeper and may be doing us much more damage in the long run. By this bias, nonviolent stories are not so much suppressed as they are plain not observed.

This cultural bias is a paradigm that embraces all aspects of human knowledge, like an embrace with only one arm. Some years ago, when I was serving as a dean, I got a call from a graduate student who was looking for some leads on aggression among primates. No scientist myself, I was known around campus for my interest in this area, and the student had been sent to me by one of the best behavioral scientists at Berkeley. There was something odd about our conversation, and I was shocked when I realized what it was: he had not the foggiest idea that the theory of innate aggression was controversial. He just assumed—his mentors had led him to assume—that our primate cousins behave with raw aggression, competition, and win/lose struggle—period; though, as Gandhi observed, if nature was set up to work that way it would not have lasted very long. In the words of Frans de Waal:

> I speak from years of frustration with the literature
> on human behavior. . . . Except for reports on pre-
> school children [as we saw in the last chapter] and an
> occasional anthropological account, I am unaware of
> data in this area. . . . I recently asked a world-
> renowned American psychologist, who specializes in
> human aggression, what he knew about reconciliation.
> Not only did he have no information on the subject,
> but he looked at me as if the word were new to him.[41]

Traces of the Future

A few years after the execution of Jesus, in 39 C.E. to be exact, the emperor Caligula conceived the insane idea of having a statue of himself as incarnate Zeus installed in the great temple in Jerusalem. To Caligula, for whom excesses in the pursuit of egotism were no vice, this must have seemed a wonderful idea, but for once his excess was going to blow up in the imperial face. As his Syrian legate, Petronius, advanced on Jerusalem to carry out the disastrous order, people of all kinds and stations began flooding into the capital—men, women, and children—collecting together in their alarm from cities, villages, and farms from the whole area west of Galilee. They came without weapons in their hands, some of them holding emblems of allegiance to the empire, but they told Petronius in no uncertain terms that this sacrilege could not be allowed. Petronius of course threatened to unleash his troops on them. They replied that they were perfectly willing to die rather than see such an outrage to their religion.[42]

Petronius, no particular friend of the Jews, was nonetheless at a loss about how to handle this unarmed resistance. Unable to persuade them, and loath to massacre them wholesale (something that legates had done enthusiastically with violent uprisings), he backed down and took the risk of writing to Rome to make some excuses for stalling the emperor's less-than-brilliant scheme. Caligula, true to form, immediately sent orders for Petronius's execution. But at this point fate intervened. Caligula was assassinated, which saved Petronius, and, for now, the Jewish religion in its homeland.

This successful Satyagraha, however much it took Petronius unawares, was not an isolated occurrence. Apparently, there was something in Jewish culture at that period that evoked this response from masses of people even though the "normal" kind of resistance, violent resistance, as we well know, was not ruled out and would finally prevail, with disastrous results. Jesus was without doubt on the nonviolent side to the extent that his teaching bore on any kind of social action. In any case, scholar John Crossan finds no less than seven popular uprisings of this very different type between 4 C.E. and 65 C.E., and reports that "all . . . were nonviolent, all had very specific objectives, and four out of the seven achieved those objectives without loss of life."[43]

Now *that's* history. If nonviolence is a law, as we have been suggesting, it should have left traces all over the historical record. And we find—now that the bias toward violence is beginning to relax—that it did. Its history, more forgotten, more overlooked even than the history of women's experience, with which it is in several ways interconnected, is beginning to be recovered. This vital work is being done not just by historians of nonviolence per se—and here we can acknowledge our debt to Peter Brock, Thomas Weber, Staughton and Alice Lynd, among others—but by mainstream historians like John Crossan who are beginning to show greater sensitivity to the role played by organized nonviolence in the stream of human events. This is essential. Our object must be to elevate nonviolence from the tiny, specialized field it now occupies and show that it is the concern not of activists, not of the downtrodden, but of everyone. It is our heritage. It is something every one of us can use, and if we want not just to reduce a particular type of crime or protect some particular victims but to get *violence* out of our path, it is probably the only thing we can use.

If we put the temple statue Satyagraha alongside the much smaller action of Karen Ridd that we began with (smaller in terms of how many people were involved), we see that the same driving force lay behind each of them, and we can understand why many have not hesitated to call that force love—meaning not the emotion that we usually call by that name, but a self-sacrificing devotion such as Karen had for her friend (and her cause), which was so strong that it overcame her fear for her own life, just as the Jewish masses' intense love for their religion, their culture, caused them to put their own lives without hesitation at the mercy of the Roman swords. And this force, for which *love* seems to be a reasonable term, is always there in human consciousness. It is unfortunate that, particularly in times like ours, we find it so hard to see that force beneath the surface of events. But that is changing.

Nonviolence is law, not luck. Satyagraha is not hit or miss. There are undoubtedly, as Pepinsky says, elements of "perversity" and surprise outcomes when we're dealing with something so subtle as a "living force" (as Gandhi called it); that does not mean that we can't learn more about that force and begin using it more systematically. Because a computer goes down, for reasons known only to itself, that doesn't mean there is no such thing as electromagnetic energy or that we'll never succeed in putting it to work. Even though we can't always predict exactly how a nonviolent intervention will turn out on the visible surface of things, we can still develop nonviolence exactly as we would a force of nature. In fact, nonviolence *is* a force of nature—only it happens to be a force of human nature, which is the trickiest kind. We human beings are, as science writer Louise Young put it, "complex, volatile, and impressionable." But to repeat, that does not mean that no laws govern our behavior. Or that only negative ones do.

> The message that comes down to us from Easter Island is the way violence breeds more violence. Acts of cruelty become progressively easier to commit when they are reinforced by example and supported by tradition. On the other hand, acts of kindness and compassion can be reinforced in a civilized society. Human nature is complex, volatile, and impressionable. Capable of both good and evil, it can be influenced by life experiences. An education in violence uncovers the beast in the human nature.[44]

And an education in *non*violence? We have the pleasure of exploring that right now.

CHAPTER THREE

NO POWER TO DESCRIBE:
THE "NONVIOLENT MOMENT"
AS PEAK EXPERIENCE

Either I don't give in to my rage, which means going crazy . . .
or give in to it, which means I go to jail.

—Franklin Smith, American teenager

WHEN MY SPIRITUAL teacher was still living in India, on the Nilgiri Hills, he had a friend who was very much like himself: a compassionate, sensitive nature and strong feelings about justice and fairness. One morning the two of them were walking through the bazaar and came upon a villager with a caged bear. The cage was so small that the poor beast could hardly turn around; it seemed to Sri Easwaran and his friend to be crying out with its eyes. They walked off without speaking. Later that day, Easwaran went to call on his friend and found him trembling with anger. "I'm going to take my gun to the bazaar," he burst out. "I'm going to set that bear free, and shoot anyone who tries to stop me."

"Wait a minute," Easwaran put in hastily, "hold on just a bit; let me see what I can do."

First, he went to the owner to try to reason with him. It turned out that the man, a simple villager, was from his own state of Kerala, so it wasn't hard to broach the subject after chatting awhile in their native language: "Look here, don't you think that creature is suffering in such a small cage?"

"Do you think I like to keep him penned up like that?" he explained. "But what can I do? A new cage would cost me more than a month's earnings."

"Would you be willing to use a decent cage if I could get one built for you?"

"Of course."

Next stop: the local carpenter. By luck, he turned out to be a Kerala man also. Easwaran explained the situation and then came to the point: "You give me your rock-bottom price for a new cage."

"Brother, I have a family to feed, but for you . . ."

Then back to his angry friend: "Suppose we could get a better cage built for so-and-so many rupees and the owner agreed to use it, would you put up the money?"

"Gladly. . . . But that owner will never agree."

"He's already agreed."

Sri Easwaran was as angry as his friend at the sight of the dumb animal's suffering. It's important to realize that, but equally important is the key difference in approach. One saw a path to a solution, and quickly took it, while the other was hung up between the choices we're all too familiar with, the dilemma that teenager Franklin Smith called "living a crazy man or dying a sane one." And so he fumed, while Sri Easwaran set about writing a happy ending for the bear, for his friend, the carpenter, the owner—and doubtless himself.

Only a minor event, if you want to look at it that way. But you could also look at it as a parable. How many crises does our government face every year to which it reacts with either violence or capitulation, either imposing sanctions, as with Iraq, or fuming helplessly, as with Bosnia, East Timor, and Tibet?

It is all rather reminiscent of the two kinds of students—or rather two kinds of training given to students—in the Davitz experiment. The nonviolent are not people who don't feel anger—on the contrary, they can often prize anger (at least, the kind of anger Sri Easwaran and his friend felt) because, first of all, that capacity to feel for others, which sometimes means getting angry over what is happening to them, is one of the things that makes us fully human. Second, and more important, that kind of anger is potentially the emotional power to correct the situation. For, in light of the Davitz experiment, we would not say that Sri Easwaran did what he did in spite of his anger; he did it *with* his anger. By not giving in to his angry impulse to do something to that bear owner but instead looking for a constructive way to help the bear and its owner, he unconsciously converted the energy he was feeling as anger into constructive effort. Emotions are power. By themselves, however, they are not necessarily wisdom. Wisdom was for him to choose, which he did. In that choice, when he blocked one path, the other opened.

This impromptu "shuttle diplomacy" was actually a fairly obvious solution, when you think about it. The trouble is that when we get angry, most of us can't think about it. Just when we're motivated to do something, we lose sight of the obvious thing to do: as an old proverb puts it, "Anger is a wind that blows out the lamp of the mind"—unless our mind is alert enough to set its sails for a better course.

If you still think this was a small event, think back to one that had exactly the same dynamic, but changed the course of history. I am thinking of the anger Gandhi experienced that fateful night of May 31, 1893, when he was thrown off the train at Pietermaritzburg a week after his arrival in South Africa. This was no minor irritation; according to his own testimony, Gandhi was furious. That, along with the fact that Gandhi is more than usually articulate about his inner experiences, is what makes this event (among millions of similar insults human beings endure at one another's hands) such an important window into the dynamics of nonviolent conversion. The first clue as to how he finally succeeded, after a night of bitter reflection, to see the creative way out is that he didn't take the insult personally; he saw in it the whole tragedy of man's inhumanity to man, the whole outrage of racism. Not "they can't do this to me," but "how can we do this to one another?" The second clue is the state of his faith in human nature. Already at that period he believed that people could not stay blind to the truth forever. He did not yet know how to wake them up; he just knew they could not want to stay forever asleep. That is how he was able to find the third way between running home to India and suing the railroad company.

Imagine the old-fashioned locomotive carrying this "coolie barrister" from Durban up the mountains to Pretoria, standing at the station in Pietermaritzburg with a good head of steam. You could shovel in more coal and just bottle up all that power and even pretend it wasn't there, until finally it exploded, or you could just open the valves and scald everyone on the platform—but surely you would want to use it to drive the train. This is what Gandhiji was going through with all the emotional power built up in him by the accumulated insults he had met since his arrival at the Durban pier. He chose neither to "pocket the insult," as he said, nor to lash out at the immediate source of the pain. He launched what was to become the greatest experiment in social change in the modern world.

Within a few years of this event, Gandhi was working fifteen hours a day, seven days a week, at a pace that would frighten even an advanced workaholic. Two secretaries could not keep up with his correspondence any more than they could keep up with his breathtaking "walks," when he scampered off down the road each evening like a sandpiper. On a lecture tour in Gujarat, taking him to two, sometimes three, villages a day, he had to remind those arranging his punishing itinerary that he was only mortal. He would keep up this pace for fifty years, taking breaks only when conveniently detained in "His Majesty's prison." What untold damage that energy would have wrought if it had been stifled inside him, as it was in millions of other Indians groaning silently under the heel of imperialism, or vented as raw violence, which was dangerously close to happening with many of them.

PEAK EXPERIENCE

The escape from violence is often experienced as a kind of strange joy. You pay a price, often a heavy one, but the sudden discovery of the creative path out of the dilemma between fear and anger, capitulation and counterattack, comes with a great feeling of release. It has been called, as in Buddhism, the "middle way," but the best expression for it comes from someone who experienced it under extreme duress, Andrew Young, who used the words of an old spiritual, "the way out of no way."

An episode that beautifully illustrates this way occurred during a march for voter's rights in Birmingham, Alabama, in 1964. The marchers, mostly black, were converging on the city hall when they suddenly found their way blocked by a phalanx of police and firemen. They hadn't prepared for this eventuality, and not knowing what else to do, they knelt down to pray. One of those marchers reported what happened next:

> [After awhile, we] became "spiritually intoxicated," as another leader described it . . . . This was sensed by the police and firemen and it began to have an effect on them. . . . I don't know what happened to me. I got up from my knees and said to the cops: "We're not turning back. We haven't done anything wrong. All we want is our freedom. How do you feel doing these things?" The Negroes started advancing and Bull Connor [the notorious segregationist police commissioner] shouted: "Turn on the water!" But the firemen did not respond. Again he gave the order and nothing happened. Some observers claim they saw the firemen crying. Whatever happened, the Negroes went through the lines.[1]

Political power, we hear, grows out of the barrel of a gun, but in this case the police had all the guns, while the marchers, it would seem, had all the power.

Whether we call it "integrative power" or say this was an "act of love," the experiences of Joan Black in her emergency room and of the marchers confronted with threat power in Birmingham, different as those experiences are, give a sense of how potent a force is involved here and how many ways it can manifest itself. What overtook the Birmingham marchers would seem to be as strong as mob violence, only somehow its reverse. What is the source of this power?

In both cases, the source is an intense fear reaction, *which was not acted on.* It was acted *out,* you could say, the way Sri Easwaran did not act on his angry thoughts but channeled them into creative action. The marchers could have given up and gone home, or they could have attacked the police and firemen. But they didn't want to just react, like automata. They were on a higher plane just then. Shortly before, one of their leaders had said, "We're going to win our freedom, and as we do it we're going to set our white brothers free." The vision of unity uplifted them. They breathed the heady air of freedom, and walked on.

And the firemen whose hands were frozen on the nozzles of their hoses? In them, as Gandhi would put it, their dormant reason was "compelled to be free." A confrontation like this, where feelings are intense on both sides and one side undertakes a clear and clarifying act of courage that precipitates a successful outcome, is what one scholar calls a "nonviolent moment."[2] From the point of view of the nonviolent actor, we can call it a *peak experience.* A peak experience is one in which we are thrown back onto deeper resources by an emotional challenge.

One of the participants in the Freedom Rides who was beaten by a racist mob offers some clear insight into the psychology of such an experience. "You feel the pain," he said, "but you don't become bitter, you don't become hostile . . . you sort of lose yourself . . . you become involved in the circumstances of others."[3] There is nothing supernatural about this kind of struggle, and there is certainly no guarantee— given the world we live in—that it won't cause us some suffering. But like a mountain climber pushing forward into the thin, bitter air of an icy peak, or a ballet dancer pushing her or his body beyond limits, there is such a thing as rising above pain. In the 1996 Olympics Kerri

Strug gave her coach "one more jump," though she had a badly sprained ankle, and the whole world winced watching her face twitch at her otherwise perfect landing. There is this difference: the nonviolent actor is deliberately seeking to manifest the pain that others are trying not to see. So in his or her case, the pain is not just something to put up with along the way; it's part of the point.

The fact is, even if you *don't* stick your neck out in today's world, pain happens. It's very important to remember this when people say, and they're perfectly right, that nonviolence is risky: people get attacked when they're minding their own business and not even dreaming of changing the world, and there is a nonviolent way to respond to that kind of pain as well, as the following story illustrates.

One day in 1992, an eighty-year-old woman was mugged and badly hurt in New York City. Eileen Egan, however, was not your typical mugging victim. She was a lifetime peace activist, a coworker of Dorothy Day and Mother Teresa, who naturally saw things a little differently than most people. A good writer, she was also able to articulate her vision, for example, in a pithy interview with *Parade* magazine two years after the attack, called "I Refuse to Live in Fear." Egan is another insightful spokesperson for the kind of experience I'm talking about, and its long-term results. Without using the word *nonviolence* (a wise move, since so few understand it correctly), she managed to describe precisely what makes this principle work, and all in everyday language anyone could follow. She started from the assumption, she tells us, that the worst result of the attack was not her broken bones but the potential "brokenness" of her fellow feeling toward the man who attacked her. Like the effect of TV violence, the effect of real violence will, if we let it, spread into our feelings toward all our relationships. Egan was extremely concerned not to let that happen. Instead of letting herself get vindictive, then, she tried to make friends with her attacker, staying in touch with him as he wended his way through the prison system, and she describes how it helped her avoid the post-traumatic stress that might have followed such a brutal attack. Note that at this point *he* didn't seem much affected by

her generosity, but that didn't prevent her from benefitting from it.
She explains:

> I've forgotten about the attack completely. I used to
> get nervous when somebody came up behind me, but
> that's gone now. There are so many more important
> things to worry about in the world.[4]

But wasn't she angry? Of course, but she had something to *do* with
her anger, so it left no scars. How did she manage it? Remember
Nurse Black? "I saw a sick person and had to take care of her." We saw
this early on in the case of Karen Ridd, and we'll continue to see it
behind every example of real nonviolence we meet. One of the things
that accompanies the peak experience, that maybe makes it possible,
is a higher vision. It is because, in the nonviolent person's outlook,
even an attacker is a person; he or she will not dehumanize another
human, even one who has dehumanized himself (or herself).

That vision has another aspect. Practically all the rescuers who
risked their lives to help Jews and other refugees during the Holocaust
felt "that what an individual did, or failed to do, mattered," that "they
could influence events . . . [and so] what they did, or failed to do, mattered a great deal."[5] Along with the vision that we are all human
together, each of us equally real, there is a sense that human action and
our own emotional struggle to act well is meaningful; we're deeply
aware that our efforts have an impact on the world. As Egan says, "If
somebody has chosen a life of violence and doesn't get the result he
expected from his victim [i.e., fear and anger], it may help him to see
life differently." Kindness begets kindness; visions communicate;
mood affects mood. Advertisers exploit our impressionability all the
time—why can't we? As of 1992, Egan had not seen much of a
response from her former assailant. Not a problem. Very likely he was
touched, but not ready to let on; in any case, *she* certainly reaped
benefits from her attitude, benefits that a professional counselor
would be thrilled to impart.

Berta Passweg was a Jewish refugee who had escaped to Egypt. One day, a friend in Alexandria said, "Berta, you should pray for Hitler." Seeing Berta's shock, she explained, "Not that he succeeds with his evil intentions, but that God changes his mind." When Berta was finally able to do this, she found that "I don't think it had any effect on Hitler, but it had an effect on me: . . . all hate and bitterness against the Germans had just vanished and I could meet and talk with them without resentment."[6]

For Berta Passweg and Eileen Egan, unlike Joan Black or Karen Ridd, the violence had already happened. In the former cases we are talking about healing, not preventing, violence—healing and not letting it spread. We are also talking about an individual rather than a group, compared to the Freedom Riders or the Birmingham marchers. These would seem to be incidentals that don't affect the basic principle or the way the peak experience feels and works: either way, purpose overrides pain. Given a higher purpose, physical pain can leave us humanly deeper.

I mentioned that we can see the same dynamic in groups or in individuals. Yet it is important to start with the individual, rather than the big march or the strike, even though most people associate nonviolence with big group actions. Actors can, of course, get swept up in a wave of group enthusiasm, but the real source of nonviolent power is still coming from within them, and neither they nor we should lose sight of that. Groups don't have emotions; only individuals do. The founding moment of Satyagraha, in my view, is the famous oath taken in the Empire Jewish Theater of Johannesburg on September 11 (interesting date!), 1906, when a packed audience of Indians swore not to obey legislation that was about to deprive them of their basic human dignity. Gandhi's explanation of the oath's meaning for each one in that vast crowd sheds light on the roots of its power in the individual:

> It is quite unlikely, but even if everyone else flinched
> leaving me alone to face the music, I am confident
> that I would never violate my pledge.[7]

He asked all of them to "search their hearts" and take the pledge only if it were really a matter between each of them and God, notwithstanding what anyone else or the group as a whole would do. In other words, though the oath taking was to be done en masse it was not a mass action; it was a summation of individual actions. That was to remain its sustaining power.

Eighty years later, Cardinal Jaime Sin would say this about the huge "people power" uprising in the Philippines:

> It was amazing. It was two million independent decisions. Each one said, in his heart, "I will do this," and they went out.[8]

Since violence and nonviolence come about subtly, long before they are seen in outward action, it should not be too surprising if certain traits of character or norms of a whole culture are causing violence without our being aware of it. Our modern culture has quite a few of these, and one of them is the way "we've started to understand every human encounter as a symbolic clash of group interests," as writer Louis Menand points out. "Violence can be talked about in the abstract, but violence, like sex, never occurs in the abstract. . . . Groups are essentially imaginary. Souls are real, and they can be saved, or lost, only one at a time."[9]

As with labels, there is a certain dehumanization inherent in the temptation to see people as a group—be it a corporation, a state, a race, even a gender—instead of seeing them as individuals. In nonviolence, at any rate, you never do this. How could you? For "soul force" you need souls. In a group act of soul force, numbers can be handy, but they're never essential. "In Satyagraha it is never the numbers that count," Gandhiji said. "Strength of numbers is the delight of the timid. The valiant of spirit glory in fighting alone."[10]

Developing Nonviolence:
Making the Moment Last

A few years before Karen Ridd's team got to El Salvador, Sue Severin, a Marin County, California, health educator, found herself so frustrated and angry over the terror imposed on Nicaraguan villagers by the policy of "low-intensity conflict" during the Reagan era that she set aside her career and volunteered for a highly dangerous project: to join a faith-based citizens' group going down to document terrorist activity along the Honduran border. It was an effective way of converting her anger to useful action, and, like many nonviolent projects, it led further than she anticipated. It was on this mission that Sue and the other North American team members stumbled onto the power of *nonviolent interposition,* or more specifically the technique that is now called *protective accompaniment:* wherever they went, particularly during their longish stay in the formerly besieged village of Jalapa, there were no Contra attacks.

So on their return to the States, Sue and others decided they had no choice but to go back and offer the protection of their presence to the people among whom they had lived, and to do it in as many areas as possible. Naturally, this was a frightening prospect, and she was as frightened as anyone while sitting in her comfortable, safe home in Marin County reading about what "the Contra" was doing in those remote jungle villages. But, as Dutch child rescuer Cornelia Knottnerus also found, "the best antidote to fear is action."[11] Strangely enough, while Sue and the others were actually in Nicaragua, fear was never a problem.

> While I was there I never felt fear. I think the main reason was, I was there out of choice. . . . I found— much to my surprise—that I became very calm in danger. I'm a Quaker and don't go very much with "God" language, but the only way I can explain it is, I felt I was in the hands of God: not safe—that I

wouldn't be hurt—but that I was where I was supposed to be, doing what I was supposed to be doing.
And this can be addictive. Maybe that's why we kept
going back.[12]

We began this chapter with a story that illustrates the conversion
of anger. Now we've seen that fear, too, can become fuel for the fire
of unsentimental, active love when one chooses the nonviolence
response.

Sue Severin's reminiscence offers a number of other insights. She
clarified something about the feeling of empowerment, almost of
invincibility, that sometimes comes over nonviolent actors and enables
them to face and often overcome danger with preternatural
courage—the Birmingham marchers' "spiritual intoxication." As she
pointed out, it is not a naive feeling of invulnerability, as though they
were temporarily teenagers again. It is something both subtler and
more realistic: what empowers you is the conviction that what you are
going through is *meaningful*. In Sue Severin's words, this is what you
are "supposed to be doing"; these words are echoed by Marge
Argelyan from Chicago, who did very similar work in Hebron in
1996: "This experience had the most integrity of any work I've
done."[13] They were echoed by Solange Muller, daughter of the assistant secretary general of the United Nations, at a meeting in New
York: "When you find work like that, you never go back."[14]

In times like ours, when life has become meaningless for so many,
it's not hard to understand how the taste of nonviolent struggle can be
"addictive." Just listen to these testimonies from a subgenre of history
that can add much to our understanding of nonviolence, the words
of women and men who risked their lives to save victims of the
Holocaust.

Professor and Mrs. Ege played a prominent role in one of the
most successful group examples of the rescue of the Danish Jews. In
Mrs. Ege's words: "We helped the Jews because it meant that for once
in your life you were doing something worth-while. . . . I think that

the Danes should be equally grateful to the Jews for giving them an opportunity to do something decent and meaningful."[15] A trapeze artist, Speedy Larking, said it with less restraint: "I feel . . . hang it . . . I feel like throwing myself down on the road and saying, 'thank you!'"[16] But it is a physician, Dr. Strandbygaard, who really takes our breath away: "Isn't this strange . . . . It's almost like experiencing again the overwhelming love of one's youth."[17]

Heady stuff. These intense, fulfilling moments, as we have seen so far, come from the inner struggle to control our built-in fight-or-flight response. Such a struggle can lead to a peak experience that often has its effects on our opponents. It *always* has effects, like those we've just been hearing about, on the doer—on ourselves. In the next chapter, we'll focus on the obvious question: how and with what degree of reliability can we expect our opponent to "get it"? But there's a bit more to be said about the world of the actor's own inner experience.

In the grip of nonviolence, people experience more intensely; life feels more "real." It is like the strange feeling of Yeats's Irish airman, who has no earthly reason to be risking his life fighting for the British except for that feeling.

> Nor law, nor duty bade me fight,
> Nor public men, nor cheering crowds,
> A lonely impulse of delight
> Drove to this tumult in the clouds;
> I balanced all, brought all to mind,
> The years to come seemed waste of breath,
> A waste of breath the years behind
> In balance with this life, this death.[18]

It is like that experience, of course, but rather different. In war you are risking your life to kill others; in nonviolence you're risking your life (if necessary) so that no one else will be killed, ultimately so that no one will ever have to face death again at the hands of their fellow humans. Nonviolence is what psychologist William James was looking for: the moral equivalent of war.

In our own "nonviolent moment," a flash of spiritual light momentarily rends the darkness of the prevailing image of ourselves as a separate, competitive, neo-Darwinian animal who knows nothing but threat force. This leads us to a very important question: how can we keep that light switched on? If nonviolence is "addictive," how do we feed the habit?

Psychiatrist M. Scott Peck gives a good description of just this process:

> I do not know what creates a mystical experience. I know that fatigue can loosen "ego boundaries." I also know that I am *now able to do voluntarily what happened to me then involuntarily:* to see, whenever I remember and choose to do so, that all my enemies are my relatives and that all of us play roles for each other in the order of things.[19] (my emphasis)

One time or another, I think we've all had glimpses of a peak experience. Though it happened over thirty years ago, I vividly remember one afternoon in Berkeley when I was playing basketball with five other guys in Live Oak Park. All of a sudden—maybe one of us had just sunk a really pretty shot—my teammates and I were in a rally. We were invincible. It was magic; every pass connected, every shot sank—it was more like a ballet than three guys playing ball. Then it ended. The spell—or whatever it was—broke. We went back to being our bumbling selves, and I don't even think we won the game. An actor, an athlete, a dancer, even a professor has peak moments when suddenly he or she "gets it" or "it clicks." The difference is that a professional actor or athlete learns how to reenter that state on demand, so that with enough training he or she can make it happen whenever it's needed. There is nothing particularly mysterious about this, even though the "learning" that's involved has to be more than just at the conscious level. The training of a "career *satyagrahi*," who will need to keep certain "natural" reactions under control when he or she is on that picket line—or of someone who wants to stay alive in a dark alley—is very similar. We learn to be calmly alert under stress, and then the magic happens.

The fact is that neither Joan Black nor the Birmingham marchers nor Karen Ridd nor Sue Severin nor Eileen Egan was totally unprepared for a nonviolent moment. Joan Black was on duty in an emergency room; her medical training and her setting predisposed her to see a distraught person as a person—someone who needed help. Karen Ridd and Sue Severin were carrying out a nonviolent mission for which, again, they had had a modest amount of training. The Birmingham marchers were in the midst of a long, drawn-out nonviolent struggle, in which they had perhaps some training and certainly the rare benefit of inspired leadership.

This was also the case with Jawaharlal Nehru. Like thousands of his countrymen, the future prime minister of free India was drawn to the Mahatma's nonviolence, but there was more to it than just getting the idea, as he discovered when he was caught in a *lathi* charge by mounted police during a peaceful demonstration in Lucknow in 1928 (a *lathi,* or *lathee,* is a metal-tipped bamboo staff that Indian and British police used liberally in those days).

> And then began a beating of us, and battering with lathees and long batons both by the mounted and the foot police. It was a tremendous hammering, and the clearness of vision that I had had the evening before left me. All I knew was that I had to stay where I was and must not yield or go back. I felt half blinded with the blows, and sometimes a dull anger seized me and a desire to hit out. I thought how easy it would be to pull down the police officer in front of me from his horse and to mount up myself, but *long training and discipline held,* and I did not raise a hand, except to protect my face from a blow.[20] (my emphasis)

Training I: Outer Work

What was that long training and discipline? This was one of the most misunderstood aspects of Gandhi's leadership. When he asked his close coworkers to live simply, identify themselves with the poorest in the land, make their own cloth—even observe certain dietary rules— he was not laying down moral precepts in our sense of the word. He was actually training them to be a little "spiritually intoxicated" all the time. He knew real nonviolence is not the kind that just happens when the chemistry of the situation is right. He would have applauded the words of the popular Buddhist leader Thich Nhat Hanh:

> If you wait until the time of crisis, it will be too late
> . . . even if you know that nonviolence is better than
> violence, if your understanding is only intellectual
> and not in your whole being, you will not act nonvi-
> olently. The fear and anger will prevent you . . .[21]

If you know in your whole being that "your enemies are your relatives," you can have a spectacular effect on those around you. One of my close friends, David Hartsough, who is white, was sitting in with a small group of civil rights activists at a segregated lunch counter in Virginia in the early sixties. They had been sitting there without getting service for close to two days, harassed almost without letup by an increasingly angry crowd. As neither the sitters nor the proprietors backed down, tension increased. Suddenly David was jerked back off his stool and spun around by a man who hissed at him, "You got one minute to get out of here, n—— lover, or I'm running this through your heart." David, a birthright Quaker, stopped staring at the huge bowie knife held at his chest and slowly looked up into the man's face, to meet "the worst look of hate I have ever seen in my life." The thought that came to him was, "Well, at least I've got a minute," and he heard himself saying to the man, "Well, brother, you do what you feel you have to, and I'm going to try to love you all the same." For a few frozen seconds there seemed to be no reaction; then the hand on the knife started shaking. After a few more long seconds it dropped. The man turned and walked out of the lunchroom, surreptitiously wiping a tear from his cheek.[22]

Not all nonviolent moments are this harrowing. This one shows, though, what a difference you can make when you see life differently *and* practice what you see, so that your love of nonviolence starts putting down roots below the mere intellectual conviction Thich Nhat Hanh refers to, and starts to occupy "your whole being." David is a committed Quaker, as were his parents. They practiced acting out their peace convictions as their lifestyle, thereby reinforcing their conviction that there is "that of God" in everyone. And he had undergone a fair amount of special training, as far as one can ever be trained to respond creatively to such an emergency. Like policemen, even soldiers, he had learned through belief and practice that when someone opposite you is upset, you don't have to be.

These, then, are the ingredients for developing nonviolent responses so that they become part of one's personality: a deep conviction about the unity of life; the inspiration of real nonviolent leadership; practice in real, or failing that, in "role-playing" situations; and finally—Gandhi's special legacy—a life lived by nonviolent principles. One would be really lucky to have all of these—leadership is especially hard to come by in today's world—but with some combination there's no reason to doubt that anyone could deepen her or his innate capacity to become an effective "actor of love."

Because this capacity is an innate response, there's really no reason to fear that we're repressing anything when we set out to develop it. On the contrary, when we find the "way out of no way" between anger and fear, we are disinhibiting a natural capacity we all possess but of which most of us are not aware. Most of us don't try to develop it, for the simple reason that we don't know we have it. But that is due to our cultural conditioning. I think in fact that it's violence that's artificial; it's violence that is a mechanical "solution" that cheats us out of an opportunity to grow—to grow as individuals, by mastering an important part of our mind; to grow as a people, by working out a real solution to what divides us. A nonviolent response originates in the struggle to master emotional forces inside ourselves; and my guess is that this very struggle is what feels so meaningful and makes the nonviolent peak experience "addictive." Conflict is an opportunity, because negative emotions are an opportunity, for conversion.

A black teenager gave perfect expression to this after he had had a loaded gun held to his head by someone who robbed his backpack. His first reaction was pretty knee-jerk: "I should have been packing." A moment later he realized that carrying a gun would hardly have made him more secure in that situation. Finally, on really mature reflection, he realized that if he had had one, "I'd have gripped the handle instead of coming to grips with my fear."[23] Speaking for a small group of American volunteers in Hebron, where they were trying to stand between Israeli bulldozers and Palestinian homes and orchards, Randy Bond said, "We were a small group of ordinary people doing some rather extraordinary things in a hurting part of our world. We had to stretch ourselves and our capabilities to do these things; that's the only way we grow."[24]

Isn't growing what life's about?

TRAINING II: INNER WORK

Emperor Ashoka ruled most of northern India from around 269 B.C.E. to 232 B.C.E., and he ruled as very few in human history have done: by nonviolence. His rock edicts, a number of which are still to be read all over India, tell us how his guiding principle was not aggression but the moral order, or *dhamma* (in Sanskrit, *dharma*). This meant, among other things, the renunciation of wars of expansion, tolerance toward all religions, protection of the helpless, even hospitals for animals. The mute rocks speak in a voice that can "resonate in our ears across two millennia or more, evoking a liberal vision with an incredibly contemporary ring."[25] Following is Edict Forty:

People can be induced to advance in the Dhamma by only two means, namely moral prescriptions and meditation. Of the two, moral prescriptions are the lesser, meditation the greater. The moral prescriptions I have promulgated include rules making certain animals inviolable, and I have established other rules as well. But even in the case of abstention from injuring and killing living creatures, it is by meditation that people have made the greatest progress in the Dhamma.[26]

Meditation may be the only word in the English language with a less agreed-upon meaning than *nonviolence*; and as we see from the close connection Ashoka draws, that may not be a coincidence.

The classical definition of *meditation* is provided by a famous text thought to be roughly contemporary with the Buddha, the *Yoga Sutras,* which begins, "Meditation is the obstruction of thought waves in the mind."[27] By "thought waves," or *citta-vrtti,* Patañjali, the otherwise unknown sage who composed this text, includes any mental event— a feeling, an image, a desire—not just a linguistic thought. It could be, for example, a wave of anger or fear—which shows us immediately the connection of meditation with nonviolence, and why Ashoka felt that meditation was better than rules and regulations, even moral regulations, for creating a nonviolent regime.

Getting the mind under control—that's a tall order! Meister Eckhart put it beautifully:

This needs prodigiously hard work. . . . A man must be closeted within himself where his mind is safe from images of outside things. . . . Second, inventions of the mind itself; ideas, spontaneous notions or images . . . he must give no quarter to on pain of scattering himself and being sold into multiplicity.[28]

Patañjali's definition of *yoga* (meditation, in this case) comes, as I said, from his famous collection of sutras, or aphorisms. Such texts were meant as scientific manuals, if you will, consisting of bare formulas meant to be expounded by a competent authority. So in practical terms, a few things have to be added to his aphoristic expression to show us how to actually do this, especially in the modern period. First, as Eckhart said, meditation is not a state you slip into but a discipline you work at. Clearly, you have to have a tool to do this "prodigiously hard work." In my case, that has meant that I practice at regular times every day, under the guidance of a superb teacher, and I do it by concentrating with all the willpower I can muster, minute by minute, on an inspirational passage that I've previously memorized. This allows me to keep spontaneous thought waves from arising, and/or to not pay them any attention when they do.

To describe it this way, meditation may seem like a dreary exercise, hardly the thing to make heroes and heroines out of any of us, but that would be because we know so little about the capacities of the mind. "So far as we know," wrote neuroscientist Robert Livingston, "the usefulness of cognitive processes such as consciousness, perception, judgment, and volition have not begun to meet any limits."[29] Our first examples in this book were of individuals or groups of individuals who were thrown into a deep state of concentration by an emergency, like Joan Black or my friend David Hartsough at that lunch counter. We are talking here about learning to reach deeper states of concentration even without an emergency. Once when Gandhiji visited the ashram (spiritual community) of a well-known sage in southern India, the sage remarked to his students after he left, "Today we have been blessed by the presence of a real yogi." They asked him how he knew that, and he said:

> When you look at him you can see that he is absorbed
> in yoga, for whenever he looks at something he pays
> all his attention. He never glances at anything else.
> Many other leaders came with him, but they were

looking everywhere, as if they had five or six pairs of eyes.[30]

So let us not overlook this seemingly humble, if not irrelevant, capacity: one-pointed attention is the psychological key to nonviolence. And to illustrate its power, and at the same time its accessibility to non-mahatmas, let me borrow a description of a peak state of performance from a more familiar, not to say unlikely, source:

> Despite his off-field manner, which is often ordinary, even prosaic, Montana is special because when he faces danger, he is . . . completely concentrated. What we don't know is how he does it. . . . Sometimes things happen in slow motion for Joe at the most crucial time. The world slows down and things get big and he feels as if he has total control. He was in that world when he threw the winning pass to John Taylor [in the crucial game of the 1989 season, against the Cincinnati Bengals]. Montana simply went about playing quarterback as if the 49ers were ahead and there were still two quarters to go. "It happened sort of in slow motion," Montana admitted. He had dropped back to pass and suddenly everything slowed down and became totally clear. Joe saw two defenders go after Roger Craig and he saw Taylor break into the clear and he threw his pass. Then he lost sight of the ball, heard the screams of the fans and the world returned to normal speed.[31]

Strange as it might sound, this is a precise description (minus the stuff about pass receivers and fans) of a state of consciousness that Indian sages call *dharana,* or "firmly held attention." They taught that *dharana* was the first of the three stages—attention, meditation, and complete absorption in the Supreme Reality—in the long journey to complete fulfillment. In this first stage, *dharana,* our attention is often on something outside (like whether Craig or Taylor is in the clear); the second stage, meditation proper, is the systematic control of the activity within our mind (remember the two areas of control Eckhart talked about); and the third stage, or *samadhi,* is—well, hard to describe.

Joe Montana put his unusual gift to rather different uses than the sages in their forest ashrams—or Gandhi in his modern one, but like them, he must also have tried to get some kind of permanent grip on the capacity he had glimpsed in peak moments. There is nothing particularly Eastern or Indian about the capacity for meditation, or one-pointed attention. It was more systematically and continuously cultivated in India than with any other civilization that I know of, but it is hardly unknown to others. Some of the "heaviest" meditators in the world, like Meister Eckhart or Teresa of Avila, sprang up in the West. Nor has its discovery, or periodic rediscovery, always happened in the context of a religion, as we've seen. Following is a remarkable insight of William James about education, which he described in his *Principles of Psychology:*

> The faculty of voluntarily bringing back a wandering attention over and over again, is the very root of judgment, character and will. No one is *compos sui* if he have it not. An education which would improve this faculty would be the education *par excellence.* But it is easier to define this ideal than to give practical directions for bringing it about.[32]

I doubt James was consciously aware that he was paraphrasing one of the names for meditation in ancient India, which is *brahmavidya,* or "supreme education." Yet his description of bringing back a wandering attention "over and over again" is precisely what meditation is. It is indeed difficult to find practical directions for bringing this about! In both civilizations, this once-cherished legacy has all but disappeared behind the glitter of materialism.[33] But materialism can never keep its hold on us indefinitely, as we can see from the dramatic way that interest in and knowledge about meditation has exploded since Swami Vivekananda dramatically introduced India's ancient legacy at the Parliament of Religions in Chicago in 1893 (the very year, interestingly enough, that Gandhi went to meet his destiny in South Africa).

Today, many people are familiar with William James not as the author of the above remark, but from his classic essay, "The Moral Equivalent of War." That he had both interests is hardly a coincidence. "War begins in the minds of men," after all. The Bhagavad Gita, the beloved Indian scripture that so deeply influenced Gandhi, not only confirms this insight but gives us a clear sense *why* the untrained mind spawns violence—and what to do about it. This teaching is dramatized in a famous interchange between the hero, Arjuna, who represents you and me, and his friend and charioteer, Sri Krishna, who happens to be God. There's nothing wrong with the mind that training won't cure, Krishna tells Arjuna; one must simply learn to "still the thought waves in the mind," in accordance with the ancient wisdom. Arjuna laments, in language we can all appreciate, "But Krishna, the mind is so shaky and agitates so violently—you may as well ask me to control the wind." Krishna's answer is, "I agree, but it will come under our sovereignty—with a little detachment, and constant practice."[34]

The moral equivalent of war is the "war within," because in that "war"—our individual struggle to pacify our minds—no one gets hurt, and on the contrary, our innate, powerful capacities for nonviolence come into play more and more as we succeed. It has always been much harder to recognize this war than the wars we wage outside. Today we are enjoying a growth industry in behavioral training to reduce violence; we find versions of it in classrooms, in prisons, in workshops for peacemakers, and in corporations. It's a good first step. Practicing active nonviolence is another step that's open to all of us, and helpful to all of us, even in daily interactions. Meditation is the next step. For those who care—and dare—to undertake it, meditation is the deep training that the Dalai Lama recently called "internal disarmament," which enables us to intervene right where violence starts, at the very root of hostile thoughts—our sense of separateness. There is no question that whichever way we go, whether it's working on our behavior or through the direct and most difficult regime of meditation, or both (my personal formula), the mind is subtle and resists correction. That is its nature; this is not easy for any of us. But through training, as the Gita says, it is doable, and as we make progress in this line, one of the rewarding results is that nonviolence can become second nature. That is a two-edged reward: training pacifies the mind, and a mind of peace cannot but project a harmonic force into the world around us. That effect on others is what we can turn to next, but this has been a pretty dense introduction and could do with some summarization.

WRAPPING UP

Nonviolence begins in inner struggle—specifically, the struggle to keep anger, fear, and greed from having sway over us. It's a struggle that has immense benefits for the individual and leads to an exhilarating sense of purpose that is very often lacking in modern life. A Dutch couple named Vos was among several who took in Jewish children during the Nazi occupation, putting themselves and their own children at considerable risk. The inevitable day came when Mrs. Vos's mother came to visit, and was understandably upset to find refugees there in the house, endangering her grandchildren. Her daughter explained:

> We find it more important for our children to have
> parents who have done what they felt they had to
> do—even if it costs them their lives. It will be better
> for them—even if we don't make it. They will know
> we did what we felt we had to do. This is better than
> if we first think of our own safety.[35]

And her mother agreed.

This rising to heroism by perfectly ordinary people, this empowerment, can also be achieved outside such acute crises, especially with, but even sometimes without, meditation or other kinds of special training. One hears this constantly from former gang members or troublemaking students in the many programs dotted around the nation's schools and neighborhoods run by those who've bothered to reach out to these kids with an alternative. The young people often discover they've always had the skills to be mediators, for example, but no one showed them how to use them, and when someone does, they feel an exhilarating sense of self-worth, as one of them put it, like "hidden gold mines."

While the feelings of fear and anger that come over every one of us from time to time are "natural," it is also natural for us to want to master them. The dilemma of violence, whether felt in the mind of teenager Franklin Smith or acted out by a nation that can see only an ugly choice between doing nothing or doing harm, is itself some indication that the "natural" reaction of fight or flight is not all that nature has in store for us. The existence of a "way out of no way," and above all the deep sense of emotional reward people have felt on following that way, would seem to say that this is a path, if not *the* path, nature has had in mind all along.

When we think of nonviolence as a peak experience precipitated by certain conditions, though, we are just scratching the surface. It is like discovering that some bread mold in a petri dish has inhibited bacteria, or that some new kind of energy coming out of a Crookes tube has printed the picture of a key on a nearby photographic plate: the work of discovering what that force was and getting it into useable form then has to follow. Peaks have valleys. The occasions for potential nonviolent moments can be totally unexpected (like Eileen Egan's mugging) or a calculated risk (as at Birmingham or Lahore) or pretty much staged (as at the Dharasana salt pans). But they're still *occasions*. What we want is for the practices of integrative power to become sustained and habitual—as somehow did the practices of threat force over the years and centuries of human evolution.

In this chapter, we went on to talk about the two levels of training that we can apply to integrative responses: the training of behavior (and we'll have more to say about the role of culture at this level) and then of the mind itself, where the seeds of behavior lie.

Gandhi was, once we understand what he was up to, probably the one person in the modern world who most conspicuously and most systematically made this training a way of life, fine-tuned by relentless scientific experiments. While much has been written about his shrewdness and the results, positive and negative, of his great campaigns, the inner dimensions of his struggle and *its* results have been relatively passed over. They are, of course, more difficult to document. When he went into the Round Table Conference on September 15, 1931, for the "day in court" that he had worked up to for thirty years, he had nothing but a few notes to speak from. When Ronald Duncan, who had the honor of driving him to parliament that morning, asked him what he was going to say, Gandhi answered, "How do I know? I'm not there yet." His impromptu speech is said to have been a masterpiece (the authorities didn't allow it to be recorded). How do we explain this uncanny ability of his? Where did he get his boundless energy, his ability to go on in the face of disasters that would have floored an ordinary person, carrying his titanic pace into his seventies? How on earth did he divest himself of so much of his personal desire, and "unnecessary" possessions? And fear? And there's another intriguing mystery. The father of a friend of mine happened to be in India in the forties, a time of high tension, and was asked to carry an important message to Gandhiji. I asked him, what was his main impression of the Mahatma as a person? He said, without hesitation, "Health." He had never seen such ebullient good health, even though, from a medical point of view, some of the numbers on Gandhi's blood pressure were in the danger zone at that desperate time.

While Gandhi is best known for his resistance to the industrial lifestyle through simplicity and the "reduction of wants"—shock treatment for modern economies of consumption—he was also constantly advocating a deeper resistance to the culture that produced those economies, the culture of consumption, external achievement, and conquest. Though he rarely used the word *meditation* itself (it had become so unknown even in India that to mention it would bring on clouds of misconception), his enthusiastic practice and recommendation of allied techniques like prayer and the repetition of a mantram (a name of God) thread through his teaching from the earliest period. Yet even if he had never said a word about these disciplines, we would have to assume that he had practiced them, just from looking at his life and its achievements, neither of which could be explained otherwise than by the assumption that this was a man whose mind was utterly at peace. His life was his message, and the message was, "Here I am, the consummate activist, but the first field of action is my own mind." Clearly, he belonged to those who return to the inner struggle that humanity forgets age after age.

His own testimony on how the conversion of anger affected him personally is therefore a fitting wrap-up to this discussion of the source of nonviolence. It reveals, I think, one of the most important secrets of Gandhi's life.

> It is not that I am incapable of anger, for instance, but I succeed on almost all occasions to keep my feelings under control. Whatever may be the result, there is always in me conscious struggle for following the law of non-violence deliberately and ceaselessly. Such a struggle leaves one stronger for it. The more I work at this law, the more I feel the delight in my life, the delight in the scheme of the universe. It gives me a peace and a meaning of the mysteries of nature that I have no power to describe.[36]

CHAPTER FOUR

"WORK" VERSUS WORK

Remember, violence works; big violence works better. No revolution ever got off the ground without massive violence.

—Tom Metzger, White Aryan Resistance

People try nonviolence for a week, and when it doesn't "work" they go back to violence, which hasn't worked for centuries.

—Theodore Roszak

NONVIOLENCE MAY GIVE us a deep sense of purpose that's missing in our modern life; it may be a healthy way out of the "fight-or-flight" response to danger, but if it doesn't work, we may as well quit right now. Theodore Roszak jogs us into realizing, however, that whether nonviolence works or not—whether anything works or not —may be a little less simple than it first appears.

In this chapter I want to do two things: the first and most important is to understand what it really means to say something has "worked," in other words to get from a simplistic to a realistic sense of action and consequences. The second is almost as important: to enlarge our field of vision concerning the various forms of nonviolent action. As we build on the events we've already considered, it will be more and more obvious that nonviolence is much more than a form of protest. After these two recalibrations, we will be able to see past what Gandhi once called our "inane" conception of nonviolence to appreciate more realistically "the greatest force mankind has been endowed with."[1]

But first, let's turn the tables on our friends the cynics and ask, how well does *violence* work?

Sociologists Robert Jewett and John Lawrence analyzed American thinking about violence in an instructive book in the seventies called *The American Monomyth*.[2] The two writers studied popular entertainment and advertising, looking for what they called a "monomyth" about violence, and they found it summed up in one figure who epitomized the heroes of popular culture at that time: Superman. Superman stories, they found, uniformly propagate three beliefs about how violence works, meaning how it preserves law and order and protects the innocent:

(1) Violence is never misused: Superman is incorruptibly good, omniscient, always on the right side.

(2) Violence doesn't really hurt; it's "clean": when Superman swoops down in front of a car full of fleeing crooks and stops it dead, the crooks tumble out chastened but not wounded. Maybe one of them ends up with a little bandage on his forehead, but there is no pain, no suffering—and of course there is no "collateral damage." No bystanders are accidentally hit, even in a high-speed car chase.

(3) Above all, it never, never rebounds. No "blowback," as the CIA calls it. Superman is invulnerable (except for the occasional Cryptonite-induced dizzy spell), so even if the criminals wanted to, they could never hurt him back. But they don't want to. They are always successfully neutralized. Putting them in jail is the happy ending of the story; we never hear about what happens to them in jail—for example, that they learn more violent techniques in prison and come out to seek revenge on the community.

Wow.

Incredibly enough, these were the narratives that shaped our way of thinking about violence then—and other versions of it still do so now. We keep thinking that with one more clean weapon, one more restraining device, one more prison, the police will be able to get an edge on crime and restore our security. But that thinking is as unrealistic as the comics on which it is, perhaps, partially based.

In the real world, violence does, at least sometimes, to be sure, achieve its immediate purpose. There is no question of that. In Santa Rosa, California, recently, a man who had been terrorizing elderly people in a certain neighborhood entered one home too many. The owner got out his gun and turned the tables on this poor wretch, who is now safely behind bars. Or take a very different example: in February 1991, the "international community" bombed Iraq until dictator Saddam Hussein was forced to pull the remains of his shattered army out of Kuwait—and off our oil supply. Violence *can* get things done: this is true, but is this all there is to it—does this cause-effect arc really exhaust the effects of violence?

Because the media present and re-present this one side of the story, we plain do not notice that a raft of other results, some of them much more important in the long run, ripple out as the "event cone" of violence widens. We do not notice that most of the homeowners who go to get their guns are overcome or even killed by their much more professional intruders, just as many people who pull out a gun or a knife in some kind of quarrel end up the victims of "victim-precipitated homicides." We rarely think about the number of guns stolen from homes or the number of children who use them on their friends. Above all, we do not notice that every time an act of violence "works"—and let me repeat, some of them—there's trouble somewhere down the road.

If we knew where to look, we would see the trouble every time. Does the criminal who is "safely" behind bars plan to go better armed next time? Does the dramatic story in the paper send other homeowners out to get guns, which four out of five times end up hurting someone in the family instead?[3] If you count up all the accidental deaths and other mishaps that result from keeping a gun at home, they are almost *forty times* more common than the scenario where an intruder is scared off. And finally, does the violent solution, despite its satisfying "conclusion," which is really only a step toward many other conclusions, ratchet up the level of violence in the community as a whole? We usually don't even ask these questions, yet they are the ones that determine which way we're really headed: toward safety or toward death, chaos or community.

During the Gulf conflict more bombs fell on Iraq than were dropped in all of World War II. This incredible punishment "worked": Saddam Hussein did indeed withdraw what was left of his forces from Kuwait. Yes, but what else happened? About 100,000 people died; millions of gallons of oil were burned in the open air or poured into the waters of the Gulf, creating an unparalleled ecological disaster. It has been estimated that the war cost Iraq alone $77 billion.[4] And now for the really bad part. Over 200,000 Iraqi children died either during the bombing raids or in the aftermath, when infant deaths in Iraq during the first eight months after the attacks rose 300 percent. Then they went on dying, the children, as continued economic sanctions were kept in place to force the unrepentant dictator into line—for evidently all that bombing did not cause President Hussein to have a change of heart, only to harden it. In order to thwart the Iraqi ruler's intentions by violence, we have brought about the greatest humanitarian crisis—some, like former attorney general Ramsey Clark, would say the greatest crime against humanity—since World War II. That consequence cannot be brushed aside. It is not irrelevant to our destiny.

Let us pause here to ask, in the name of what kind of logic have we inflicted this appalling suffering, year after year, on this people and these children? Dictators by definition do not care about the well-being of their subjects. So by hurting their subjects . . . ? In fact it has been pointed out often enough that our sanctions weakened the Iraqi people to the point where they could no longer resist their harsh leader even if they wanted to. We did his job for him.

We could have predicted both these results, if only we understood the dynamics of violence. We would then have realized that in terms of the *type* of force applied, harsh sanctions are only quantitatively different from bombing. We would have realized that we ultimately strengthened the ruler of Iraq's hand, not because we wanted to, but because we used the same kind of force he does. He relies on violence. We didn't come up with an alternative.

When President Bush launched Operation Desert Storm with the ringing words, "The liberation of Kuwait has begun," he wanted us to think of the liberation of Europe from Hitler's armies (the official line had been all along that Iraq was bent on, and somehow capable of, world conquest). He might have been a little more careful about his historical precedent. The massive air attacks ordered by the Allied leaders who met at Casablanca in January 1943 were an experiment that was designed to achieve the destruction and dislocation of the German military and the undermining of the morale of the German people sufficiently to undermine their capacity for armed resistance. Since the Germans who remained alive did give up, it is easy to convince ourselves that the bombing had the desired effect. Yet, as the great pacifist writer Vera Brittain pointed out early in the game:

> The "experiment" has demonstrated, so far, that mass bombing does not induce revolt or break morale. Victims are stunned, exhausted, apathetic, absorbed in the immediate tasks of finding food and shelter. But as they recover who can doubt that there will be, among the majority at any rate, the desire for revenge and a hardening process, even if, for a time, it may be subdued by fear?[5]

According to many studies done after the war, and after other wars, her prediction was quite correct.[6] Particularly interesting is the bombing of civilian targets in the North-West Frontier Province of India by the British in 1930, which we'll have occasion to return to: "500 tons of bombs were dropped over the Pathans, but their spirits remained uncrushed. The number of Red Shirts increased from a couple of hundred to 80,000."[7]

So the untoward results of the massive bombing of Iraq were not incidental, or unpredictable. They were the results of very general and predictable rules: in principle, bombing does not lead to unmixed good results; in principle, violence itself does not lead to simply good results, even if it leads to some results that one side considers good. Violence is, in principle, a destructive force, and there is no way to get around that. In May of 2000, *Newsweek* published a previously suppressed NATO report making it clear that instead of crippling the Serbian military the year before (only fourteen tanks were destroyed, for example, not 120 as earlier claimed), NATO had terrorized the civilian population by bombing generating plants, bridges, and other infrastructure of daily life.

As Professor Pepinsky said, human beings are embedded in "crosscurrents of violence and responsiveness" and we are always, at every moment, influencing our surroundings by our "profoundly religious choice between violence and democracy." There were obviously still other eddies and crosscurrents released by our choice of violence in the Gulf: the demoralization of the Iraqi people, including a "deep hatred" among the Iraqi youth for us, spasms of violence unleashed against the Kurds of the north and Shiites of the south—and we must think also of the wider world. Shortly after the Gulf War, Serbs and Croats unleashed unparalleled violence against their Muslim neighbors. Was that a coincidence? Or could they have picked up a resonance from the brutality visited on the Iraqi people by the American and European states acting under UN auspices? The heartless bombing, the massacre of Iraqi soldiers trying to flee Kuwait, the brutal entombment of others in their trenches (not to mention the continuing sacrifice of the children) were all examples of Muslims not being treated as human beings. Was the bombing of the World Trade Center in New York by Islamic fundamentalists a few years after the Gulf conflict also a coincidence?

The Gulf conflict had another, extremely bad result that is not controversial, once we give it a moment's thought: every time we use violence to solve a problem we send the signal that violence is the way to solve problems. In the present case, it is hard to ignore the desensitization of the CNN-watching American public for whom the war was turned into a video game. In the world of violence, as we've seen, nothing is more dangerous than trivialization, than losing our human sensitivity. This is why the task in *non*violence is often to awaken sleeping consciences by making people aware of the pain they're causing—making them feel it empathetically. That task is becoming ever more difficult. Since the Gulf debacle, the U.S. military has increasingly been using video games to train military personnel. They claim—and I'm sure they believe—that they're doing this because video games have become as realistic as real combat, but I claim that consciously or unconsciously they are doing it *to make combat seem as realistic as video games.* Which is to say, not real at all. Unconsciously they are training their personnel not just to use weapons—that's the easy part. What has always been more difficult is getting soldiers not to feel what they're doing when they use their weapons on live targets. "Once I met a Vietnam veteran on an airplane," Henri Nouwen wrote.

> He told me that he had seen so many people killed on
> television that it had been hard for him to believe that
> those whom *he* killed would not stand up again in the
> next movie.[8]

So intense are the unrealities of war that we may well conclude, as Simone Weil once said, "War is unreality itself."

I won't dwell on the media's role here because it's been so graphically laid before the public by the books of Lt. Col. Dave Grossman.[9] But the point to remember is that whenever we prepare minds for war we unprepare them for life, and that hurts all of us. This is a severe hidden cost of the war system—and to some degree, of all violence.

Earlier, I used the handy image from physics of an "event cone." This is how physicists describe the fact that even the tiniest event— say, the emission of a gamma ray from a decaying particle—ramifies into the future, changing patterns and altering seemingly unrelated events at a great remove in time and space. When you see its event cone, the working of violence begins to look a lot less "surgical." It too can create a "butterfly effect" of cascading disorder. If you share the widespread intuition that violence is a disruptive, not constructive, force, that intuition begins to look a lot more plausible.

In his classic study *Man, the State and War,* Kenneth Waltz tried to show that however deplorable war and violence are, they sometimes preserve "order." You would certainly think so. Ironically, though, he cited the bloody suppression of the last Moro rebellion in the Philippines as an example (this caught my attention: my grandfather served in the unit that brought in the famous Philippine resistance fighter, Emilio Aguinaldo, in 1901). The war may have been an ugly business, said Professor Waltz, but it paved the way for a "stable regime" for that country—under Ferdinand Marcos![10] The "stable" Marcos regime collapsed unceremoniously in February of 1986, and its successors had trouble with the Moros for ten more years. In Professor Roszak's happy terminology, the war "worked" but it didn't work. It didn't have successful long-term results. Gandhi frequently said, "Violent revolution will bring violent *swaraj* [regime]." Not maybe, not sometimes: he meant it as a law. Sometimes it may take a long time for these unhappy results to mature, and then we have to be ready to see the connection, but it's there.

The problem isn't with war only. To repeat, it's in the very nature of violence. The majority of Americans believe, for example, that the death penalty deters homicide; but in one of the few reliable studies on the actual results of capital punishment, it was found that introducing the death penalty seems to *increase* homicides, by about 2 percent. The state destroys a human life to "send a message" to would-be murderers; but in reality it's sending not one message but two somewhat contra-dictory messages. On the conscious level its message is mainly about retribution, about warning, but on a deeper level it is unfortunately more about the expendability of human life—and the impossibility of bringing a violent person back into the community. The title of the study is "Deterrence or Brutalization."[11] Evidently, the deeper message, as usual, is slightly more effective.

Or more than slightly. As Sister Helen Prejean points out, Texas executes more people than any other state, "yet its murder rate remains one of the highest in the country."[12] New York, which does not have the death penalty, reduced its crime rate dramatically in the first four months of 1992, largely by expansions in other, more preventive, areas of crime control. These other areas are, incidentally, ones that a state can afford to institute when it is not spending $2.3 million on every capital case.

The closer we look, the more problematic our reliance on violence for security appears. Violence is a slippery way to go, with as many bad repercussions as desired ones. The feeling that tells us that violence works is not based on facts, and I suspect the reason we don't look at those facts too closely is simple: if the facts say that violence doesn't protect us very well *but we don't know what does,* those facts are disturbing. The rules of cognitive dissonance take over, and facts are forgotten. A teen I quoted earlier, the one who had his backpack robbed at gunpoint, said, "I'll never get caught slipping again. The next guy who tries to run up on me is getting blasted." Then he came to his senses—partway—and corrected himself: "I'm glad I didn't have anything that day. I would have killed that fool."[13] Really? With a loaded handgun pointed at his temple? Would he not rather have become—like a Sonoma County, California, woman who carried guns for protection until she got killed reaching for one—yet another case of victim-precipitated homicide?

. . . AND IT EVEN "WORKS"

Anyone who does what I do becomes by turns frustrated, despairing, and amused at the certitude with which people tell me that nonviolence doesn't work. If nonviolent volunteers tried to interpose themselves between hostile forces in former Yugoslavia, one person told me, they would just be wiped out—martyrs. "They'd all be machine-gunned," said another with equal certainty. Yet at the time they made these statements (at a meeting of the U.S. Institute of Peace in Washington in the spring of 1993), only one person had been killed and three wounded in the whole history of nonviolent interposition, a history going back to the early part of the century and involving tens of thousands of not overly trained volunteers. In Haiti, in ten or so months of accompanying threatened people, seventy volunteers from Peace Brigades International defied the ruthless para-military, FRAPH, without taking a single casualty. As I write this, not one volunteer (knock wood) has ever been killed in one and a half decades of doing the kind of high-profile, sometimes quite confrontational, work of Karen Ridd and Sue Severin in Central America, nor has anyone been abducted or killed while being accompanied by them.[14] (How many heavily armed soldiers and guerrillas have been killed in that period?) Once, after I gave a talk some years ago at a local college about the Indian freedom struggle, a student challenged me, "What about the tens of thousands who got killed?" When I asked him what he was talking about, he started spinning out scenes of atrocious massacres he had seen somewhere. It turned out that he had seen them, all right—in his imagination. Outside of the real massacre in 1919 at Jalianwalla Bagh in the Punjab, and what happened in Peshawar in the thirties (which this student could not possibly have known about), almost no *satyagrahis* were killed in the thirty-two years of intense struggle Gandhiji conducted in India. Fewer died in ten years of civil disobedience across the south than in three nights of rioting in Watts. None of the former deaths occurred during a nonviolent demonstration.[15] It is time for a culture-wide reality check.

"Acts of love" that arise in a peak state of self-control *do* work, beyond the psychological work they do within the actor. They work, generally speaking, on three levels:

(1) They persuade people to change in the ways that we want them to—and often.

(2) Contrary to all expectations, they don't get you killed nearly as often as violence does. There are no "victim-precipitated homicides." In other words, nonviolence can be dangerous, but not nearly as dangerous as violence. And finally,

(3) They work on the much deeper level that is precisely where violence fails most reliably: every time someone uses real nonviolence, things get better, and the system moves forward toward stable peace, whether or not the actor achieves his or her immediate goal.

For the rest of this chapter we'll be exploring these claims as we try to fill out our picture of what nonviolence looks like in the "real world" of politics and history. So let's open the file.

DOWN TO CASES

I want to begin, despite some misgivings, with an event of high drama. Misgivings because I know how easy it is to get entranced by a spectacular climax and miss the years of preparation that went into it, which is to miss the essential ground from which a nonviolent moment springs. A friend of mine who was quite the ballet dancer in his early life told me that Margot Fonteyn was once being gushed over by some admiring fans. Ms. Fonteyn said, "You see all this 'effortless' grace, this 'spontaneous' beauty; little do you realize the hours of sheer torture that went into it." I don't want us to miss the years of careful training, but let's start, nonetheless, at the climax of the freedom struggle in India on May 21, 1930, when more than 2,000 unarmed volunteers walked up to the gate of the Dharasana salt factory in Gujarat and were beaten to the ground by guards whose vehemence went on without relenting throughout the day. This event, brilliantly reenacted by Sir Richard Attenborough in the film *Gandhi,* was, as many agree, the climax of the Salt Satyagraha, and in large part of the freedom struggle itself. When American correspondent Webb Miller saw wave after wave of unarmed volunteers, in bands of twenty-five, walking into a hail of beatings without even lifting an arm to protect themselves, he wired, "In eighteen years of reporting in twenty-two countries I have never witnessed such harrowing scenes." Yet on they came, walking deliberately into the blows, taking only a short break during the afternoon heat, with their crude first-aid station patching up the fallen and splinting their broken bones.

Now the fact is that not only this "raid" but also the entire Salt Satyagraha campaign were, technically, utter failures. Outside of a few minor concessions wrested from the government in the existing salt laws, nothing seemed to change. Yet now we know that this bloody climax made India's freedom inevitable, because it showed what the Satyagraha volunteers were made of, and what the oppressive system of government that the British had imposed on India was made of. When freedom came, sixteen years later, the agony of the 320 hospitalized marchers, and the two who died, had borne its fruit.[16]

If Gandhi noticed the delicate irony—that the campaign that did the greatest work didn't "work" at all—it did not faze him. It illustrates perfectly his formula for successful action, which comes straight from the Bhagavad Gita: use the right means in a just cause and leave the results in the hands of God. In another idiom, if you put good energy into a situation, good results have to follow, somewhere.

Anyone who works for nonviolence has seen this phenomenon, though usually on a smaller scale. Before all-out war broke out in Kosovo in March 1998, a group I work with sent six observers to the region to give moral support and some nonviolence training to the ethnically Albanian students demonstrating against their already harsh mistreatment by the Serbian regime. I happened to be coming back from Denver the day after they reached Prishtina, and by mere chance I ran into our board president waiting for the same plane back to San Francisco. Steve greeted me with some alarm. "Have you heard the news? David [our executive director] is arrested: they're all in jail." We read the details on my laptop: we had failed. The whole group was arrested on a minor technicality and sentenced to ten days in a Serbian jail, followed by expulsion. What we did not know was that the American attaché was at their hearing, and events had already taken a course of their own. Within hours, pictures of the six Americans, with their shaved heads, started appearing on world news services. By the time we reached San Francisco the press was on full alert. Our friends were released the next morning and back in Washington soon afterward, giving press conferences and visiting senators. Camera crews were knocking down the door to our tiny office a day later—and Kosovo was world news. In the event, there was no big turnaround. The "international community" (I always put that in quotes, because it isn't much of a community) completely failed to stand up to President Slobodan Milosevic and just left the Kosovars to their fate until matters got much worse and they could use bombs (which made matters *much* worse). But you have to be realistic—and humble. We were a handful of unknown locals 10,000 miles away, operating on a shoestring, and yet we succeeded beyond our wildest dreams in bringing an egregious situation to world attention.

I sometimes think that the reason we can't easily understand nonviolence is that the "non-inane" reality of the thing is so enormous that we're like ants crawling over a colossal Gulliver. No one, not even Gandhi, could grasp the whole thing at once. You have to sketch in the picture of how it works from various angles, like that popular form of Hindu worship called *arati,* where you take lighted camphor or an oil lamp in your right hand and move it in slow circles around the head and neck of the god you're worshipping, be it Ganesha or the Divine Mother, or whomever. You are garlanding him or her with light. When this is done in the sanctum sanctorum of a temple, or the worship room deep inside a nonelectrified home, the shadows shifting as you illuminate the divine image from every angle give a distinct impression of movement. Ganesha comes alive.

To illuminate the worshipful picture of peace, we, too, have to move reverently around her, seeing her beauty from every angle. That's why I made bold to put one of my own small experiences side by side with the mighty "experiment with truth" at Dharasana. Both illustrate, even in their disparity, how deeper forces seem to take over and conduct nonviolent efforts to good, but not always foreseen, conclusions. I will share with you some examples of nonviolence (three big ones and a few extras I couldn't resist) that are as different from each other as can be—spaced pretty evenly around the wide circle of the possible. With some imagination, peace can come alive for us at the center.

Calling Hitler's Bluff:
The Rosenstraße Prison Demonstration

"It never would have worked against the Nazis." This routine objection has to be taken seriously, because what people really mean by it is, since nonviolence wouldn't have worked against the Nazis—i.e., since it's too weak to work against powerful opposition—we have to keep violence around to fall back on. But if we do this, nonviolence *cannot* work: nonviolence plus violence, nonviolence with violence held in reserve, is no nonviolence at all. That makes the objection, if it were true, serious indeed.

There are several things wrong with it, however. One is, how can something not work when it hasn't been tried? With a very few exceptions, one of which we're about to consider, the only weapons people knew to use against Nazism were either passivity, which, whatever the reasons for adopting it, was a disaster; or violence, which, as we're beginning to learn today, was a flawed success. The objection that nonviolence would not have worked is based on sheer speculation. But worse than that, it's false.

In Berlin in 1943, on a gray weekend at the end of February, police and Gestapo swept through the cold streets and arrested the remaining Jews, mostly men, who had been left more or less at large because they were Jews "of Aryan kin," i.e., married to non-Jewish wives.

There was little resistance to the unannounced roundup, as may well be imagined. The arrestees were brought to a large, recently converted building on the Rosenstraße, a few blocks from a major Gestapo headquarters, without incident. Only two weeks earlier, in Munich, the student-led "White Rose" conspiracy had been betrayed to the Gestapo, and virtually all its youthful members were on their way to the guillotine. However, in Berlin the "Jewish Radio," as the still-remaining Jews' informal phone network was called, was buzzing, and within hours the wives and, in some cases, mothers of the arrested men learned where they had been taken. What then took place was like nothing that had ever happened under Nazi rule. By the following morning, from every part of the city, "as though in answer to a call—as though prearranged," the women converged on the Rosenstraße detention center, demanding the release of their loved ones.[17] All day they defied orders to leave. As their numbers swelled to more than 6,000, the prisoners themselves took courage and began clamoring through the barred windows to be released. It was an acutely embarrassing display. Gestapo headquarters, as mentioned, was but a few blocks away. One or two machine guns could have swept the street clear of these troublemakers—if there were nothing in the world but threat force.

For many years this episode provided an answer to the inevitable "it never would have worked," etc., because in fact the demonstrations worked. They created an impossible dilemma for the regime, and within a few days the Gestapo, not the women, blinked. By Sunday the men were free. Some of them had been already deported to concentration camps. They were told never to talk about what they had seen there, and hastily put on trains to Berlin, so hastily that some of them couldn't get back their own clothes.

Until recently I thought, like everyone else who knew about the episode, even most Germans, that the "Aryan-related" sons and husbands were no doubt quietly rearrested later in twos and threes, and then there was no one to save them. So the demonstration had a spectacular but not a lasting success; it "worked," but it did not work. It did not have much lasting effect on the whole system. Or so we thought.

In 1996, a full-length study appeared, with the superb title *Resistance of the Heart,* documenting what actually happened, not only in Berlin but Paris and other cities that also had the *Mischling,* or "mixed-breed," problem, while each local headquarters watched anxiously for guidelines from the German capital. The book is full of fascinating details about the insanity of Nazi logic, and the contradictions of violence—for example, that the führer himself refused to make any decision. He whose "fanatical will," he once boasted, had "rescued the German nation" was paralyzed. Nonviolence paralyzed him. The big surprise, however, is that virtually everyone snatched back from the jaws of death by their loved ones out in front of Number 1–2 Rosenstraße survived the war. As did their colleagues in Paris and other capitals under Nazi control. In other words, tens of thousands of people were rescued by this impromptu demonstration by untrained women, women who had been living for more than a decade under a regime of authoritarian terror, the likes of which the modern world had rarely seen. Nonviolence was almost never tried against the Nazis, but when it was, it scored a resounding victory.[18]

The very success of the demonstrations raises a somewhat embarrassing question: why did they stop? Why did no one see the holes in the Fascist armor this episode revealed? As the study pointed out, probably a reason the episode has been so well ignored lies in this implication, that if one demonstration worked, others might have done more. And imagine if they had started sooner. . . .

Rather than conclude that the event was passed over in silence because some were embarrassed by its very success, I prefer the charitable, and more practical, view that it's been ignored not so much out of moral cowardice as cultural ignorance. You just don't see what's coming at you from another paradigm, even if it's right before your eyes.

The resistance at the Rosenstraße detention center did not noticeably slow the Nazi juggernaut all by itself. Would we have expected it to? It's unlikely that more than a handful of those involved even knew the name of the force that they were wielding, much less how to build on it. As a full-fledged insurrection, it was of course too little, too late—as if the women had had any such intention. Still, the events of that dramatic weekend reveal a solid nonviolent principle: through a courageous act of self-sacrifice, the demonstrators brought about a momentary rehumanization of the Jewish prisoners—their loved ones—in the hardened hearts of the Gestapo. The large crowd of women demonstrators were not only somewhat awkward to massacre in broad daylight, but the incident also gave a salutary yank on their captors' ideological blinders.

But they were, needless to say, totally untrained for such resistance. Nonviolence training was scarce in Berlin in the forties! The chances are that few of them were aware of what was really going on in India or would have dreamed they could apply the Indians' methods in their own circumstances. Some of them may have been there when the führer deigned to appear briefly with a most un-Gandhian Indian freedom fighter, Subhas Chandra Bose, whose way of fighting the British was to join the Axis forces. Thus, without leadership or a sense of how to proceed, they were naturally not able to capitalize on their discovery. Their spontaneous demonstration therefore "worked," i.e., it accomplished the desired result right there at hand; apparently, it did not do much work (without quote marks) to change the system, because whatever the peak of courage reached by the demonstrators on that occasion, they had no idea how to turn it into a movement, either by bringing about a more enduring conversion within themselves or some kind of outward organization. For that reason, we can assume, it had no noticeable long-term effect. That was not the case with the next event I would like to consider.

The Saint of Auschwitz

At Auschwitz one day during the summer of 1941, a Polish prisoner from Block 14 managed to escape. The routine punishment for such an event was to take the entire block, several hundred men who were themselves hanging onto life by a thread, and force them to stand at attention until the escapee was hunted down. If he were not found, ten others would be culled out and put in "the Bunker," a bare underground cell, without food or water, to slowly die. It was considered the worst thing that could happen to you at Auschwitz. Guards and prisoners alike strained to catch the occasional sounds from the soldiers and dogs searching the surrounding swamp. Hours went by. Gestapo Commandant Fritsch paced back and forth in front of them like a pendulum of doom. The miserable daily soup ration was brought out, but Fritsch ordered it poured down the drain before the eyes of the starving men. Finally, toward evening, the search was declared a failure. One after another, ten men were pulled out of formation to pay with their lives for one man's desperate escape. "Long live Poland!" shouted one; another, a father, broke down and wept, "My poor wife, my poor children. Goodbye, goodbye!"[19]

Then, once more, an unheard-of thing happened: a prisoner stepped calmly out of line and started walking toward the commandant. For some reason, no one shot him; Commandant Fritsch instinctively pulled out his pistol but only shouted, "Who is this Polish *Schwein?*" Word shot around: it was him—Father Kolbe of Niepokalanów. For the last two years, Father Maximilian Mary Kolbe had been a living symbol of human endurance and dignity for the whole camp. Now he walked up to Commandant Fritsch and calmly said to him, in good German, "I have a request." When Fritsch recovered from the shock, he barked, "Well, what do you want?" and Kolbe quietly said, "I would like permission to die in place of one of these men." A priest was almost as low as a Jew in the grotesque ideology of the Nazis, and Fritsch scornfully granted the request, totally misunderstanding its power. The husband and father who had wept, Sergeant Franciszek Gajowniczek, would live; after eight brutal days, Father Kolbe was put to death with an injection of gasoline. (Franciszek Gajowniczek died recently at the age of ninety-three in his home city of Brzeg, having testified at the papal institution of Kolbe as a Martyr of the Church).

We'd be justified to call this act the climax of Father Kolbe's spiritual career. What was the effect of his final, unpremeditated sacrifice? What good did it do? Here is the testimony of an eyewitness, George Bielecki:

> It was an enormous shock to the whole camp. We became aware someone unknown among us in this spiritual night . . . was raising the standard of love on high. Someone unknown, like everyone else, . . . went to a horrible death for the sake of someone not even related to him. Therefore it is not true, we cried, that humanity is cast down and trampled in the

mud. . . . Thousands of prisoners were convinced the true world continued to exist and that our torturers would not be able to destroy it. . . . To say that Father Kolbe died for one of us or that person's family is too great a simplification. His death was the salvation of thousands.[20]

The "salvation of thousands" here is not metaphorical. For you and me, a mood swing up or down is not a matter of life or death, but to a prisoner at Auschwitz that is exactly what it was. As every doctor knows, when a person is critically ill, the will to live can make the difference between life and death, and in the death camps everyone was critically ill. A prisoner who lost his or her will to go on visibly collapsed and was generally dead within two weeks.[21] It's quite possible that thousands, not just Sergeant Gajowniczek, who would otherwise have died in that man-made hell, got the courage to live on, in some cases long enough to see the day of liberation.

So it seems that nonviolence did work against the Nazis—not to save Father Kolbe's life, of course (which wasn't his purpose), and not *only* to save the life of one other person (which was), but to release a forbidden ingredient—hope—into the nightmare of dehumanization in which the Nazis had tried to entangle the minds of millions.

This was done by a single man with no external resources whatever, yet in a sense it was even more effective than the Rosenstraße demonstration that was carried out by 6,000 citizens who were technically free. It is the degree of the sacrifice, not the number of the sacrificers, that gives a nonviolent act its power. Consider what Father Kolbe was up against. Hitler's stated ambition "to prepare a generation of young people devoid of a conscience, imperious, relentless, and cruel" had succeeded with many like the guards at Auschwitz, some of whom had been systematically dehumanized since they were children. But Father Kolbe had been systematically training himself since *he* was young. At Auschwitz he had endured extreme abuse without succumbing to hatred; he had intense faith that there was a supreme, compassionate reality behind all appearances, which in his case was Mary, the Mother of God, and that this reality was present even in his oppressors, though they were entirely unaware of it. He was, therefore, literally a match for them. His humanity was, to use a phrase of Gandhi's, "mathematically proportionate" to their inhumanity.

Once we know what to look for, the underlying forces that determine the outcome of a nonviolent act are not too difficult to discern. Perhaps, if we knew this science somewhat better, we would be able to assess such cases still more accurately, or even predict their outcomes. One thing is certain: nonviolence *did* work against the Nazis. It worked proportionally to the balance of the human power over the dehumanization trying to hold it in check. It will always work against oppressors—provided we've trained ourselves as well as they have.[22]

It should be clear now why Theodore Roszak put the word "work" in quotes when he wrote that people say nonviolence doesn't "work." It's extremely important to be clear about what we mean when we say that any act did or did not "work." If we mean, did it do just what we wanted, visibly, immediately?, then yes, nonviolence sometimes doesn't "work." It did not, for example, save Father Kolbe's life. But if we mean, did it have a long-term positive effect on the whole system, perhaps one that the actor didn't foresee?, then we get a very different answer. In these terms we can make a central proposition about nonviolent versus violent effectiveness that's key to understanding the whole subject:

Nonviolence sometimes "works" *and always works*
while
violence sometimes "works" but never works.

Sometimes we hear a common variation on "It never would have worked against the Nazis," namely, "It sure didn't work against the Nazis!" People who say this are assuming that the millions who went to their deaths in the Holocaust were being "nonviolent." As we've seen before, it's extremely important to be clear about the difference between passivity and nonviolence. Was father Kolbe "passive" when he stepped forward to die for another human being, thus setting the whole Nazi lie on its ear? Outside of the isolated, little-known events like the two we've just considered, active nonviolence was rarely tried against the Nazis or anyone else in the Western hemisphere. The Munich students of the "White Rose" conspiracy, for example, issued leaflets calling for "passive resistance," but they had little notion what passive resistance was, not to mention the subtle but important difference between it and active nonviolence. No, it was passivity that was tried against the Nazis. Harsh as it may sound to say this, when one is passive in the face of such aggression, passive out of fear, one is going along with the violence, obeying its logic. This is not to condemn anyone caught in such a trap. To say that someone was passive out of ignorance of an alternative is not to say he or she was morally wrong, which in any case is language I rarely use. It is not to condemn those caught in such a tragedy; it's to understand the choices so that people will not be caught in them again.

The trap that sprang shut on the "Aryan-related" Jews of Berlin on February 27, 1943, was the result of an evil that had gone on practically unopposed for two decades; the power that forced apart the jaws of that trap long enough to let some victims escape must have been, at least for that moment, just as strong. What gave these women—leaderless, unorganized, untrained, and probably unaware that what they were doing has a name—strength enough to face down the Gestapo? It was love for their husbands and sons. Perhaps we can think of the bond between husband and wife, and mother and son—the force of love that holds together the "nuclear family"—the way we think of the "strong force" that holds together the nucleus of an atom: sometimes it shows its strength only when pulled apart.

These considerations bring us to an important element in nonviolent science that is often forgotten by those who object that it "never would have worked" against a very violent opponent: it makes a lot of difference that Nazism went practically unopposed for so long.

I have found it useful to think of the way violence feeds on itself, the escalation of conflict, as a steep curve, where time is plotted against intensity—intensity measured not by the number of weapons but the degree of dehumanization, the single most telling parameter of hostility. The important thing to bear in mind is that nonviolence, like violence, also comes in degrees. In the case of violence, time turns up a rheostat and progressively more energy is activated. Therefore, when a conflict has been allowed to go on and on untended, the degree of nonviolence we need has to "escalate" accordingly. The longer we wait, the more soul force we need to apply.

For practical purposes, we can say that conflicts escalate in three stages:

In the first phase, on the low "foothill" of the curve, conflicts can be successfully handled by the art of conflict resolution: there is a worsening dispute, perhaps, but the parties can still work things out, either directly or through a mediator, by representing grievances and negotiating them; give and take is still possible. But a time comes

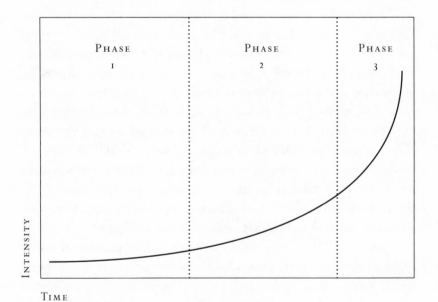

The escalation of conflict

when it is not. As anger increases, "hearing" gets dim. Then a different level of force has to be used. Gandhi, drawing as usual on his own experience, defined this psychological boundary very well:

> Things of fundamental importance to the people are not secured by reason alone but have to be purchased with their suffering . . . if you want something really important to be done you must not merely satisfy the reason, you must move the heart also.[23]

We have now crossed the border, in other words, into phase two, the zone of Satyagraha. In this region the "law of suffering" that Gandhi discovered in South Africa applies, because we need to reach the other party at a deeper level than reason. One party has to "give when it hurts" and reawaken the now seriously alienated opponent by voluntarily taking on that hurt—the hurt, or at least the risk of being hurt—not trying to avoid it. The women at the Rosenstraße detention center showed that sometimes just risking pain, which involves the mastery of one's fear, can be extremely effective.

Father Kolbe carried the same principle to the extreme degree. Here the dehumanization had become so intense, the power relationship so unequal, the time for acting so short, that he had to lay down his life to make it work. He illustrates how to apply nonviolence at the really steep section of the curve, phase three, when there's nothing for it but the final sacrifice. Again the power comes, as Gandhi often stated, from the *satyagrahi's* being *willing* to die. Whether or not he or she will actually die depends on various external circumstances, but he or she is not bluffing. When Gandhi fasted unto death, it was not a ploy. He made the supreme renunciation and put his life on the block, leaving his opponents to respond as they would. (In his case, they always yielded, but sometimes at the eleventh hour.)

I find that this graph settles "would never have worked" objections very well, for almost without exception, those who make the objections are thinking of an extreme situation in which they have to imagine themselves suddenly invoking nonviolence very late in the game—for example, when an entire nation has gone on dehumanizing its consciousness without hindrance for decades. Naturally, this stacks the cards! We in the "international community" were helpless in Yugoslavia because we stood around doing nothing while Mr. Milosevic used his state-controlled media to drive nationalist Serbs into a frenzy of hatred. Nonviolence in Germany would have been much less costly in 1918 or 1920—as in fact it was, during the Kapp Putsch—or 1932. Nonetheless, that there is a way for nonviolence to work even late in the game is what the Rosenstraße women and Father Kolbe begin to show us. *How* nonviolence would have worked against the Nazis depends on when we imagine it might have been applied and by whom; *whether* it would have worked is not in question. Assurances to the contrary notwithstanding, it would have worked—in fact, it did.

Some years ago—but his judgment still applies—the well-known activist and scholar David Dellinger, who titled his autobiography *From Yale to Jail*, deemed that we understand nonviolence about the way we understood electricity in the days of Marconi and Edison. This strikes me as an apt comparison. Marconi and Edison knew they were dealing with a natural force, and that it must have a great untapped potential, but little else. Gradually, they figured out the manner of this force (despite its mysterious nature: to this day no one really knows what electricity *is*) and started learning how to use it without getting hurt. Which is exactly what we're talking about here.

Comparing, for example, the Rosenstraße demonstration with the episode of the Birmingham marchers, we can further refine our sense of what makes a nonviolent interaction tick. The Berlin women (like the mothers of the disappeared in Argentina or the Women in Black in Israel or Serbia) had one powerful thing going for them: the "nuclear power" roused by the extreme threat to their loved ones. This power was not there to sweep aside the fear in the Birmingham marchers, but several things *were* there to enhance the nonviolent power of their impromptu action. They were being proactive, for one thing. It was they themselves who were on the march, not passively overtaken by surprise events. They did have the advantage of inspired leadership. And most importantly, they had gone through a certain amount of preparation. Moreover, they were a community of faith and (thanks again to the leadership they enjoyed) were able to draw inspiration and ideas and wisdom from the Indian freedom struggle with which, we now know, they had fairly extensive contacts.[24] All these things helped them rise beautifully to the unexpected opportunity for their nonviolent moment, even though they were not thrown back on their deepest resources quite as much as the women of Berlin, whose sheer desperation we may well imagine. The modest training—and impressive leadership—of the Birmingham marchers also enabled them to do the critical thing the Berlin wives could not do: follow up. This may be the most important difference in terms of a major, systemic effect on the future. Like a number of spontaneous nonviolent episodes, Birmingham succeeded. Unlike many others, it was part of a movement that also, in large part, succeeded, and that succeeded against a resistance comparable to Nazism in its ideological vehemence.

Taking It from the Top: The Holy Experiment

The events we have described at Berlin, Birmingham, and Dharasana share a similar structure, and they are the kind of event most of us associate with the word *nonviolence:* a protest movement by an oppressed group resisting abusive authority. Even there, on familiar turf, we found many myths and misconceptions that needed chipping away before we could appreciate how even rudimentary nonviolence can be surprisingly effective against determined and serious opposition, that is, against people with a very dehumanizing outlook whose bullying has gone unchecked for a long time.

Now we can push off into less familiar territory or, if you will, widen the lens. Nonviolence can't be only a weapon of the oppressed, any more than can electricity only appear as great flashes from the sky, or gravity only work on falling apples. We have tended not to *look* for nonviolence anywhere else, because we think that the powerful don't need nonviolence while the weak have no other recourse. By now we should begin to suspect that both of these assumptions are wrong.

Nonviolence can of course come "from below," but it can also be offered from the high seats of power. Colonial America can boast one of the best-known examples. Almost a century before the revolution, in March 1681, King Charles II gave William Penn governorship of the vast territory that today bears his name. Unlike most colonists, Penn crossed the Atlantic with a double mandate: empowered by his king to administer a colony, he also came with the blessings of his spiritual mentor, who was one of the greatest dissenters of British history and one of the most effective promoters of radical nonviolence ever in the West —George Fox, founder of the Society of Friends. Penn used his mind-boggling opportunity to carry out what history now calls the "Holy Experiment"—seventy years of governance by nonviolent principles.

Even before leaving England, Penn wrote a now-famous letter to his new subjects, the Delaware Indians, which witnesses to a tolerance far ahead of its time (and, sadly, often ours). He said, in part:

> I am very sensible of the unkindness and injustice that hath been too much exercised toward you by the people of these parts of the world . . . but . . . I have great love and regard toward you, and I desire to win and gain your love and friendship, by a kind, just and peaceable life.[25]

Penn actually carried this out to a remarkable degree. In all ways that were possible, given the growing inequality of the situation, he tried to prevent the indigenous peoples' exploitation by Europeans. "The result was to be an unparalleled record of some seventy years of almost completely unbroken peaceful association" between them.[26] Of course, from our own perspective, perhaps Penn should have refused to rule over the native peoples at all. That is easy to say nearly 300 years after the fact, and perhaps *perfect* nonviolence would have said it then. But life doesn't become perfect all at once. The beginnings of nonviolence in the colony made a relative paradise for the indigenous and the conquering peoples compared to the bloody shambles of a relationship that obtained elsewhere and whose legacy we have still not overcome.

In the Holy Experiment, nonviolence (needless to say, still an unknown word at that time) was no rebellion against established authority; it *was* the established authority. Nor was it spontaneous, accidental, or ad hoc as so many nonviolent episodes still are today. It "trickled down" from the mind of George Fox, the founder of Quaker theology and social teaching. America has been home to many utopian experiments, but not too many utopian *regimes,* especially regimes that furnish a model—if we would only use it—for governing on a national scale.

The colony experienced problems of every kind, including friction with the Crown, but despite them the house that nonviolence built on early Quaker lines showed that nonviolence could work in every department, from defense to criminal justice. It also showed that a regime based on this principle of order is robust. The experiment endured until the vision faded and the Quaker party lost its mandate at the ballot box. It was not overwhelmed either by the world around it or by the power of the Crown above it, both of which were based on depressingly conventional principles. For seventy years it housed under one judicial roof a diverse collection of colonists from many parts of Europe and several religions who lived in a relatively high state of harmony under the "Great Law" their governor had set up in 1682. This law was in many ways more humane than the crime bill of 1991. Under the Great Law, capital crimes were reduced from 200 to exactly two—treason and murder—a tremendous step forward for its time, which we are now reversing.[27] The Great Law even abolished war—on December 7, 1682. (Why not celebrate *that,* instead of Pearl Harbor?) The Quaker regime produced both internal and external kinds of security: the colony remained an island of peace when storms swept over surrounding territories, traumatizing the relations of the red and white races down to our own time.

In this way, despite its problems, the seventy-year Quaker regime "laid the foundations for what became some of the . . . guiding principles of an entire nation."[28] America as a whole owes something to the Holy Experiment, which was based squarely upon ideals and principles that we would recognize today as nonviolence and which tried to carry those principles out in social policy, criminal justice, religious toleration—even national defense.

As Gandhi was later to declare, "Nonviolence that merely offers civil resistance to the authorities and goes no further scarcely deserves the name."[29] Under his leadership, it went much further indeed, and in terms of power relationships it went in three directions. While the Indian *satyagrahis* were resisting the Raj, they were also, on Gandhi's insistence, trying to be nonviolent toward the Muslim community that shared the British yoke with them, and toward the "scheduled castes" who were beneath them in the ancient Hindu social hierarchy. If their anti-British resistance came from below, in terms of political space, they were also nonviolently working sideways on the communal question and downward toward the former untouchables, renamed by Gandhi *harijans,* or "children of God." He came to feel very early on that these two relationships were, if anything, more important than nonviolence toward their rulers, that relationships of truth with their equals and with their social "inferiors"—with the underclass they themselves had created—were an essential prerequisite to loosening the British hold. Nonviolence was the rule of life, not the rule of only one kind of relationship.

Gandhi himself never showed the slightest inclination to take public office. But there was a long tradition in India of the ideal ruler, who would hold sway over his or her subjects by integrative power instead of threat power, and that ideal came close to being a reality in at least one famous case I've already alluded to—when Emperor Ashoka, whom H. G. Wells called the greatest emperor in history, built his rule on Buddhist principles in north-central India. Ashoka had ascended the throne of his father's sizable kingdom probably in 269 B.C.E. After he had exercised power for about eight years, he won a famous victory, but instead of rejoicing, he recorded that the horror of war was borne in on him by the scenes of death and suffering. That vision turned an ordinary conquest into a personal crisis, a demand for self-conquest, that was to change history. As the emperor described it:

> When the King, Priyadarsi [Ashoka], Beloved of the Gods, had been consecrated eight years, Kalinga was conquered. 150,000 people were thence taken captive, 100,000 were killed, and many more died. Just after the taking of Kalinga the Beloved of the Gods began to follow Righteousness [*dharma*, i.e., he adopted Buddhism], to love Righteousness, to give instruction in Righteousness. When an unconquered country is conquered, people are killed, they die, or are made captive. That the Beloved of the Gods finds very pitiful and grievous. . . . Today, if a hundredth or a thousandth part of those who suffered in Kalinga were to be killed, to die, or be taken captive, it would be very grievous to the Beloved of the Gods. If anyone does him wrong it will be forgiven as far as it can be forgiven. The Beloved of the Gods even reasons with the forest tribes in his empire, and seeks to reform them. But the Beloved of the Gods is not only compassionate, he is powerful, and he tells them to repent, lest they be slain. For the Beloved of the Gods desires safety, self-control, justice and happiness for all beings. The Beloved of the Gods considers that the greatest of all victories is the victory of Righteousness.[30]

Ashoka reigned from 273 B.C.E. until he died, of natural causes, in 232 B.C.E., having considerably enlarged the already great territories he had inherited from his famous grandfather, Chandragupta Maurya. As this edict makes clear, he had no intention of abdicating the responsibility of securing his realm; indeed, he enlarged it, but he was never again to practice violence as an instrument of conquest. He showed that one in power could be pragmatic and yet compassionate. He showed, if you will, that compassion not only comes from strength—it begets strength. William Penn was a major contributor, through an important essay, to the tradition of "perpetual peace" thinking in Europe, but Ashoka's influence went even further, for it was he who spread Buddhism to much of Southeast Asia.

It is interesting to compare these two real experiments with the fate of a utopian regime in Aldous Huxley's novel *Island,* which so captured the imagination of the sixties. Its somewhat psychedelic version of mysticism and its escapist picture of a free life spoke to that generation's hungers, but in one important respect it perpetuated, unconsciously, the very worldview it was trying to escape. The novel ends with doom hanging over the island paradise, which is about to be overwhelmed by a neighboring state. The outside world is jealous of the island. That's realistic enough. And because the islanders are unaggressive they have no defense. That isn't. Neither the Holy Experiment of Emperor Ashoka nor of William Penn was defenseless against outside pressures, as we have seen. Neither was the weapon-less Tokugawa Shogunate nor contemporary Costa Rica—one of twelve national states without a defense force, and one of the very few that does not rely on a defense arrangement with any other state—nor other smaller and lesser-known regimes that have renounced the protection of violence in some way or degree.

In fact, we can check the validity of Huxley's imaginary finale in another way. At dawn one day, the Gaviotans who provided us with the opening image of this book were getting ready to go to work when they found themselves "visited" by an armed unit of the *Fuerzas Armadas Revolucionarias de Colombia.* The uniformed brigade tried to explain to the utopians the need for armed struggle. "There is no neutral ground in Colombia," the commandant argued. "You're either with us or against us." But the Gaviotans replied, "We're with people, not politics." The guerillas left them in peace. They had been ordered not to hurt *los gavioteros* because the latter's experiment was so valuable.[31] On a small scale, the episode shows again that when it comes to the power of nonviolence, even Huxley's imagination did not go far enough. The novel does allow us to discern that, yes, non-violence doesn't "work"—in novels; but its alleged defenselessness is not borne out by the logic of science or the facts of history. With non-violence we can protect the good as well as disrupt the schemes of the tyrannical.

Springtime in Prague

In the late spring of 1968, the Soviet high command became alarmed by the "dangerous" liberalizations of party secretary Aleksander Dubcek, which were threatening to create a different kind of Communism in Czechoslovakia. Their response to "socialism with a human face" was to order massive Warsaw Pact armies into the country. Soviet military experts predicted it would take four days to bring Czechoslovakia to heel, and by military criteria they were right. But those are not the only criteria on which the real world runs. Lacking a military way to defend themselves, the Czechs somehow came up with a rough-and-ready civilian resistance that was nonviolent in character. They could not keep the Soviets out, but they could and did refuse to obey curfew orders, using that time to stroll about in the streets and plant flowers in soldiers' rifles or engage them in heated discussions. They turned street signs around and watched armored columns rumble off aimlessly into the countryside; in one such episode, an entire Polish army that tried to invade was fooled into spending a whole day circling back to the Polish border. (A friend of mine was in a Prague bookstore when a Russian tank pulled up outside. One of the soldiers came in and patiently waited his turn at the cash register, then asked for a map of the city, which he politely paid for in Czech money.) They published alternative media to replace banned papers and radio stations, with Czech police often delivering outlawed newspapers in their squad cars. They defended not their territory but their institutions, and they did this not with weapons but with a characteristic Czech blend of humor, courage, and solidarity. As far as possible, life went on as if the occupation forces were simply not there.

Remember, they were not dealing with the dispirited Russian army, which was to bog down in Afghanistan and Chechnya; they were dealing with half a million determined troops under orders to put down what they were told, and many must have believed, was a full-fledged counterrevolution. For eight full months, from August 20, 1968, to April 17, 1969, these armies were frustrated by untrained citizens who kept on fraternizing with them as people while determinedly noncooperating with them as invaders. As a KGB agent ten years later confided, after a few drinks, to my friend Gene Sharp of the Center for Nonviolent Sanctions at Harvard, "My boy, it was a complete disaster!"

Later, when the ghastly Soviet empire collapsed from inside, taking most of world Communism down with it, jubilant Western analysts would call it the "end of history." What are we going to learn from all this history, then? Should not the spontaneous Soviet collapse (not unlike the Rosenstraße demonstrations) have prompted a sobering reflection—that we could have dealt with the Communist menace all along in an entirely different mode, without that expense of human life, that mortgaging of the hope of half the world for a decent development, not to mention the psychological trauma endured by all of us when all life on earth hung at risk? "Prague Spring" showed the innate weakness of such an oppressive system, and the glimmer of a way to exploit that weakness. It is one of the best-known examples of spontaneous nonviolence in Europe but, like all examples of nonviolence anywhere, is scarcely known to any but a small band of prophetic enthusiasts.

In the eight months that it took for Moscow to reassert control over Czechoslovakia, whole armies had to be rotated out of the country and replaced with troops who had not been "corrupted" by contact with the civilians. Resistance sputtered on even after the civilian leaders were coerced into accepting a shadow compromise. Most of the new recruits were brought in from remote parts of the Soviet empire and could not understand a Slavic language. An armed resistance that held off such an overwhelming force for eight months would have passed into folklore—a new Thermopylae, which we remember after 2,000 years. But in 1968 there wasn't even a name for the type of resistance the Czech civilians were carrying out, and so we were left with the irony of Prague Spring—that because an untrained people were able to offer successful resistance for eight months without shedding a drop of blood, the world hardly noticed anything was happening.

Now, however, we do have a name for this kind of resistance, thanks in large part to Gene Sharp's pioneering work.[32] What the Czechs did is now known as Civilian-Based Defense (CBD). CBD is one of two main forms in which nonviolence has emerged as an alternative to war, and I'll give both a thorough review later, in chapter 8. We should note, for now, two principles of CBD by which a determined and reasonably united people can withstand an invasion, as in Prague, or an internal takeover, such as the failed proto-Fascist Kapp Putch in Weimar Germany in 1920; or even resist within the context of an occupation, like the Norwegian schoolteachers' strike, which prevented the Nazification of the Norwegian school system. One principle is: a people who will not submit cannot be ruled. They can be killed, but they cannot be ruled. The other is: if a people can steadfastly discriminate between a group of people and their agenda—between the sinners and the sin—resolutely resisting the latter while just as resolutely acknowledging the humanity of the former, they develop an almost irresistible force. Did the Prague resistance "work"? No, it did not save the Czech liberalization. And yet, I would say, it "worked" extremely well, considering that it bought the country eight exhilarating months, even though it was an impromptu reaction by people who—as usual—had no training and no real leadership for this kind of social action, most of whom probably could not have told you what it's called, not to mention how to apply its principles with flexibility and appropriateness. It "worked" well enough to allow us to think that it might have finally prevailed, had the Czechs been determined to go on until the peace was won, had they understood what they had stumbled upon.

And did Prague Spring work (no quote marks)? Let me draw on the testimony of an eyewitness, my late friend Petra Kelly:

> During the summer of 1968, when nonviolent citizens in Prague were resisting the occupying Soviet forces, my grandmother and I were there in a hotel near Wenceslaus Square, under house arrest. Even after Dubcek and his close associates were arrested, the people remained steadfast in their resistance. Eventually . . . the Soviets were able to reassert their authority and delay the reforms of the Prague Spring by twenty-one years. But through their sacrifice and suffering, the people of Czechoslovakia . . . later did indeed succeed in their "Velvet Revolution." These events demonstrate the power of nonviolent social defense.[33]

The power, in other words, to change things for the better, to solve unforeseen problems down the road—and sometimes those at hand as well. Prague Spring did not last long. But then, neither did the mighty empire that seemed to win that unequal struggle.

SAY IT WITH FLOWERS?

The stories of many Holocaust rescuers have been coming to light in recent years—fortunately, since a few of the rescuers are still alive. Oskar Schindler, who is not, was made world famous by the novel and Steven Spielberg's film about his "list," but in peace circles one of the best-known stories unfolded in the village of Le Chambon-sur-Lignon in the Haute-Loire, not far from Marseille, which is to say, in Vichy territory. But it was also Hugenot territory, where a Protestant minority had endured persecutions in centuries past. When the occupation came to Le Chambon, Pastor André Trocmé and his wife, Magda, inspired their whole parish to set up an underground escape route that went on sheltering refugees or spiriting them out of the country, under the noses of the Vichy government and the nearby Tatar Legion of the SS, throughout the war. If our previous examples showed that nonviolence can work against bitter opposition, or from the political top, or against whole states—if they began to give us some sense, in other words, of the variety and range of its applications —then the resistance at Le Chambon tells us something about its inner consistency.

The resistance of the Chambonnais is one of the few cases that is not a leaderless, "amateur" effort: Trocmé had come to his convictions early and knew of Gandhi through the Fellowship of Reconciliation (FOR), a venerable peace organization begun by two Quakers, a German, and an Englishman, who found themselves on a railway platform in Cologne at the outbreak of WWI and swore never to let the enmity of their countries come between them or their joint longing for peace. FOR has today one of the longest track records of an existing peace group, and one of the best foundations in nonviolent principles. Outside of the Danish underground's rescue of that country's entire Jewish population, the resistance at Le Chambon was the largest such operation in Europe and has been relatively well known to a general public since ethicist Phillip Hallie wrote his study *Lest Innocent Blood Be Shed.* One interesting question is, how did an operation of that size escape the attention of the Germans?

And the interesting answer is, it didn't. Many years after the events of 1940 to 1944, Hallie found out that the commandant of the region, Major Schmehling, had known what *les responsables* of Le Chambon were up to the whole time, but he was so moved by the villagers' courage that he actually defied the SS to protect them: "I am a good Catholic, you understand, and I can grasp these things," he explained to the Trocmés twenty years later.[34] At the time, the

Chambonnais had no idea that Schmehling was protecting them at such risk to himself. If it had not been for Hallie's research, neither would we. Imagine how many things of this sort we *never* find out—how many such stories are hidden in history, a science that until recently was not concerned to look for them.

Le Chambon is an example of nonviolence that both "worked" and worked; it saved 5,000 people (i.e., it "worked against the Nazis") and it created an enduring light in the midst of vast darkness. It was Schmehling, who had been impressed by the sincerity of one of the Chambonnais at his trial testimony, who explained to SS leader Colonel Metzger, "This kind of resistance has nothing to do with violence, nothing to do with anything we can destroy with violence."[35]

The Chambonnais carried on their work for three years, daily sticking by their choice to risk death rather than abandon the responsibility they had accepted. Therefore, in addition to Trocmé's astute leadership, they had the advantage of passing through the crucible of sustained experience. One result of this was that they moved past the stage that's reached by most of the events we consider as nonviolence or peace activity in the world: the stage of symbolic resistance. Things began at Le Chambon the way they begin very commonly when the urge to resist awakens—as symbolic defiance, but they did not stop there: "The saluting of flags, the ringing of bells, the giving of oaths dissolved as important issues for the Chambonnais. . . . What was left was the one *activity* that made Le Chambon a village of refuge: the saving of innocent lives."[36] (my emphasis) This important point is so often misunderstood that it must be stressed: in nonviolence, you don't say it with symbols. When Sir Richard Attenborough's film brought the phenomenon of Gandhi to public attention, one startled journalist, I recall, said that *Gandhi* was about "the mystery of a man just sitting, holding a flower." I have seen, I believe, every still photograph and every foot of film of Gandhi that's in public domain. He never holds a flower in any of them. He has a staff, a spinning wheel, a microphone, but never a flower. The man used tools, not symbols.

It is important for us to realize that just because people wear ribbons or have marched from point A to point B with placards, it doesn't mean they have been nonviolent. Not yet. And, therefore, if their demonstration doesn't "work" (or work, needless to say), we have no right to say that nonviolence failed. There hasn't *been* any nonviolence until there has been personal struggle or sacrifice, followed by outer work—both things that are, in their respective ways, quite concrete. They are not requests or signs; they are acts. They may be symbols *also,* but first and foremost they are real.

But what about the protest marches Gandhi led in South Africa and India? Let's look at those famous marches a little closer. The first, now known as the "Great March," was launched in South Africa on November 6, 1913, when Gandhi found himself in charge of several thousand striking mine workers and their families. It was first of all a deliberate act of civil disobedience undertaken by the miners-turned-*satyagrahis* from Newcastle in Natal province, who entered the Transvaal to court arrest. It was, in other words, an illegal act. Indians who did not live there were not allowed to enter the Transvaal. It was not about going from point A to point B to show they cared about something. These mine workers had lived on company property; when they walked off the job, they lost their homes, and there was nothing to do but march to the Transvaal where Gandhi would try to accommodate them at his ashram. Thus, the march was not a mere symbol. They were not merely voting with their feet; they were going somewhere they had to go—and defying the law in the process.

Now recall the most famous march of all, the one that launched the climactic Salt Satyagraha of 1930, when Gandhiji and seventy-eight ashram volunteers undertook a 200-mile "pilgrimage" to the seacoast town of Dandi to take illegal salt from the ocean in defiance of the government monopoly. Along the way, some 70,000 people fell in with the civilly disobedient "pilgrims." You may know the scene from Attenborough's film: what you see is real people going down to a real sea to get real salt that had been cruelly withheld from them for the purpose of rank exploitation, and once again they were breaking an unjust law to do it. What could be more basic, more concrete, than salt? If anything, it was the absurd monopoly over salt taking that was smoke-and-mirrors, a construct that millions had taken for real until Gandhi's brilliant gesture broke the illusion. Of course, Gandhi could have taken a train—but then how would he have brought with him those tens of thousands? Call it theater, if you will, but not symbol.[37]

Let's look again at the Gandhian definition of power that I cited in chapter 2, and mark the precise language:

> Of power there are two kinds. One is obtained by *fear*
> of punishment and the other by *acts* of love.[38] (my
> emphasis)

I emphasize the difference between *fear,* on the one hand, and *acts* to again point up the greater concreteness of nonviolence over violence. Symbols can play a role in the initial stage of a movement; they can encourage people to stand up and be counted, to show solidarity. But once they're all there and counted, what will the people *do?* If they keep on waving flags and marching from point A to point B, they will be going against the spirit and the deepest reality of nonviolence. You could almost say, at that point symbols perpetuate the very thing the actors should be trying to dispel: the belief that only threat force has real power, and thus nonviolence is merely an appeal to the other's sentiment, not, as Gandhi insisted, an awakening of his or her awareness. This contradiction may be why in practice many symbols backfire in nonviolent action—for example the "Goddess of Liberty" put up by the students and other protestors at Tienanmen Square, which infuriated but did nothing to incapacitate, much less dissuade, the authorities.

Threat power, on the other hand, does not come from punishment, in Gandhi's instinctive word choice: it comes from the victim's *"fear of* punishment." No fear, no power: it has even been argued, I think cogently, that the scariest "what if" scenario of modern times— "What if Hitler had gotten the bomb?"—is really not as compelling as it may sound. OK, what if he had used atomic bombs on one or two cities *and what if we said,* "Do your worst: we will not give in"? Would he have wanted to rule over a radioactive wasteland? In actual legal and political experience, threat is a much less reliable way of getting people to comply than it seems.[39] We have to react to the threat as it was intended or it won't work. Tyrants rule by fear much more than by the actual power they have to inflict harm. To repeat, if we have no fear we cannot be deterred. This is why Gandhi said that Satyagraha "compels reason to be free," while punishment only works on those who emotionally cooperate by fearing it. The Nobel Prize–winning biologist Albert Szent-Gyeorgyi brought this out very well in an appreciative summary of Gandhi's historical significance (like most people, he used the word *force* for what we would call *threat force*):

> Between the two world wars, at the heyday of Colonialism, force reigned supreme. It had a suggestive power, and it was natural for the weaker to lie down before the stronger.
>
> Then came Gandhi, chasing out of his country, almost singlehanded, the greatest military power on earth. He taught the world that there are higher things than force, higher even than life itself; he proved that force had lost its suggestive power.[40]

Violence can hurt us, but it can't make us change our minds or even our behavior. Only *fear* of violence can do that. Nonviolence, too, works on the emotions, but those of us who have used nonviolence successfully know that its native mode of operation is quite concrete.

The Washington-based Search for Common Ground is one of the most successful international conflict-resolving organizations in the world, to my knowledge. They began by simply trying to get people who are bitterly opposed to each other, who think they have no common basis of agreement—for example "pro-choice" and "pro-life" people—to identify some common ground to build on. John Marks, the president of Search, has told me that "while dialogue is important, it should lead to something concrete." Ideally, opponents should work together on shared problems, like ethnic Slavs and Albanians cleaning up religious sites together.

"Working together on shared problems" is precisely the formula discovered by a well-known team of psychologists who tried all kinds of ways to resolve conflict in a summer camp, and found that simply having the two parties work together to fix the truck or get the well working did the trick. Seeing movies or eating ice cream together didn't do it.[41] In fact, some of the world's most bitter conflicts are over symbols, and some of the sweetest resolutions have come when the nonreal conflict was confronted with the reality check of concrete truth.

If nonviolence had no inherent power, then signs and ribbons and statues would be about the most effective things you could do—but then, if nonviolence had no inherent power, there'd be no reason to write a book about it.

SOCIAL WARMING

For all the ugliness of his message, white supremacist Tom Metzger made an unarguable point in the first epigraph to this chapter: violence comes in degrees. There's such a thing as "big, massive" violence, and indeed it "works"; the bomb that destroyed the Murrah Federal Building in Oklahoma City on April 15, 1995, had more impact than a lone protestor railing against the government from a soapbox. This would be a trivial observation were it not for the fact that the corollary, which I have been trying to demonstrate, is somehow less obvious: that nonviolence, too, comes in degrees. Any amount of love we launch in any situation will do work, but if we want it to "work," i.e., to have a specific effect then and there, then it has to wield *enough* love to outweigh the hate that's operating in that situation. The hate set loose at Auschwitz was extreme; therefore, the tremendous power of a supreme sacrifice, such as Father Kolbe made, was required to counter it when the moment came for him to act decisively against it.

Gandhi said of his followers and himself that the success of their efforts in the last Free India campaign in 1942 was "mathematically proportionate" to the purity of their nonviolence; I believe he meant it literally, and I for one believe that it was—it is always—literally true. If we had some idea how to measure the forces I'm here calling love and hate, we would probably see that there were no accidents or surprises in the long process that finally gave India her political independence. We know how deep, how second nature in people and how institutionalized in society, was the distortion of race relations when Rosa Louise McCauley Parks refused to give up her seat on a Montgomery bus on December 1, 1955. In the years that followed, much of that dehumanization was exposed and released; the institutions it had built, dismantled. *How* much, if we could measure it, would give us the sum total of the force set in motion by Parks's training at the well-known Highlander Folk School, by her courage, by Martin Luther King Jr.'s genius and the power of sacrifice and the sustained work that he inspired in so many?

The weather is notoriously unpredictable. But something about it, as we know to our cost, is only too predictable: if we keep pouring fluorocarbons into the atmosphere, if we keep on burning up the rain forests and all the fossil fuel we can get our hands on, we will continue heating up the planet. Global warming is a man-made phenomenon we have never before experienced. Because of global warming, small perturbations in the atmosphere that are themselves perfectly normal and unavoidable—maybe as small as a little updraft, causing a small eddy somewhere over the Atlantic—can cascade into terrifically destructive storms. When and where these will occur we cannot predict, but we can predict *that* they will occur, more and more, if we continue heating up our planet. There will be other effects of global warming, too. We can safely predict only one thing about the changes wrought by such an unnatural development: they will hurt us.

It is just this way with violence. We cannot predict *who* will lose it and walk into which high school with what kind of weapon, but we know sure as anything that as generation after generation watches more violent TV and movies, plays more dehumanizing video games, there *will* be more suffering from violence. Here is the judgment of the American Psychological Association's Commission on Violence and Youth in 1993, which was echoed over the next few years by the U.S. surgeon general, the American Medical Association, and virtually all of the country's most prestigious health organizations: "There is absolutely no doubt that higher levels of viewing violence on television are correlated with increased acceptance of aggressive attitudes and increased aggressive behavior."[42] When we're boiling water, we can't predict which molecules will vaporize when, nor do we need to. Just turn off the flame.

The media not only elicit violence, but they incapacitate us from solving it, as we've seen, by directing our attention to the part that we cannot predict, namely who will "lose it" when. If we are to be a free, responsible people, we shall have to put 90 percent of our attention back on the basic fact we *can* predict: violence begets violence. And on its converse: nonviolence begets nonviolence.

Nonviolence is a science if there ever was one, but it cannot make predictions as neatly as mechanics or electricity, for Satyagraha is what Gandhi called "a living force," not a physical one. Those "crosscurrents of violence and responsiveness" Pepinsky referred to as running constantly in all of us help to account for episodes of violent behavior but cannot predict them exactly. They do not put a formula in our hands that would let us say, "If we get thirty hours less violent programming per week, there will be 3,000 fewer homicides per year." It would take some sort of chaos theory to gain exactitude in predicting how a person or a mob will react. Sometimes we're nice to people and they nonetheless blow up at us. That is life.

But there is one thing about violence/nonviolence that is very simple and very predictable, and again it may be the only basic thing we have to know about it: somewhere, somehow, violence will always hurt, while somewhere, somehow, nonviolence will always heal. To ring a slight change on the formula we arrived at earlier, *violence some-*

times "works" but it never works; nonviolence sometimes "works" and never fails to work to make human life somewhere somewhat better.

So nonviolence is, like the weather, at once mysterious and predictable. When Gandhi said, "Nonviolence is not the inanity it has been taken for down the ages,"[43] I take him to mean both that it is far less limited in scope and far less arbitrary in its effects than we still believe. My Peace Studies colleague, Professor Gordon Fellman, has accurately described the way nonviolence is portrayed in, for example, *High Noon*—a far more influential piece of fiction than Huxley's *Island*. In this iconic film we see a leading lady with scruples about killing, but this "nonviolence" of hers is portrayed as "undeveloped, a simplistic, weak alternative with no program, no imagination, and no real integrity."[44] As soon as we see that nonviolence is first of all not a kind of outcry but a kind of power, strong in its own right, and that it can be offered by anyone toward anyone, whether one is in a concentration camp or a president's suite, we begin to break out of the "inane" limitation of nonviolence to a mere tactic that may possibly "work," if our opponent is nice.

That said, I've broached a daring proposition, which I'll develop more fully later on: when we have sufficient knowledge of how nonviolence works and can think of the appropriate way to mobilize it, it can even be used to make obsolete the scourge of war.

And yet, we have just begun to explore its possibilities. Despite the variety of the fields in which we've so far seen nonviolence in action, we have looked at only one modality of this "matchless weapon." It has two. It should be clear the minute we realize that nonviolence is a primary reality, not a non-something, that its classic expression may not be in the protest mode at all, real *or* symbolic. It is true that Gandhi once called himself a "professional resister" when he was asked his profession in a British-run court, but out of court he gave a rather different account of his life's work: "My real politics is constructive work."[45] Nonviolence is not only a method of struggle against wrongs (as Penn and Ashoka demonstrated) but also—indeed primarily—a force that builds things right in the first place. For most of us, who are not protestors, this takes nonviolence off the shelf and puts it right into our own hands as an entirely new tool that we can use every day to design the future we and our children get to live in; and to this intriguing prospect we can now turn.

CHAPTER FIVE

A WAY OUT OF HELL

How much more delightful to an undebauched mind
is the task of making improvements on the earth, than all
the vain glory that can be acquired from ravaging it.

—George Washington

Put the lover of justice to shame with your compassion.

—Saint Isaac of Syria

MUBARAK AWAD HAS been a guest speaker in my nonviolence class as often as I can get him. A big, gentle man, an extremely engaging and sincere speaker with a keen sense of nonviolence, he speaks in vivid, Arabic-inflected English that always adds a note of authenticity when we discuss one of the world's most important nonviolent uprisings, the first Palestinian *intifada* (literally, "shaking off," or "shaking up"). Mubarak, after all, founded the Palestinian Center for the Study of Nonviolence, which I suspect had a lot to do with that movement. The Israeli government certainly thought so. His most dramatic visit was undoubtedly in 1990, when he came in fresh from his expulsion from Palestine. Along with the glow of martyrdom, Mubarak had real inside information to share with us. My students already knew enough not to accept uncritically the media image of the *intifada* as a violent, even "terrorist," uprising, but what we didn't know was what it was like to be there "on the ground" facing riot-armed Israeli soldiers. Mubarak, a trained psychologist, was the ideal person to share that with us.

The *intifada* began in 1987, when it became clear that the terrorism and guerilla tactics of the Palestinian exiles had not worked and
that it was up to the Palestinians actually living under Israeli occupation to do something about their destiny. What they did was resist with
Gandhian techniques of selective boycotts, shutdowns, and the like
(mostly learned from Gene Sharp via Mubarak) plus some indigenous
ideas of their own with a dash of highly confrontational stone throwing—an uneasy mix of what I call "non-dash-violent," i.e., refraining
from (serious) violence against one's opponent without trying to love
him or her out of the opponent category with positive energy. This put
the Palestinian youth, in particular, under a lot of pressure: because so
many adults were being arrested, teens were forced to take up respon-
sibilities and face dangers—beatings, imprisonment, death—that
most of us don't have to cope with even as adults. This, of course,
impressed my students greatly. But what surprised Mubarak, and all of
us, was that when the *intifada* got under way, the youth of the occupied territories stopped taking drugs. Drug and alcohol abuse, until
then a serious problem, virtually disappeared.

We asked him to go on. In the Gaza Strip and Israel proper, there
was the same class of youth, ethnically and economically, as in the
occupied territories, he explained, but these young people had no way
to participate in the uprising. Sure enough, there was no such change
in this "control" group: where there was no *intifada,* drugs and alcohol
continued their destructive course.

You may be wondering at this point what I'm leading up to. Am
I saying that the way to get rid of the drug problem is a nonviolent
revolution?

Of course not. What I'm saying is much more outrageous. As far
as I can see, we can get rid of *all* problems with a nonviolent revolution. Not just drugs; not even just crime itself—just about everything
but death and taxes. How can I make this extravagant claim? If we start
from the streets of Ramallah and Beit Sahour, we can thread our way
to the answer.

ADDICTED TO MEANING

By coincidence, shortly after Mubarak told us about all this, the papers carried a surprising report about substance abusers in the United States. Three researchers, working quite independently of each other, all found to their surprise that the conventional wisdom about who takes drugs in America is wrong. The "typical" drug abuser in America is not a black male, not strapped by poverty in a ghetto. All three scientists turned up a totally different profile.

> The same person who gets ahead in the workforce and is more of a risk taker, is more daring, [and more] susceptible to drugs. . . . [They have] a far more active lifestyle, are much more engaged in political campaigns, are much bigger users of information.[1]

They are, in short, the most upwardly mobile people in American society, the "cutting edge."

None of the three scientists could explain why being more capable than average made someone more, rather than less, vulnerable to drug abuse. One said it's because of "some hidden factor"; another wondered whether "there's something in the basic personality" of the higher achievers, without proposing what it might be. The third scientist was at least on to something: these people are "high sensation seekers," he observed. Accordingly, he prescribed a program of terrific sensations for them: skydiving, bungee-cord jumping and disco dancing, with MTV-style jumps from one thing to the next under a barrage of heavy metal music. This sensation blitz indeed helped them stay off drugs—better than bumper stickers that "just say no." But this only begs the question: what made these talented, energetic young people think they could find happiness in sensations in the first place?

I propose to you that these active, intelligent people are not really looking for more sensations. They *think* they are, because that's what the mass media condition all of us to think. What they are really looking for is some meaning in life.

> The Cooperative Institutional Research Program recently surveyed the brightest young people in the United States. It found them overwhelmingly materialistic [with] an unprecedented concern with money, power and status. The biggest declines involved altruistic interests and social concerns.[2]

These are clear signs of people without a purpose.

The Americans and Palestinians who got out of drugs in such different ways—a "high sensation" program, on the one hand, and a largely nonviolent revolution on the other—had both gotten into drugs for similar reasons: despite the striking contrast in their outward circumstances, both had succumbed to hopelessness about their lives. The Palestinian youth faced a stark future, where every chance to grow was blocked by an overpowering, often contemptuous, oppressor. The North Americans were facing a life of temporary, external satisfactions they already knew to be hollow from personal experience. They were rich, but in a way they were very poor; they were what Mother Teresa called "the spiritually poorest of the poor" because they could not see their way to a life of service and meaning.

So they were both looking for a purpose in life, which, I'm afraid, is not to be found in bouncing on the end of a bungee cord. I would safely bet that after awhile the swooping sensation in the belly, the rush of being a human yo-yo to jarring music will wear thin, and the sensation seekers may even find themselves going back to the needle. Materialism and sensationalism are part of the problem, not the solution—and it's a much bigger problem than that facing this group in particular. It's everyone's problem. If we had the whole country bouncing on bungee cords, would it solve crime, homelessness, and despair? In Roszakian language, high sensations may "work" (for some), but they don't work.

Here is where the *intifada* was different. It didn't just give young

Palestinians something to do; it gave them something *meaningful* to do. True, bungee cords and the *intifada* both offer danger and excitement (as does combat), but nonviolent resistance offers danger, a sense of risk, for an overriding purpose. In the other cases danger, or rather the thrill of facing danger, *is* the purpose. And that's not good enough. I can't help recalling once again the words of Sue Severin, the Marin County health professional who went down to Nicaragua with Witness for Peace:

> The only way I can explain it is, I felt I was in the hands of God: not safe—that I wouldn't be hurt—but that I was where I was supposed to be, doing what I was supposed to be doing. And this can be addictive. Maybe that's why we kept going back.

Almost uncanny that Sue should use the word *addictive* in this connection, but that is how powerful meaningful work can be—strong enough to overcome chemical dependency. Recently, *Youth Outlook (YO)*, a San Francisco–based youth newspaper interviewed a young addict in San Francisco who gave a heartbreaking explanation of why he takes heroin: "I want quiet peace to inject my soul with forever."[3]

He was looking for peace. Who is not? He looked for it in drugs because he was conditioned—and today who is not conditioned?—to think that what we need comes from outside us: peace is something we inject; security, health are things we buy. Yet some of us know that what we're looking for *isn't* outside us, that it's the inner peace that can lift us even out of potent addictions, the peace that comes when we've found a convincing purpose for our lives.

Is my outrageous claim starting to make some sense?

CRIMINAL INJUSTICE

Over the years, I have seen hundreds of young people working on projects that are similar in spirit to the *intifada* uprising, if not as dangerous. This has been one of the great privileges in my life. Some months prior to the NATO bombing of ex-Yugoslavia I served as moderator for a Berkeley "teach-in" on the sufferings of ethnic Albanians of Kosovo. On the panel were two of the young people I mentioned earlier who had just gotten back from two days in a Serbian jail. They spoke with quiet passion. They spoke from the deep security of having found something to do, however small it seemed, about the suffering in the world. They spoke cogently, without anger (though some Serb nationalists in the audience were charging the atmosphere with plenty). They spoke with love. I remember thinking how I would want all my students—in fact, I would want every one of us—to have such a sense of quiet fulfillment.

I'm not saying this in the spirit of "let the kids do peace work; it's good for them and it may keep them off drugs." I'm saying that these young people have hit upon something—a principle. It is a principle we too can apply in our own ways, individually, and then corporately. To illustrate that, I want to enlarge our focus to a problem that is arguably the biggest we now face as a society, perhaps as a civilization.

At the present time, roughly half of the juvenile detention and incarceration in America is for drug-related crimes. The amount Americans pay for illegal drugs is staggering—officials noted with naive satisfaction that it came *down* to $57.3 billion in 1995.[4] In response, we throw on another $17.9 billion to wage a "war" on mind-altering drugs. And that war is failing. On that point, scores of analysts who have studied the hapless war in detail all agree. Under these circumstances, we cannot afford *not* to follow up on the implications of cases like those we've just been considering, cases of "spontaneous remission" of drug abuse in America and Israel-Palestine. They seem to open up the suggestion of an entirely different approach, one that is not a war on drugs, not a war on crime—odd as it may sound, not a war at all.

Drug abuse, like violence, could be looked at through various lenses, as we've already seen. In most of the West we have chosen, rightly or wrongly, to look at it as a crime. There are other possibilities, but all right, let's call it that for now, and let's take this as an opportunity to look at the whole question of crime. The war on drugs (which somehow often comes down to a war on victims of drug abuse) is part of our war on crime in general, and that larger war is also a drastic failure. The National Criminal Justice Commission reported in 1996 that "the prison population has tripled since 1980 and expenditures on law enforcement have quadrupled. Yet crime rates are essentially unchanged and fear is higher than ever."[5] And since then? Matters have gone on deteriorating. "Let us begin with a fundamental realization," wrote criminologist Richard Quinney at the head of an important book called *Criminology as Peacemaking.*

> No amount of thinking and no amount of public policy have brought us any closer to understanding and solving the problem of crime. The more we have reacted to crime, the further we have removed ourselves from any understanding and any reduction of the problem.[6]

In a word—the word of Ruth Morris, in her landmark book *Penal Abolition*—our whole criminal justice system, not just the war on drugs, is "an expensive, unjust, immoral failure."[7]

This double failure—the rise in crime and violence and the nation's inability to contain them—has brought our civilization to a defining moment. In April 1967, when we were in the grip of the Vietnam War, Martin Luther King Jr. made the prophetic observation that for every nation there comes a time like this when it faces a defining moral crisis. "Though we might prefer it otherwise," he said in his famous speech at the Riverside Church in New York, "we must choose in this crucial moment of human history."[8] We did not rise to that challenge, we did not find an honorable end to the war, but in my opinion we did not altogether sink below the possibility of redemption. Rather, as always seems to happen when such problems are not resolved, we have lurched on to another crisis, or perhaps the same one in a different guise.

> This is a watershed moment in California's history, a
> moment when we can take a path toward becoming a
> healthier society, or when we can consign every
> penny of future funding toward a failed system of
> human warehouses.[9]

This language of Vincent Schiraldi, former director of San
Francisco's Center on Juvenile and Criminal Justice, was echoed by
former Attorney General Ramsey Clark in a fund-raising letter some
time in 1998, when he said that our country is confronted with a
"stunning moral crisis." At that time (it's much worse now) there were
1,366 people on death row in the United States and we were adding
more every week. Only three countries—South Africa, China, and
Iran—were executing nearly as many.

Shortly after Ramsey Clark made this statement, South Africa
dropped out; the new, anti-Apartheid regime under Nelson Mandela
abolished the death penalty along with racist ideology. That leaves us
and China now leading the industrial world in penal severity, as we are
in crime (the number killed by guns in the United States each year is
on another order of magnitude from that of any industrialized nation).
In recent years the World Court has twice appealed to the United
States to postpone or commute a sentence of death, in vain. That's a
hard statement to have to make about the world's oldest democracy—
that we're leading the world back into punitive violence.

But crime is a crisis that has "opportunity" to it as well as dangers.
To see the opportunity amid these many negatives we have to look at
things in a different light.

CRIME AND RESTORATION

Following is part of a story from a special news group on positive
developments as it came streaming into my computer one day back in
1992:

Reference: Latin America
Title: ENVIRONMENT: OUTLAW POACHERS BECOME NATURE
RESERVE GUARDIANS
an inter press service feature
by roberto herrscher

buenos aires, nov (ips) — in an argentine nature
reserve, poachers who once hunted endangered species
have been converted into the conscientious guardians of
the animals they once stalked.

the remarkable conversion took place in the ibera
nature reserve, in corrientes province, 700 kilometers
north of argentina's capital.

in 1987, pedro perea munoz took over the directorship
of the ibera reserve. munoz met two poachers, "mingo"
cabrera and ramon cardoso, who had lived in the reserve
for as long as they could remember.

their life was difficult. cabrera and cardoso lived deep
in the swamps of ibera and survived by fishing and hunting. from time to time they would travel to the small
village of pellegrini, on the southern border of the
reserve, to sell carpincho, deer and alligator hides.

instead of adopting an antagonistic attitude, munoz
understood that these men knew ibera better than anyone
and that hunting was their only means of survival.

"they couldn't believe it when i offered them a job.
now they are the most dedicated and conscientious
guards (at ibera)," munoz told ips. . . .

"to understand nature, one must be peaceful. these men
were born with this. they were hunters by necessity,
and now, as guides and guardians, there is no one better.

by just looking into the eyes of people entering the
reserve, they know who the poachers are," munoz said....

amongst the clear crystal wetlands of ibera live the last
700 members of a rare south american swamp deer—a large
mammal, whose hooves end in toes united by membranes.

ibera's residents also include the "aguara guazu," a
small wolf in serious danger of extinction. a variety
of rodents, lizards, alligators and multicolored birds
complete the population of this unique and delicate
ecosystem. cabrera and cardoso are just two of six
guards in the reserve, but they are the favoured guides
for researchers, photographers, and members of ecological expeditions.

"now that we understand the importance of the reserve,
we see that, without realizing it, we were spending our
whole lives preparing for this," cabrera said.

This event turns our expectations wonderfully upside down.
Cabrera and Cardoso were technically "criminals," and warden Muñoz
certainly could have treated them as such. Yet what an opportunity he
would have lost! Instead, he somehow decided that rather than look on
the two men as the *cause* of the problem, he would turn to them for the
solution. They solved it. And notice two other results: (1) The whole
affair changed from a conflict to a classic "win-win" configuration in
which everyone gained: Muñoz got the job done, and Cabrera and
Cardoso changed from outlaws to employees, harmers to helpers;
everybody won—even the animals. (2) Cabrera and Cardoso got
something of profound, permanent benefit that we're starting to
recognize as a signature of nonviolent activities, namely, a sense of
meaning: "We were spending our whole lives preparing for this."
Pedro Muñoz is not the only person ever to have such an outlandish idea about crime and "criminals." About the same time as this

breakthrough, two American schoolteachers came up with the idea, quite independently, of taking young offenders who were in detention and putting them in charge of some severely handicapped youth. Sharon Roberts was one of the teachers. As she admitted, she was asking a lot of the Los Angeles school board to let her "put the most dangerous people in LA in charge of the most vulnerable."[10] The paradox worked brilliantly. Again, both the disabled youth and the offenders "won." "I was used to being a thug on the street," says Alfred, age sixteen, member of the Cripps, on probation for being accomplice to a shooting, "but now when my home boys come around . . . I tell them I have other things to do." Things like taking a disabled girl named Star to class, while he earns high school credits and work experience. "This shows I can do something. It's the first time I've felt like that. I feel more kind-hearted and stuff than I thought."[11]

Note how in Alfred's mind now, being helpful is the only thing that counts as "doing something." He has already come a long way from the attitude in the prevailing paradigm that to "do something" you should be helping *yourself,* if necessary by hurting others. But the big winners are now you and me—society as a whole. Young detainees who would have caused worse trouble down the line, almost without exception, were given a way out of this desperate spiral by the only method that can ever do that: they were enabled to find good in themselves.

In ancient Rome there was a saying, "*Curruptio optimum pessima,*" "The corruption of the best people is the worst kind." We might flip this around and say, "*Redemptio pessimum optima,*" "The reinstatement of the worst people makes them the best." This is not too paradoxical, since as we saw in the case of the high achievers who got into drugs, it's often the most capable people with the highest expectations who get the most frustrated with modern life. They feel most keenly the lurking emptiness in the modern definition of achievement, and at the same time they have great capacities, which have been turned to nonconstructive ends. In the worst troublemakers lies, logically enough, the most creative potential. The trick is knowing that it's there, then having the courage to reach for it.

"Peer mediation" programs have been catching on in many schools across the country. Teachers and administrators have been thrilled to find that not only do the programs "chill" a lot of the fighting, but a peculiar pattern emerges wherever they try it: the biggest troublemakers turn out to be the best mediators. How perfectly natural, really, when you know what's going on.

After his "conversion," one of those young troublemakers told a friend of mine that to be a mediator you have to "check your ego at the door." You're not just in it for yourself, is what he meant; you have to put your own feelings aside. Then he added, still more significantly, "I've always had the skills to be a mediator, but I didn't use them before because I had no one to show me how." Nor is he that special; everybody has this capacity that so very few learn to use. "We're all like hidden gold mines."

His statement is a textbook of conflict resolution condensed into three sentences:

(1) We have to "check our egos at the door," get a little above our own personal feelings. Some kind of spiritual sacrifice, large or small, is the basis of any action that can result in peace.

(2) All it would take for most of us to learn this skill is a little training—which, unfortunately, we rarely get.

(3) And finally, given such training, we would discover that there's a "gold mine" in every one of us. If we don't find a way to mine our inner resources, it causes the greatest trouble for us and society; when we do, we can find ourselves becoming the most creative peacemakers. Whether we start out as poachers in an Argentine game preserve or youth offenders in Los Angeles, the most difficult among us are often the ones most capable of helping to create loving community, if we would help them out of their difficulty.

So what the AP writer called the "remarkable conversion" of Cabrera and Cardoso is no more remarkable than the changeover of the *intifada* youth who stopped taking drugs, or the "most dangerous" of Los Angeles who discovered the satisfaction of taking care of another, helpless human being. In all these cases the "worst" had gotten that way because they saw no way to use the good that lay—often quite unexpected—within them. All that benefit would have been lost if the prevailing approaches to crime had been adopted.

CUNNING AS SERPENTS

The possibility of "hidden gold mines," of course, does not mean that we should immediately put offenders in charge of the disabled, endangered species, and peacemaking. Let us be idealistic, yes, but not naive. Quite a few "troublemakers" might rise to the occasion, but some would not. Writer Norman Mailer discovered this to his cost. In 1981 Mailer was, quite understandably, repelled by the hypocrisy of labeling people as "criminals" when we ourselves create the conditions that promote crime. He had been in correspondence with a particular violent offender, something of a writer himself, Jack Henry Abbott. As a kind of personal protest, Mailer used his influence to get Abbott released into his custody. Six weeks into his parole Abbott murdered Richard Adan, a twenty-two-year-old Greenwich Village waiter. Mailer realized with added shock that he had several times left his eighteen-year-old daughter alone with this man. Abbott hanged himself shortly afterward in prison.[12]

Mailer was perhaps naive, but it was a special kind of naivete many of us fall into when we become aware of something very wrong and react impatiently: we reverse the wrong instead of resolving it. In his eagerness to get rid of the "victimizer" label society had put on Abbott, Mailer swapped it for a "victimized" label: this person had been made bad by society, so it wasn't his fault, therefore he was innocent, therefore he was "good." Reversing labels doesn't get us closer to reality. What we really want to do is get *rid* of labels. That's the only way we can see each other as people. When a label falls, like one of those gels they use on theater lights, between us and real people, it is the beginning of violence. Sliding that gel out of the way is rehumanization. In the world of criminal (in)justice, rehumanization is being able to look at people realistically and see how they became lawbreakers. Then we can begin to understand what to do with them *and*—much more importantly—what to do so that others do not go through the same process.

Mailer's first impulse was absolutely correct; as Ruth Morris says, "Let's be clear that the dangerous few [in prisons] are used by all those who want to keep the other 99 percent in our present expensive, unjust, immoral system."[13] This is the logic by which a handful of militants can be used to discredit a whole struggle—all ethnic Albanians, for example, even grandmothers, were labeled "terrorists" by the Serbian regime. Mailer was only applying a well-known principle of nonviolence, that noncooperation with evil must never shade over into animosity toward evildoers—not even into labeling them as such. It may seem like a small thing—*criminal* is just a word, after all —but with that word comes the whole dehumanization response, and in the case of criminal justice that means the whole system Ruth Morris spoke of with such stinging accuracy. Gandhi was against using the word altogether:

> The word criminal should be erased from our vocab-
> ulary; or else we are all criminals.[14]

But then, Gandhi, Christian that he was, felt that "man is not capable of knowing the absolute truth and, therefore, not competent to punish" in the first place.[15] We want to stay away from such dangerous radicals, of course. Let's stick with some reliable professionals, like Dr. Arnold Trebacher, criminology professor and head of Washington's Drug Policy Foundation. Speaking from his own professional experience, Trebacher said, "The English and Dutch have taught me . . . that you can disapprove of drug use, but you don't have to hate users."[16] But if we don't want to hate them, we have to stop labeling them. Dr. Trebacher is only echoing one of the most important principles in Satyagraha—or for that matter Christianity: the definition of a

Christian, Augustine said a millennium and a half ago, is: "We hate the sin but not the sinner."

Today this ancient creed is providing the underpinning of a new outlook, called *restorative* as opposed to *retributive* justice. Let's give Harold Pepinsky the space to spell this out:

> In decades of sampling millennia of literature across traditions, and everyday attempts in any facet of life's attempts to become more socially secure and safer, I see everyone applying one of just two social control systems: peacemaking, or what I call "warmaking." In the context of governmental efforts to control domestic social disorder, Ruth Morris calls "warmaking" "the retributive justice system." . . . When one chooses to make war on a social problem rather than to make peace with it, one adopts this system of thought: The first order of business is to identify and assess blame against those personally responsible for the danger and insecurity we face; these are our enemies. Next we try to isolate them and subdue them —stamping out the enemy's will to fight. The process entails passing judgment on enemies and punishing them (i.e., taking power away from them by locking them in cells).
>
> If you decide to regard threatening social disorder in the *peacemaking* social control system, blame gets in the way of cleaning up the social mess and restoring antagonists' capacity to get along safely together, as in being able to turn your back without fear on someone who has attacked you. While the preeminent task of the warmaker is to be the biggest, baddest combatant you can be, the preeminent task of the peacemaker is to *weave combatants, weakest victims first, back into a social fabric of mutual trust, mutual safety, mutual security.*[17] (my emphasis)

This "new" way of thinking (as we'll see later, it was widely practiced in some indigenous societies) is not only a sentiment but has a pragmatic principle behind it. Jeremy Bentham said, in one of his essays, "Sanguinary laws have a tendency to render men cruel, either by fear, by imitation, or by revenge while laws dictated by mildness humanize the manners of a nation and the spirit of government." Today, to be accused of "mildness" around crime is probably the fastest way to lose an election, yet some practices are beginning to tap precisely that power to make huge improvements in and around the grim prisons built by the alternative.

Building the Way

A friend of one of my students, a petite, attractive young woman, was sitting one day doing a workshop in a circle with a dozen or so prisoners in a concrete, windowless room in San Quentin when the lights went out. In the dark, she could hear the men shuffling around her and whispering—and the blood pounding in her ears. What seemed like a long time later the emergency lighting came on. The men were standing around her in a circle, arms linked, facing outward, protecting her.

One of the most successful restorative justice projects in the United States was started in 1975 at Greenhaven State Prison in New York. Significantly, it was started not by scholars or social workers; it was initiated by prisoners themselves. Calling themselves the "Think Tank" (an intentional pun, I assume), they contacted a local Quaker group to help them find nonviolent alternatives to prison life and what it was doing to them. What emerged from that collaboration quickly spread to fifteen states and Canada and is now widely known as the Alternatives to Violence Project (AVP). Many similar projects sprang up, like the one for which the woman in the previous story was working. What is AVP? Essentially, it is a set of workshops designed to provide a rehumanizing environment and a set of tools that allow the prisoners to unlearn aggression. The idea is simple, and slowly becoming more familiar.

> Social learning theorists have demonstrated that
> aggression and violence are learned behaviors. They
> can, therefore, within biological and genetic limita-
> tions, be altered by utilizing social learning principles
> such as [role] modeling. . . . Research has demonstrated
> that utilizing positive responses which are incompati-
> ble with the act of violence (e.g., smiling; state of
> muscle relaxation; open, clear, direct communica-
> tion; active listening; the development of trust, etc.)
> renders the likelihood of aggression and/or violence
> much more improbable than do negative sanctions
> such as punishment, shame or guilt.[18]

We might want to query those "biological and genetic limitations" (was Gandhi of another species?), but we can certainly accept, indeed applaud, the "basic premise of AVP, as explained at the beginning of every workshop . . . that human beings don't have to be violent with each other, that human violence is not a given, even in prison." Teaching nonviolent techniques, therefore, "can . . . greatly profit assaultive people." For example, teaching them (or any of us) verbal skills reduces their need to react to a provocation with violence (as Winston Churchill once said, "It is better to jaw, jaw, jaw than to war, war, war"). More than this, being more articulate helps them preserve their integrity and self-esteem in embarrassing situations. "This sense of worth," University of South Dakota's Lila Rucker reminds us, "is tied to our sense of connectedness to other human beings."[19]

That premise is basic to the nonviolence worldview. We are not talking only about getting some assaultive people back in line with "normalcy," but getting them over some of the spiritual isolation that has been accepted today as normal. When they can channel some of their considerable assertiveness into social competence, reorienting their drives for "power over" somebody to "power with" others, they are having the kind of growth experience that even us "nonassaultive" types could do with.

As Rucker says, it "can bring tingles of excitement if we allow ourselves to conjure up images of transforming *correctional* centers into *healing* centers."[20] Frankly, I agree. I admit, I feel tingles of excitement about programs like AVP. Imagine if we could convert the entire criminal justice system from warehousing and punishment to restoration and social healing. And this happens, often. One of the best formulas is when progressive-minded reformers mix in certain indigenous practices with their own innovations, as we'll touch upon in this book's epilogue.

If we could somehow convert the entire judicial system to healing projects like AVP, it would help immensely, because those projects arise from right principles. Those we label "criminals" are in reality human beings with full human potential, but who are alienated. If crime is alienation (a kind of violence), it cannot be healed by vindictive punishment (another kind of violence). The real cure must come from something that is *not* a kind of violence and does not further alienate. Instead of telling offenders, "Hey, get outta here!," as one colorful prison activist put it, restorative programs convey, "Hey, get back in here!" It is indeed mind-boggling to imagine what it would be like to convert our whole criminal justice machinery from punishing to healing.

Yet it would be dishonest, and finally ineffectual, to stop there. For think of how much damage has already been done by the time someone lands in prison. Ray Schonholtz, founder of San Francisco Community Boards, once told me, echoing the insight of Deborah Prothrow-Stith, "Our entire justice industry is after-the-fact, like our entire health industry. It's all after-the-fact." Even programs that heal instead of punishing are after-the-fact. I want to share with you a story from India about a villager who is out gathering firewood near his village and meets a holy man. The sage tells him about a forest of sandalwood trees deeper within the forest, and the villager is enchanted to find them and enjoy not only their purifying fragrance but some income. However, when he goes back to thank the holy man, the latter tells him, "Don't stop there: if you go further on you find a copper mine." The villager is thrilled, but—not being Indian, I will make this delightfully long story short—the holy man tells him, "Don't stop there," until he comes to a silver mine, a gold mine, and finally a diamond mine.

When we consider how many reform programs are after-the-fact, the sage would tell us, "Don't stop there"; go deeper into the forest. Go back down the chain of causality; go deep, go into our value system and find the changes that will prevent crime, violence, and alienation from happening in the first place. The real challenge that comes from the "conversions" of people like Cabrera and Cardoso, like the innumerable high school troublemakers who become the best mediators, like the young offenders in Los Angeles or the thousands who have been through AVP and related programs, is not to heal the wounds of alienation once it has happened but to change the alienating conditions of this world so people like them—like all of us—can live fulfilling lives. That is the only way to head off alienation of all types, those that lead to technically criminal behavior or to less formal sorrows.

Is there not a certain hypocrisy in doing anything else? After all, what is a "criminal"? Let me remind you of something we discovered about one of the most bruising conflicts of the twentieth century: "Why are they killing one another? . . . People here [in the Balkans] have always believed, and still believe, what they see and hear on television." Well, frankly, "criminals" are people who believe what they see and hear on commercial television: that people are separate, that life is a fight, that happiness is outside us, that we are all doomed to compete against each other for limited material goods.

This is, of course, a more subliminal message than the unsubtle hate propaganda of state television from Belgrade. It is more subliminal —and therefore more effective. And it has not been going on for a mere five years, but at least forty (to speak of television in particular). In a culture that puts out messages like these from every radio and television tower all day long for over forty years—messages whose underlying philosophy is the very stuff of violence—it is hypocrisy to do nothing but punish those who succumb to that message in an illegal way. And it is folly to think that when you've caught those individuals you will gain security. "I will act the way I am treated, so help me God"; this is handwriting on the wall for all of us if we keep setting loose the demons of alienation and then looking for what Ruth Morris calls the "pseudo-security" of locking "criminals" out of sight. Real security has an altogether different face.

> The retributive justice system, with its established hierarchical rituals, robed judges, armed police and locked cells, offers quite literally a concrete substitute for the deeper security we have lost. More tragic still, we take this quick fix, and it appeases our inner hunger just enough that we fail to seek true security in the caring community, where we can be certain of love and support no matter what happens. We can never lock up the last offender . . . but we can create the kind of community where we know that, whatever the future holds, we will be surrounded by love and support.[21]

THE CULTURAL IS THE POLITICAL

So let's "go further," as the wise man in the forest would say. We can use nonviolence to solve the problem of crime, but we need to start before the cell doors close. To go further here means to go three steps up the chain of causation and see where and how to intervene at each stage.

First: We need *restorative justice* for arrestees, particularly if they are young. AVP and Sharon Roberts are our pioneers, showing us what we need for the whole system. This is not a terribly radical suggestion;

it is new to the public (I first saw the term *restorative justice* in the papers in June 1998), but it is no wild or particularly new idea to social scientists. To quote Ruth Morris one last time, "When university programs become training grounds for orthodox guards, prison administrators, and lawyers and police who grind out our retributive and destructive system they . . . are out of touch with the literature of serious research that documents over and over the inherent inability of a revenge system to accomplish any positive social purpose."[22] Restorative justice is step number one, for those whom we've already failed.

Second: We need much more support for programs that can head off criminal behavior—again, especially for young people. In almost every American city, police and volunteer organizations try to give youth something better to do than run around in gangs. They organize basketball games, create places for them to spend time, and best of all get in and spend time with them. One of the biggest wounds in our society is the gap between old and young; it probably rivals the lack of communication between the genders in its destructive effects on human culture. "Big brother" and "big sister" programs are a way to overcome a part of this, but again, they are no substitute for families. Nothing is. A solid, loving family does crime prevention (or "provention") in the truest sense of the word. Barred windows and metal detectors are prevention in the most cynical sense, and they may "work" but they do not work.

By now most of us have become aware that the prison budget is draining money from the school system—absurdly, since it's been proven time and again that schooling is the second most potent way, after the family itself, of keeping people from committing crime. Still, at the start of the nineties, to cite one instance, expenditures for K–12 and higher education nationwide increased a little over 8 percent apiece while correction for youth and adults increased 18 percent— and since then educational outlays have almost always gone *down* while prison walls went up.

Wilbert Rideau is an articulate writer who killed a bank guard at age nineteen and has been paying for that mistake in Louisiana State Penitentiary since 1962. He has no reason to pretend that the prison system reduces violence and he can be pretty blunt about it. Tough anticrime measures are, quite frankly, a "crock," he says. "People don't want solutions to crime, they only want to feel good."[23] He has a point. Four-fifths of the prisoners in the long-term facility at Angola State Prison are high school dropouts like himself. Instead of society getting tough on them when the damage is already done, "I'd like to see more efforts aimed at really improving people," he says. "Crime is a social problem, and education is the only real deterrent. . . . Put your money there." A Modern Greek proverb puts it beautifully:

Όταν ανοίγει μια σχολή, κλείνει μια φυλαχή.
"When a school opens, a prison closes."

Or, to go in for some billboard rhetoric, "Open a school, close a prison." Education is very rehumanizing. It has even worked, in some bold experiments, *after* criminalization occurs. In Massachusetts a young woman who had served several "normal," i.e., punitive, sentences for other crimes was then "sentenced" to taking a literature class. Her comment was, "It's the first time anybody ever gave me a chance."[24]

Should we convert the whole criminal justice system to an educational system? You know, we could do a lot worse. Should we bring back the money that has been diverted from schools to the correctional system? We could do a lot worse. But we must also do much more.

Third: We must patiently, resolutely, take apart the culture of violence our material civilization has given rise to and replace it, part by part, institution by institution, with a culture of peace, basing that new culture on the long-overdue "revolution of values" Martin Luther King called for in a famous sermon two weeks after his New York declaration against the war.[25]

However, while it is true that education is the antidote to violence, it is not true that education means nothing more than getting youth to stay in schools. How can it, when today they are bringing violence into school with them in the form of more than 100,000 guns every day, one million a year?[26] In this country, which now has more shopping centers than high schools, if we were to go ahead and restore the money to schools that has been drained away by the prison system, that would not solve the problem by itself, because children would be sitting in those spacious, well-kept, air-conditioned schools learning almost nothing but how to get a job. The greatest enemy of education is not a lack of funds, though that hurts; it's a lack of purpose. Lack of funds is only a symptom of the present culture of materialism. It is this same culture that also makes us think it's safer to build prisons than schools—and makes the schools so unsafe that young people feel they have to carry guns in them.

Education has weathered a two-pronged attack that even good funding—and I agree it's needed—does not fully address. On the one hand, our children come to school increasingly unreachable by their teachers. Simply put, the mass media are practicing education without a license. On the other hand, the general public and—I hate to say this—educators themselves have lost sight of the purpose of education. They have come to feel that education means only one thing: getting ready for a job. Universities, as a colleague of mine recently put it, "have reinvented themselves as corporations." A very education-friendly candidate for superintendent of education in California recently dared to suggest that "we need to integrate visual and performing arts into the curriculum," from kindergarten onward. I was ready to dash out to the ballot box, but then she added, "This is important . . . because of the requirements of the new economy." Not the eternal requirements of a sense of purpose, beauty, meaning. Oh well.

So even those who, like Rideau, advocate education as an antidote to crime must realize that putting people through schools so they can get jobs is not education; in fact, defining education as such is part of the problem. As we learned about the typical drug user in America, our culture considers certain lifestyles a "success" that are actually resounding failures in terms of saving people from frustration and emptiness. Actual human needs can be strikingly different.

Man [or woman] cannot flourish if his entire world consists only of objects that he can see, hear, touch, taste or smell. Instinctively, whether he be a New Guinea tribesman or a Wall Street tycoon, a human being tends to feel that life on this earth must be subject to some sort of higher purpose.[27]

Recently, this observation was echoed by another high-level health authority:

A few years ago the Department of Health Education and Welfare in Massachusetts published a study, since replicated in France, in which scientists and statisticians looked once again at the risk factors for heart disease. They found that the number one predictor of fatal heart attacks, initially described as job dissatisfaction, was more precisely pinned down as lack of meaning or purpose in life.[28]

At the beginning of this book I suggested that meaning and purpose, namely their absence, explain the suicides of teens in south Boston. But it is not just teens. In South Africa, when Apartheid finally fell, some of the whites who had clung to that system to give meaning to their lives felt the bottom dropping out from under them. In one or two cases, whole Afrikaner families committed suicide because they felt that there was "no way forward . . . no future for whites in this country."[29] One authority said of the Heaven's Gate cult suicide in San Diego in 1997 that the cult members fit a "typical pattern" of people who "sought a consuming purpose" for their lives.[30] Typical of whom? According to the medical evidence just cited, every single one of us seeks a consuming purpose for our lives. When the predominant cultural message is that we are separate, physical objects bent on consumption and doomed to compete, that purpose is going to be hard to find.

I was involved for a while in a program that taught meditation to people who had been diagnosed HIV positive. We were prepared to discover, and we did, that meditation and the allied disciplines protected them from some of the worst effects of anxiety, including some of its effects on their already weakened immune systems. What surprised us, though, was the number of people who told us, "If I could get back my health at the cost of giving up everything I've learned from this program, I wouldn't do it."

So the full, deep solution to the crime epidemic, the solution that works *before* people do damage to themselves and others, is restorative not just for those who have fallen through the cracks, but for the culture itself. Yes, we need many more restorative programs in jails; yes, we need to rebuild schools and let them teach young people how to live (not to mention *why* to live), but we also need to develop a culture that facilitates, rather than discourages, "man's search for meaning."

The scientist I am paraphrasing with that last phrase is Viktor Frankl. Frankl, trained as a neurosurgeon in his native Vienna, passed two and a half years of his life in the living hell of Auschwitz and survived to write his best-selling book, *Man's Search for Meaning,* directly out of that devastating—yet for him strangely triumphant—experience. From the abyss of violence he rose to ask the deepest question of our existence: What is the meaning of life? What are we supposed to be doing here?

Even to ask that question was somewhat restorative, but Frankl went further. He saw that real meaning cannot be concocted; it has to be *discovered*: "I think the meaning of our existence is not invented by ourselves but rather detected."[31] Thus, while even a *sense* of meaning is therapeutic (even if we get it from bungee-cord jumping, not to mention Apartheid), real meaning comes when we get connected in some way to a purpose higher than ourselves and beyond ourselves. Ninety-one-year-old Leona, who spends her spare time using her expert sewing skills for others, says it so well: "I figure if you can't help somebody, what's the use of living?"[32]

Frankl's insight (on which his "third school of psychotherapy" is based) is that we can't simply make up something meaningful to do;

we *have* something meaningful to do. The real search is to find out what it is. Everything I've been saying in this book is meant to shed light on that search, for I believe it's possible to define what is meaningful for us who live in the present crisis of history. The task is to create loving community, and the way to understand and address that task is through nonviolence. Whoever we are, there is a way we can do this. This is the work that will give our lives purpose, individually and as a people. The most beautiful expression of this task that I know of comes from a letter Einstein wrote when he was seventy. It is no surprise that this little paragraph is becoming so well known:

> A human being is a part of the whole, called by us the "universe," a part limited in time and space. He experiences his thoughts and feelings as something separate from the rest—a kind of optical delusion of his consciousness. This delusion is a kind of prison for us, restricting us to our personal decisions and to affection for a few persons nearest us. Our task must be to free ourselves from this prison by widening our circle of compassion to embrace all living creatures and the whole of nature in its beauty.[33]

The task that Einstein speaks of is not for this age only; it is the human task for all time, part of the human condition. But that task presents itself right now with a special urgency, when loving community and "the whole of nature" are being torn at by the forces of greed and alienation. In the case of the crime problem, we are expelling people from society and locking them up in warehouses, not to mention expelling them altogether from the community of the living with the barbaric death penalty, not realizing that it is we ourselves who remain in prison—the prison of our ill will, our fear and anger that seal ourselves off from others. We shall escape from our prison of delusion when we let people of their prison of concrete and iron.

Toward the end of 1997, the still-living laureates of the Nobel

Prize for Peace made a joint plea for changing human consciousness in the coming millennium; they named their call the "International Decade for a Culture of Peace and Non-Violence for the World's Children." Humanity is slowly beginning to learn that nonviolence is a creative force that contains within itself the principle of creative order. It alone seems to be a method of conflict adjudication that contains the energy of peace in its very process. Nonviolence (and as far as I can see, only nonviolence) does this by elevating rather than depressing the human image; it alone leads to long-term, deep changes in the social system that will eventually result in the desired goals of loving community within the given society and stable peace with others—in a word, loving community all around. We can now add what may be the most important characteristic of nonviolence: it provides people with a high, inspiring goal—a task that can be implemented in endless ways to fit each individual's capacities, be it as small as turning off one's television set or as large as de-institutionalizing war.

History has not yet given us an example of a full-scale, nonviolent revolution that rebuilt a culture from the ground up. Even India's freedom struggle, by far the biggest and the purest, went out of control toward the end. But it has given us enough hints that we can see how such a thing might indeed be possible. The way the *intifada* youth turned off drugs, for example, was part of the character of the *intifada* as a whole. Because their schools were constantly being shut down by Israeli authorities, Palestinian teachers set up clandestine schools in the basements of their homes or the backs of stores. Because commercial links between Palestinians and Israelis were disrupted—some the result of deliberate acts of boycott and others part of Israeli retribution—people created systems of their own to deliver milk, fix cars, and get the injured and the sick to clinics. Particularly striking was one change that reached deep into the fabric of Palestinian life: as more and more children were left behind by jail-going parents, Mubarak told my class, "Every woman became every child's mother." In that brief period when nonviolent energy was at work, the Palestinians found themselves doing much more than rebelling against an external authority: they were reinventing themselves as a civil society. To do this, interestingly enough, they were reawakening the timeless principle of the extended family that had indigenous roots in their society. Even in this flawed, only provisionally nonviolent, struggle, loving community emerged as a by-product. And yet it was not just a by-product. It was—and always is—a direct result of choosing nonviolence. In chapter 3, we saw the psychological health that shows up in the individual who makes that choice. Now we are beginning to see the social health brought into the group at large.

Why, then, are nonviolent campaigns usually protests and disruptions? If they contain the seeds of creative order, why this popular perception of nonviolence as a kind of revolution, and why do nonviolent activists from George Fox to the Berrigan brothers go about breaking laws and generally disrupting applecarts? We will see that it is not just because protests and disruptions are the only expression of nonviolence that people tend to recognize. It is because nonviolent actors are the ones who are clinging to order in societies where some kinds of disorder have been taken for granted—like the British monopoly on Indian salt and cotton or the segregation of buses in Montgomery. As Archbishop Romero said in homily before his assassination in El Salvador on March 27, 1980:

> I don't want to be an opposition, as was said of me this week. I want to be simply an affirmation. When one says yes to one's own conviction, one is not confronting. . . . Naturally, some others don't think the same way and thus confrontation arises.[34]

Applecarts that are going blindly over a cliff must sometimes be upset by people trying to save their occupants.

The Spiritually Poorest

So "the children of the stones" (as the *intifada* youth are often, and somewhat unfairly, called) hit on something very relevant to our own dilemmas. We traced the connection step by step from drug abuse to crime itself, and finally to a lack of purpose in the industrial culture we are surrounded by, each step getting closer to the cause of our problems. At the same time, each step revealed more clearly an answering path from *restorative* programs that can heal the alienation between the assaultive person and society, to *preventive* programs that heal some sources of alienation within communities, to—what shall we call it?—the overriding *creative* program of restoring the value system whose deformation has led us into a world of so much crime, among other symptoms of disorder.

Mother Teresa shed some light on this goal in an observation of hers I referred to earlier:

> You in the West have the spiritually poorest of the poor. . . . I find it easy to give a plate of rice to a hungry person, to furnish a bed to a person who has no bed, but to console or to remove the bitterness, anger, and loneliness that comes from being spiritually deprived, that takes a long time.[35]

Overcoming spiritual deprivation is deeply personal work, but it's also a matter of building loving community with others—eventually, all others. The purpose of our life in the third Christian millennium is grounded in the personal, but how could it stop there? We want—we need—to take apart the entire house that violence has built and begin building again with the other, the opposite, kind of power.

Daunting. But we don't have to start absolutely from scratch. Along with all the other trouble he caused, Gandhi devised a social program with just this daring. And it nearly worked.

CHAPTER SIX

CONSTRUCTIVE PROGRAMME

To reclaim our colonized political spaces,
we must reclaim our colonized cultural spaces.

—David Korten

ONE DAY IN 1940, a young Indian importuned Gandhi, "What will it really take to get the British off our backs?" Gandhi replied brightly, "Phenomenal progress in spinning."[1]

I like to imagine that this was one of those revolutionaries who didn't believe Gandhi was really serious about nonviolence. He thought—he wanted to think—that Gandhi was just biding his time, waiting for the moment to launch the real revolution. But nonviolence *was* the real revolution. Really, though, we are tempted to ask, with spinning wheels? Yes, with spinning wheels and everything they stood for. At the time Gandhi made this rejoinder, he had almost fifty years of experience behind him and was no longer interested in sounding clever. We can take it that he meant just what he said. Why did he endow the humble spinning wheel with such power?

Nonviolence has two faces, that of cooperating with good and that of noncooperating with evil. These two faces, or call them two edges to the sword of Satyagraha, are known to history as what Gandhi called *Constructive Programme,* where you create things and make corrections in and on your own community, and what I like to call *obstructive program,* where you refuse to put up with others' attempts to weaken or exploit you. When to do which is largely a matter of timing, yet most people who think about nonviolence at all are like that young man who importuned Gandhi in 1940—they think only about the obstructive side. None other than Kenneth Boulding once quipped that nonviolence was good for offense but not for defense, which, humor aside, turns out to be wrong, as we will see in chapter 8. This blinkered perception, shared by activists, some scholars, and lay observers alike, has done a great deal to hinder the development of peace and nonviolence. For ironically, the constructive edge is actually far more important than the confrontational/obstructive side of which we're becoming relatively aware.

Once I met a French baron and his wife while I was working at an archeological site on the Greek island of Delos. M. and Mme Evrard-Garbé invited my wife and me to their Paris apartment for dinner, which of course we readily accepted. Madame was a superb cook, and the conversation was going splendidly when my friend Monsieur le baron casually remarked, "Oh, I completely believe in the inequality of the races." My wife blanched, knowing I was likely to make a scene. Normally I would have, but several things held me in check this time. The conversation was in French, for one, and that slowed down my repartee; then, too, I was in his home, eating his wife's gracious cooking; and most importantly, perhaps, I had a year or so of meditation under my belt at that time. I held my tongue. Some moments later, as the conversation changed course, my host said, "You know, nothing in the world matters but love [charité]." I quietly said to him, "Do you think the races are unequally endowed with the capacity to love?" He was stunned.

I probably did more to reduce the racist burden of the world that evening than I had in a lifetime of activism. And yet, I wasn't an iota less angry—tant s'en faut! Unbeknownst to me, my anger was seeking a more constructive outlet, making me more alert to what my host was saying rather than less, even though I held it back not out of conviction, really, but simply because circumstances so dictated. This was for me an important personal experience of the efficacy of anger transformed—and what I was to understand years later as Constructive Programme.

As we'll see, the seed of Constructive Programme was planted at the very beginning of Gandhi's public life, about a year after the shock of Pietermaritzburg had worn off or, rather, had sunk in. By the twenties, shortly after he arrived back in India, that seed had grown into Constructive Programme, a roster of eighteen projects designed to rebuild India from the ground up. Not only did it become more elaborate and comprehensive along the way, but it also steadily moved to center stage in Gandhi's thinking. By 1940 it was his main hope. He was fully committed to the belief that while nonviolence had an impressive power to protest and disrupt, its real power was to create and reconstruct. The tail of protesting wrongs would never wag the dog of building a society. This is what he wanted his young interlocutor of 1940, and all of us, to understand.

Today, wherever we look for successful examples of social change, it seems, it's the groups or individuals taking concrete, positive steps like the reconstructive projects we looked at in the last chapter that are making the biggest difference. Maybe it's as simple as the Environmental Defense Fund's "Safe Harbor" program, which rewards private landowners who protect endangered species, instead of punishing them when they do not. Introduced in three states, it has "worked" beautifully; Safe Harbor Texas alone has over a million acres under protection, according to their 1998 mailing. Or the Educational Fund to End Handgun Violence, which started a project called "Hands Without Guns," whose purpose is to show kids a world of fun and opportunity outside a world of fear and violence. This positive message struck a resounding chord. From Boston to San Francisco, neighborhood teens have organized a gun buy-back and made peace sculptures from the collected weapons.[2]

One of the most successful environmental programs worldwide is Dr. Karl-Henrik Robèrt's "Natural Step." Dr. Robèrt is an MD from Sweden who became immensely concerned with environmental degradation and set out to bring many others into that circle of concern. He had, fortunately, patience to match his passion. What's unique about Natural Step is not so much its superb scientific homework and scientific credentials as its approach.

> First we educate business leaders, politicians and sci-
> entists in The Four System Conditions [four things
> that have to be observed for the earth to be a sustain-
> able life-support system] and then we ask them for
> advice. Instead of telling them what to do, we say,
> "How could this be applied in your world?" This
> sparks creativity and recruits enthusiasm into the
> process instead of defense mechanisms.
>
> Any expert in her field . . . is much more clever
> than you or I. If you give her the overall principles,
> therefore, and then ask for advice, she finds much
> smarter solutions than Greenpeace or I or anybody
> else can. And we are very much in need of practical,
> creative solutions.[3]

In the early days, before Natural Step had national organizations around the world, Robèrt would go to corporations and ask to speak to their boards about the diminishing funnel of resources they were running into. Typically, they would dismiss him with a "don't call us, we'll call you," but in a week or so, they *would* call him. The secret is that if you assume people are rational, it helps to awaken their rationality. It "forces reason to be free." This sometimes works even in cases on the high end of the escalation curve, when the intensity of negative passions seems to have stifled reason. At lower levels, it works beautifully.

Long before Gandhi threw that cold water on his impatient questioner of 1940, twenty years earlier, when he launched full-scale Satyagraha against British rule in India, he did so with the daring promise of "Swaraj [freedom] in one year." It was daring, but not foolhardy. He promised freedom in one year *if* he got complete cooperation in Constructive Programme and spinning. Nothing had changed his opinion between 1921 and the early forties; if anything, he was more certain than ever that nonviolence was the only way to go and that the true meaning of nonviolence was not in the grand, dramatic confrontations like the Dharasana raid (those glittering nonviolent moments), but the slow, steady humming of the spinning wheel.

In fact, to appreciate fully how fundamental constructive work was to his concept of nonviolent change we have to go back to the very beginning, to 1894, when he had wrapped up the law case he had been hired to help with in South Africa and could now turn his attention to the "evil" that had been in his face almost from the day he arrived in May of 1893—Apartheid. For right here, where it all began, he made sure that alongside the community's direct struggle with the government "the question of internal improvement was also taken up."[4] These were to prove portentous, and understated, words. In course of time, "also" would become "mainly"; the emphasis would steadily shift to constructive work undertaken in the community itself, whether it be the Indian community in South Africa or the disenfranchised Indians in their own country, even though the drama that fascinated the world would always be the outright clashes with British power. He meant it when he said his real politics was constructive work. It was so simple that almost no one got it.

A nonviolent actor will naturally be a little nervous about putting the blame for any wrong exclusively on others. When you are the weaker party and are in fact being exploited, it's all the more important to remember that you, too, must have some weaknesses that got you into the situation. No weakness, no exploitation. Though he had no illusions about the ruthlessness and bias of Europeans, Gandhi would nonetheless tell his fellow Indians—in *Hind Swaraj*, one of the most fiery tracts he ever wrote—that India was not taken with the sword and could not be held by the sword: "We brought the English, and we keep them . . . our adoption of their civilization makes their presence in India at all possible."[5]

Whatever we may feel about the fairness or "morality" of the emphasis on correcting our own weaknesses, it is a powerful way to resist exploitation. Gandhi came to feel that it was the best way. Like most popular movements, Satyagraha originated as a reaction to an outsider's offense. That was Gandhi's first reaction, as it is anyone's. But where most movements stay fixed on "getting them off our back," he instinctively felt that this was only half the story—and maybe only the shadow half. The really powerful approach was "let's get up off our own backs." Two things give the approach power, as we've seen: the shift from "them" to "us" (think how much more accessible we are than they, after all) and the parallel shift from an *obstructive* to a *constructive* mode of operation. Is it not obvious that, other things being equal, it is far better to build than destroy?

FROM CONSTRUCTIVE PROGRAMME TO A CONSTRUCTIVE PROGRAM

How can we apply that insight today and in the West, facing the enormous changes we need to bring about? Here and there, many people like Dr. Robèrt are already hard at work at parts of this vast project: rebuilding neighborhoods, rescuing young people from gangs, doing nonviolence workshops in prisons, saving whales. What's missing, it seems to me, is that all this has yet to gel. The whole that would make much more beautiful sense of all these parts is not yet very clear. One afternoon, a student of mine asked a well-known peace scholar who had given us a beautiful talk:

> As an activist, I find it frustrating that we're trying to stop a war here, stop genocide there, stop the arms race all over, and the minute we prevent one thing, there are three more. What we're not stopping is what's causing all these things. And I'm wondering if you have any sense of what that is.

She didn't. But I think we're beginning to. What causes "all these things" is called violence, and something called nonviolence is the antidote, and something called *constructive program* would be the most effective mode of nonviolence, especially in between, and leading up to, climactic struggles like the civil rights movement. It seems to me that two things need to happen that are not quite in place: we need to have a real grasp of the nonviolent principle, which will give us an articulate understanding of how to apply it (no inanities, Gandhi would say), and we need some overall design—some coherent, but all-embracing, picture—which would help us feel that we're all working together even if we're not working on the same project. Not a whale here or a prison group there, a beat-up nose cone here and a hugged redwood there, but a total nonviolent-guided evolution.

The design of the Indian Constructive Programme offers us a model. For the program did have an overall design, which was extremely simple and could be visualized in a single, oft-repeated image: Constructive Programme was a "solar system," Gandhi would often say, and *charkha* (the spinning wheel) was the "sun."

Since Gandhi had a chance, as King did not, to develop his ideas on a mighty scale, we have the opportunity to see in him reform in action on that scale—to see, for example, the interesting relationship between *charkha,* the flagship project, the campaign to wrest back from British control India's once-proud textile crafts by cottage industry, and Constructive Programme in toto. The great advantage to this configuration was its harmonic coherence; if the whole wide-ranging program seemed bewildering, you could understand it in the spinning wheel—for example, he could say "phenomenal progress in spinning" and you would understand that it stood for the whole thing. It was not a pinch of salt here and a boycotted liquor shop there; it was the whole call to truth that those and other activities represented.

Watch your eyes; we're going to look directly at the sun.

Epiphany at Ahmadabad

In the broad, comprehensive spectrum of those eighteen projects, *charkha* (Hindi for "wheel" and shorthand for the home spinning campaign) was the sun 'round which the rest revolved. One has to remember that from ancient times, India had been a "forest civilization" whose culture lay not in the great cities like Takshishela, Pataliputra, or Kashi (modern Benares), but in villages, hundreds of thousands of them, in which people lived close to nature and to one another. The economic signature of these villages was self-sufficiency. Most village industries were carried out by families who had been organized for centuries into a system of interdependent castes. The exchange of goods and services, rather than money, was the main currency of this interdependence. Among many such industries, spinners and weavers were a part of a "village economy" that reached far beyond its villages. Indian cloth was the pride of Asia. Clearly, the absence of *central* organization does not mean the absence of any organization, whatever the European rulers would later think. Cottage industry was the hub—the network of many hubs—of a vigorous trade throughout the subcontinent and beyond. Some fragment of that trade is being revived when one sees a Kanjiveram silk sari ranking as high fashion at a San Francisco gallery opening or a Washington ball. And along with this economic self-sufficiency went a whole cultural system: religious institutions, education, and most of the governance and law and order that were based in and around the villages and in the hands of people who knew each other.

Then, in the course of the nineteenth century, city-based industrial mills started pulling to themselves the many threads of this economy. In almost no time (if you take an Indian perspective), industrial cities like Ahmadabad, and with it the British monopoly on textile making, idled millions of productive villagers, driving them off the margins of the social system. (Another, portentous aspect of the abuse was that most of these textile tradesmen were Muslims.) In 1928 Gandhiji visited those mills in Ahmadabad, the capital of his home state of Gujarat, and had an experience one might be tempted to call a vision. As he stood on the mill floor, looking at the clanking machinery, he wept. For where you and I would just see machines—noisy and unpleasant, perhaps, but just machines—he "saw" the structural violence and the greed that put them there: the city dweller exploiting the simple villager, the impersonal corporation replacing what had been a wide network of close relationships, the craze for profit overwhelming the dignity of work. Legends relate that once the Compassionate Buddha and his disciples were gazing at a particularly beautiful scene, and while they were admiring the snow-clad mountains and the clear river, he saw a river of sorrow—the flowing tears of suffering humanity—and mountains white not with snow but with the bones of the departed. Buddha's answer was to set in motion the Wheel of the Law; Gandhi's was to turn the spinning wheel of freedom: freedom from greed, centralization, and structural violence.

The *charkha* showed that we can return to the kind of life humanity lived before the craze of the machine took over. Not only cloth was involved, but an ideology—not too different from what India had known centuries before—in which the rich would voluntarily "live simply, so that others may simply live," and the socioeconomic system would be one of human scale. Again, the fact that the system was decentralized did not mean that its components were isolated. As in the past, the spinner in his or her village was joined with the farmers who provided the cotton, and with those who manufactured, who sold, and finally who wore the *khadi* (homespun cotton). Even more than the *intifada, charkha* was rebuilding the infrastructure of a free India with her own, sustainable way of life.

From the twenties onward, Gandhi urged everyone, rich and poor, to spend an hour a day spinning, if not carding, weaving, or otherwise making cloth from India's own cotton, tirelessly explaining that the point was to make cloth for those who could hardly afford to cover their nakedness, to give back meaningful work to millions who had been idled by a system of subtle but ruthless exploitation, and in so doing to bring that system to an end. Many Indians, especially Westernized city dwellers, did not *like* wearing *khadi,* or *khaddar.* It's itchy, it's rough, and it's definitely not high fashion. This kind of argument hurt Gandhi to the quick.

We must be prepared to be satisfied with such cloth as India can produce, even as we are thankfully content with such children as God gives us. I have not known a mother throwing away her baby even though it appears ugly to the outsider. . . . Khaddar is the concrete and central fact of Swadeshi.[6]

Swadeshi, briefly defined, is globalism in reverse. It means self-reliance and local action, growing outward from that position of strength to wide interdependency and global concern. *Swadeshi* embodied is homespun, as Gandhi said.

Charkha was exactly the thing to do in so many ways that it's easy to lose sight of the most important things. "Food, clothing and shelter are basic necessities of civilized life," said one of Gandhi's granddaughters recently. "Most of us, at some time in our lives, have rolled out a *chapati* [flat, Indian bread]. Similarly, every Indian should at some time in his life, feel and touch the charkha, for that is the *praan* or soul in all of us. We need cloth next to food."[7] In Gandhian economics, there is a qualitative difference between the basic needs of food, clothing, and shelter, and anything less essential. Everyone has a right to those three basic needs. If they are not met—for everyone—a society has failed.

Now recall Gandhi's other really great campaign. It's about salt—again, absolutely basic in a tropical country like India. With these two campaigns, the "obstructive" bid to get salt back from the government and the constructive project to make cloth at the village level, Gandhi sought to repossess two of the most basic life-sustaining elements of any economy, food and clothing. This makes Nehru's famous saying, that *khadi* was "the livery of our freedom," almost an understatement: in the fight for cloth and salt, India was fighting for control over the necessities of life itself.

Nothing could be more *real,* then, than a spinning wheel. Of course—thinking now of the real versus symbolic issue we dealt with in chapter 4—the wheel is *also* a symbol. In India, as anywhere else, it's an ancient symbol of the world process, the "wheel of existence, of life and death *(samsara)*"; or as in Buddhism, the "Wheel of the Law." But what brought that ancient symbol back to political life? Not a slogan that you hung on the back of your bullock cart, "You're Following a Spinner." It was people spinning very real cotton for people who really needed it. From that concrete reality came many other gains: an income for idled, often starving, people; hundreds of local networks getting raw material to spinners, and their products to market; the provision and repair of the capital equipment of *taklis* (spindles), wheels, carding bows; an ethos of simplicity; a deep sense of solidarity with the poorest; and, last but not least, political freedom once the British grip was nonviolently neutralized. A picture of a spinning wheel on a billboard or the nation's flag (where it resides today) could have done none of these things.

In addition to these three major qualifications for *charkha*'s "solar" status, namely that it was concrete (as Gandhi pointed out), constructive, and nonconfrontational, we can easily see a few of its other advantages:

(1) Everybody could do it. Working together creates a sense of shared destiny and unity, as almost nothing else does. I've already mentioned the now-classic experiment carried out at a children's camp where working together on common projects reunited rival groups of youngsters more effectively than seeing movies, eating together, or any other common activity.[8] Potentially, everyone was united by *khadi* because everyone could spin; man, woman, or child, rich or poor—no one was too humble or weak or proud or powerful to put his or her hand to *this* wheel. In the grand days of *charkha,* even congressional VIPs came home and spun their half hour every day—in fact, especially the VIPs. But *khadi* was not only something you spun; it was something you wore, and this forged another kind of solidarity, since the rich could dress just like the poor—in simple, dignified homespun. Wearing their beliefs on their bodies, many well-off Indians found out firsthand that brotherhood is more satisfying than status.

(2) You could do it every day. You did not have to wait for the right time, weather, or circumstance, or depend on a big turnout on some special occasion; the ancient rhythm of the spinning wheel was tied only to the rhythm of day and night itself. It must have reminded and symbolized to the volunteers that they were in it for the long, long haul—the "relentless persistence" that makes the difference in nonviolence, or almost anything worthwhile. It's interesting in this connection that Gandhi even claimed that daily spinning was a kind of spiritual discipline, because no Indian believes that spiritual results happen in fits and starts. You can realize them only by sustained application over a long period.

(3) *Charkha* was *proactive*. You needed clothes, you made them. This is the heart of a constructive program. Truth takes the lead, and events follow. Being proactive gives one a great strategic advantage, as any general knows. But it also involves the deepest principle of Satyagraha: truth is not a reflection or an absence of something else; it *is*.

(4) Finally—coming back now to the impatient volunteer's question to Gandhi in 1940—spinning was unquestionably an act of truth that confronted the lie of colonialism at the deepest level, and therefore constituted the most effective resistance. The whole colonial system rested on a lie: the "big lie" of dependency, which tries to make one group of human beings think it has to beg its bread from another. That is not the way God stocked the planet Earth, but the mystique of superiority is compelling, even to those on the receiving end. India had come to believe the implicit message "You are dependent on us— you need us to give you salt and cloth (not to mention, administer justice, defend you from outsiders, and keep order)." This is what Gandhi called the "sinful" and unnatural connection between exploiter and exploited; and to it the *charkha* hummed back, "Thank you, we can clothe and feed ourselves—as we did for 5,000 years before you came." In fact, if we listen closely, the wheel is saying, no one needs anyone else's manufactured goods to stay alive; in fact, people need very few factory-made goods at all. Revolutionary enough?

In a world of falsehood, truth is inherently confrontational. A truly constructive program in such a world is like a fish swimming against the current—it will bang into obstructions, even without seeking them. The Raj began as a trading company; it ended when its unwilling partners decided they would no longer go along with that kind of "trade." The British may have taught in schools and speechified in parliament about "the flag" and "destiny" and "white man's burden," but as soon as the Raj became unprofitable it lost its grip, especially since Gandhi offered the double-sided resistance that Toynbee defined so well: "He made it impossible for us to go on ruling India, but at the same time he made it possible for us to abdicate without rancour and without dishonour."[9]

So *charkha* only *appeared* nonconfrontational; it was really going for the colonial jugular. A woman in her cottage, a youngster on the verandah, sometimes a whole village gathered in a festive moment on the *maidan* (meadow), the air humming with *charkhas*—they sat slowly, steadily undermining the whole economic system of the Raj, and the government scarcely knew what was happening, or how to stop it if they did. Constructive Programme provokes confrontation simply by what it is—or rather, what the rest of the world is. One hopes that Gandhi's impatient questioner grasped that.

At the same time, there was a noncooperative dimension to *charkha* that complemented the purely constructive one of spinning— one who clings to truth never clings to just one mode of operation. *Khadi*-clad Indians burned their British trousers with as much gusto as they had turned the wheel to make their own (probably more). The boycott of foreign cloth was so successful that nearly three million Lancashire millworkers found themselves out of work, and at a time of worldwide depression, when economic tempers were already frayed. Gandhi, in England for the Round Table Conference, made a special trip north to explain his movement directly to the Lancashire workers on September 22, 1931, which has become one of the high points of nonviolent history. "I am pained by the unemployment here. But here is no starvation or semi-starvation. In India we have both. If you went to the villages, you would find . . . living corpses." He did not mince words with them: "Do not think of prospering on the tombs of the poor millions of India . . . cherish no hope of reviving the old Lancashire trade" that *charkha* was rendering superfluous. "Don't attribute your misery to India. Think of the world forces that are powerfully working against you."[10]

It was another miracle of Satyagraha: "May I say or need I say," one man wrote, "that I as a Lancashire cotton working man, who is to some extent suffering through the action of the Indian Congress leaders, have a profound admiration for Mr. Gandhi and a great many of my fellow workers share that spirit?" Said another, after Gandhi's stern words, "We understand each other now."[11] Through soul force we can divide opponents from their agendas while reuniting them with ourselves.

HEART UNITY: DIVERSITY WITHOUT DIVISION

Constructive Programme was a comprehensive agenda of projects that dealt with virtually every aspect of the injured country's condition, but throughout them ran an underlying thread, and that was to heal the "brokenness" of Indian society. The first plank on the platform was, accordingly, Communal Unity. Removal of Untouchability was the second—in other words, to restore harmony between Muslim and Hindu and to eliminate caste arrogance within the Hindu fold. No less than six others aimed at "weaving back into the community" various groups that had been marginalized either by Indian tradition itself or the disruptive influence of foreign rule.[12] Clearly, Constructive Programme as a whole was designed to build loving community; heart unity lay behind its every project.

Let's pause for a moment over this deceptively simple phrase. *Heart unity* means that I want you to be happy, notwithstanding our differences. In fact, to feel heart unity with others is to *enjoy* differences—what a flat, boring world it would be without them. And those differences can even be, for example, differences of wealth. Inequalities of wealth are an increasingly obscene feature of the global economy. The world's four richest men hold onto more wealth than about a third of the world's least developed *countries*. What else can one call this but obscene? Now, absent a concept of heart unity, the only solution that suggests itself is to wrest wealth away from the richest people by whatever means necessary and then spread it around until everyone has about the same amount. Wealthy people tend not to like this solution, and the result is bitter and unequal violence. With a heart unity framework, the approach is very different. You do not begrudge the comparative happiness of the rich (as Gandhi explained to the Lancashire workers), but you seek to awaken them to the shallowness of material wealth and the sorrow of extracting it from others who are in need. So you have to change the *minds* of the rich. This, of course, is not that easy, but it's actually easier than dispossessing them of their money. For one thing, you can demonstrate your own lack of concern for excess material wealth, even if you have access to some. This will work; in a culture that is not overly materialistic (which admittedly we don't have at the moment), it will even visibly "work."

We don't have to go on until we've made the whole world a level economic playing field. All we have to do is get the most destitute people enough to live on and nourish the hope that they'll be able to grow and express themselves like human beings. We can't stop until we've achieved that, but on the other hand the delineation of "rich" and "poor" can be tolerable as long as the poor have enough to live on, *including respect*. We can't have rich and destitute, as America does, but everyone doesn't have to be at the same economic level, only the same *human* level. There has to be empathy, which is the means and end of all heart unity techniques.

If people of different races have reached a state of heart unity toward one another, what possible difference can it make that they look different? Or have a different diet? Or taste in music? Or religion?

Heart unity is the basis of loving community. Which means, of real community.

Other projects in Constructive Programme addressed health, substance abuse (mostly alcohol), poverty, and cultural deterioration, the latter through "new education." Taken together—and they were meant to be taken together—they were to make India a viable, whole society embracing her diversity. *Charkha* was no exception, since, if you recall, everyone, big shot or peasant, was supposed to be doing the "bread labour" of supplying this basic need together—and wearing the results.

One thing is clear: if we are to benefit from Gandhi, we have to take him whole, not just try to imitate the iconic moments of high drama that punctuated his career. His trust for the future lay mostly in steady, constructive work—steady rather than occasional, work rather than protest, self-uplifting rather than obstructing others, practical and concrete rather than symbolic. No one could fight with more determination when it was needed, but no one was as willing to get back to constructive work the minute it wasn't.

What can we learn from Constructive Programme? Not the individual programs, at least not without understanding and modifying them: we don't have 700,000 villages, so "village uplift" won't make sense in our world (although people doing community building in their neighborhoods are doing a version of it). Our material resources are on a different order of magnitude from what theirs were then, so *khadi* itself won't be directly applicable. Not the structure of command, since we don't have a single leader of Gandhi's stature (but we do have an individualism that balks at giving anyone the "dictatorial powers" the Indian masses gladly gave Gandhi).

The impressive thing about Constructive Programme, the thing we can still use, was its vision and its comprehensiveness: the way it addressed every hurting problem with one inspired energy. We can take the energy, and the organizational model. The energy is nonviolence; the model is a broad range of programs with a "solar" project holding them all together, a project that everyone can take part in and that brings the other components into range of a single vision.

Perhaps it's obvious what I think that project should be.

SINE QUA NON

There is a clever Canadian magazine called *Adbusters* dedicated to exposing and often satirizing commercialism. One of its first issues came out with an extremely clever cover.

You see a flotilla of small boats carrying men in colonial dress made up as Native Americans, making for some old-fashioned three-masters sitting at anchor. Some of the "Indians" have already boarded the ships and are happily throwing boxes of cargo overboard. Sound familiar? But as you look closely, you begin to register a few anachronisms: the little boats are actually rubber zodiacs, and the cargo that the "Indians" are ditching in the harbor is TV sets. The caption is, of course, "The Boston TV Party."

There is a very serious point to this irreverent pun. In a sense, we have been "colonized" by people who don't have our interests at heart any more—and in a way considerably less—than the officials of the Raj cared for India's well-being. Our colonial masters do not come from another country; they move among us with the same skin colors and speak the same language we do (though they are butchering it by degrees), and yet they systematically victimize us, the "viewing audience," by making us buy things we don't want and convincing us to run after happiness where it cannot be found, while covering up the unity and purpose that could bring us real happiness. Unlike India's colonial oppressors, who came from a different civilization, speaking a strange language and touting an upstart religion (which they hardly followed themselves), our "oppressors" walk the streets with us and follow exactly the same religion that most of us do—materialism. Commercial television has so altered the minds of young people that teachers are hard pressed, those who still try, to convey anything to them that doesn't follow the materialist-competitive paradigm. As I put it in the last chapter, the mass media are practicing education without a license. It is time to rebel.

Let me give just one example of what David Korten, in this chapter's epigraph, meant by the colonization of our political and our cultural space. Millions of Americans watched the Clinton-Bush television debate on October 19, 1992, myself among them. When it was over, a network official came forward and announced, "We'll have the results of this debate for you in just a moment." The "results"? He meant, of course, who had "won." I'm sure this passed unnoticed for most viewers, but for me, since I virtually never see commercial television, it was quite a shock. I thought the point of a public debate was to help us make up our *own* minds, not be told by some arbitrary "authority" what we had just seen. I thought political debate was to air issues, not to sort out "winners." Many commentators before me have pointed out that the media, particularly television, have changed politics as we knew it, changed it from being at least partly a decision-making process to a popularity contest—a fight. They have reduced democracy to a power struggle. It is from the beachhead established by materialism and competitiveness that they have moved this far into our political space.

It is an irony, but it's true, that after fighting so many wars to defend our way of life from foreign aggressors we have given up our most meaningful freedom—freedom of thought—without a struggle. We will certainly not get it back without a struggle, but the method of that struggle and the manner of it must be different in kind from the forces that got us into this morass. We must put at the very center of this struggle a key project that begins in personal choice—to break the hold of the mass media over our values and culture. Where the Mahatma's rallying cry was "boycott foreign cloth," I propose "boycott foreign *thoughts*." Where he put the wheel of the *charkha* in motion, I say we should spin the dial of the mass media—to "off."

Thoughts of hostility, revenge, competition, materialism, and greed can truly be called "foreign" to our essential nature—such, at least, is my confirmed belief. It is in this sense that my late friend

Willis Harman used to use the term *pseudovalues* for making money and "getting ahead" at the expense of having deep relationships, a vibrant family. The former are goals that fade into insignificance for those who have gotten a taste of service and compassion and loving community. This hollow world of turmoil and darkness that we have devoted our ingenuity to creating is not the essential expression of our nature. Despite their long evolutionary pedigree, greed, lust, and anger are foreign to us in the very real sense that they impede us from realizing our profoundest aspirations.

Children are not born prejudiced, for example; they "have to be carefully taught," as the old song says, and they can be untaught remarkably easily, as we shall see. We can become so conditioned that it becomes second nature to respond to a different skin color or accent or belief system with hostility, but it never becomes our first nature. The opening verse of the central text of Buddhism, the Dhammapada, reads, in Eknath Easwaran's translation, "All that we are is the result of what we have thought."[13] Whoever influences our thoughts influences our destiny. Are advertisers equal to that responsibility?

Getting Real

The reclamation of our "cultural space" can be, and probably must be, an everyday, everybody activity—just like *charkha*. And while it begins, unlike *charkha*, with a "no," it's open to all of us to "spin" some time each day—the very time we save by not watching television or going to a gory movie—on constructive alternatives. Even within the "no" there are constructive, network-building aspects: writing letters, spreading knowledge, maybe organizing a media boycott in our kids' school, or church, or just among friends.

Media cleanup can be as satisfying as spiking trash alongside the freeway or dredging a toxic swamp; and though it starts in personal choice, it can give rise to a network, a campaign—a movement.

One day a few years ago I received a call from the Santa Rosa,

California, school board asking for some help. A well-known director was making a horror film in which teenagers were terrorized, complete with realistic, gory violence, and he had the brilliant idea of making it right in picturesque Santa Rosa High School. Why not let the young people participate in their own degradation? Would I come to a public meeting as an expert witness, asked the caller. Coincidentally, a former student of mine who now works with the Media Violence Project had just sent me some of the latest studies on screen violence, and horror movies in particular, so I told the caller I'd be happy to speak, little realizing that by the time I got there the meeting would be front-page news.

I arrived at the high school early to find the auditorium already thronged with an intense, buzzing crowd. Filmmaking, I had forgotten, is one of California's largest industries. The director, who shall remain nameless, had threatened to blackball our community, perhaps even our state, and the then-governor—always concerned with our (fiscal) welfare—had backed him with threatening noises of his own. But these powerful men had reckoned without their host. Over 800 people soon filled the seats, and both aisles were filled with prospective speakers waiting their turn at the mike (including "spies" from the studio—attractive young women trying to sweet-talk some of us men out of our resistance). It was a disciplined, intense, high-level meeting, one of the best I've ever seen and perhaps the closest to an old-fashioned town meeting you'll ever find outside New Hampshire. The issue was crystal clear: accept $30,000 in cash from the director, as the governor pressured us to, or protect the minds and hearts of our children.

Speaker after speaker came forward and delivered good arguments, with almost no ranting, almost all of them against the filming. One man concluded his defiance of the film company and the governor by going up to the stage and plunking down $30 from his pocket to compensate for the school's financial sacrifice. (I had pointed out that a certain infamous betrayal in our civilization had been knocked down for thirty shekels of silver, and while I wasn't sure how much a shekel would go for in today's dollars, the choice we were facing looked uncannily similar.) A woman who spoke made it onto the next day's front page: the director had sent a message that "in twenty-five years of filmmaking I have never encountered such resistance"; to which she replied, "It's about time!"

We made our point, and the filming was turned down. I had never felt so good about "the American system"—even when the film ended up being made in an old abandoned estate across the road from where I live!

Satyagraha is always a form of education. The more we can get people to focus on what the issue really is— in this case, money versus the well-being of our children—the sooner and the less abrasively we can solve it. The networks—thinking of television again—are in the business for ratings; they have no ideological attachment to vulgarity and violence as such. Even one letter that politely explains, "I have stopped watching your program because of its gratuitous violence," with a "cc" to the advertisers who support that program, makes a difference. More make a bigger one. A movement based on truth may not catch on as quickly as some, but it doesn't go away as easily either.

Boycotting television and most other media is, it is true, less than inspiring as a *constructive* undertaking: What does it build? Or, what are we "putting *in* business" with this kind of boycott? Actually, quite a bit. Families that have stopped watching television have started rediscovering each other; over and over they have found that it's far more satisfying to interact with someone, even if it's a someone you have a problem with, than to stare at pictures of someone who isn't there. "The children spent a great deal more time doing creative things," wrote Officer Brawley, a New York City policeman who turned off the tube for two weeks as part of an experiment.

> I could begin to see where the children spent more
> time doing things which would be of importance to
> them in their school work in the future. . . . For the
> first time since I had been in school, I was completely

caught up with all the reading for my courses . . . we began to visit different families who, during the winter months, we lost contact with.

The children seemed to fight among themselves more often. . . . At the same time the children became closer to us as we participated in doing things together.[14]

"The family, I feel, is pulling together tighter as a result of No TV," wrote one participant in a school's experiment in Denver.[15] Watching television can be an isolating experience—which is to say, a pre-violent experience, even before we get to the horrendous content. Conversely, whenever and to the degree that people or families or friends have abstained from watching television, they have found relationships springing back up to take its place, whether it's playing games with the kids or talking about family decisions or just talking. Five minutes of in-depth conversation is more fulfilling than five hours of vicarious absorption in images of someone else's life. People and families have just about universally reported a sense of relief, of discovery, a sense that they were better off and more "functional" when they deep-sixed their sets.

They have scientific support. In an interesting study reported by Israeli sociologist Urie Bronfenbrenner, children who grew up in new, postwar housing developments in West Germany where they were given wide yard space to play in were found, surprisingly, to have done *less* well developmentally than comparable kids in more cramped quarters in older German cities. The reason, the researchers concluded, was precisely that space—it allowed the children to run away from each other whenever they couldn't get along, instead of working out their difficulties and becoming more intimate in the process, as Officer Brawley discovered.[16] We need human space to grow up in, not physical space.

My grandchildren have grown up in a world where gas station attendants sit in glassed-in cubicles and the cashier at the movie talks to you through a speaker tube. This is a form of dehumanization, and by virtue of that fact, an indirect cause of violence—other forms of which, ironically, this separation is trying to prevent. Here we go again, making the problem a little worse in the long run, by isolating ourselves from one another at the heart unity level, in the name of "preventing" (or rather, thwarting) a certain manifestation of violence in the short term.

Since I'm digressing a little, let me make the most of it. Being a classroom teacher in this era has had its shocks, and most of them are due to the appearance of a generation who not only grew up on television but whose parents had grown up on television. Alongside the downgrades you commonly hear about—that freshmen don't know anything (that is, anything of permanent, cultural value) and that they have a terribly short attention span (so they can't *learn* anything of permanent, cultural value)—there is one you may not have realized. I remember the first time I was talking away about something and a fellow in the second row just got up and walked out. Unceremonious departures still go on—and so does my sense of shock. My students don't lack respect for me or interest in what I'm saying. It took me awhile to realize what the problem is: *they don't quite realize I'm real.* They walk out to get a snack when the tube is on, and they're not totally aware that now they're listening to a real live person.

Remember my observation in chapter 4, that when the military uses video games to train combat soldiers, it's primarily training them not to shoot straight but to shoot without remorse, to suppress their awareness that what they're shooting is alive. It is also true that those who kill within our own society, in our streets and workplaces and homes, often testify that they did not see their victims as real human beings, but like moving dolls, or images—"virtual" people, just targets. Just as Nurse Black overcame violence by seeing the person behind the would-be killer, reversing that process keeps those who would kill or injure from seeing the person for the label, or something even more dehumanizing: Susan Atkins of the Manson cult literally said that her victims "didn't even look like people. . . . I didn't relate to Sharon Tate as being anything but a store mannequin."[17] No, I'm not personally afraid of violence happening in my classroom, but I'm quite afraid that our culture has, by making us progressively less real to each other, planted the seeds of violence in students before they get there.

The Action Guide at the end of this book will suggest ways we can reconnect more vividly with one another. That's the most constructive way to tackle depersonalization. The other is to use discrimination in what we see and hear. Create your own human image impact index. In the early years at our meditation community we saw every Ian Carmichael comedy available; we saw *Casablanca* almost as often as *Gandhi* (well, not quite). If we all support films like *Groundhog Day* or *Mr. Holland's Opus,* it will help convey to producers that not everybody likes dialogue dripping with cynicism or thinks that people betray each other and use guns to solve problems with one another as a matter of course. When producers or newspaper editors say, "But this is what the public wants," they overlook the simple fact that they trained us to want it. It has been a two-way street, and the same two-way street will lead us back out. If we refuse to be an audience to bad programming and the media have to endure a period of lower ratings until the general public is retrained, we will shape a healthier, less "toxic" culture, with a higher human image and better values.[18]

If someone were to ask me, "What is it *really* going to take to get violence off our backs?," I would answer without hesitation, "Phenomenal progress in culture."

LOVING COMMUNITY

Constructive Programme was, as the name implies, constructive rather than obstructive. The central projects sought to weave back into the community the economically depressed, marginalized, or rejected, using the simple but potent concept of heart unity that informed all of Constructive Programme, as it informed—or was supposed to inform—all of Satyagraha. The healing energy gave people a self-transcending purpose and in the end worked some of its magic even between the rulers and the ruled. We have every reason to believe that the coherence of such a "solar system" model would give us a way to follow our individual passions (save whales, perch in redwood trees, educate about the death penalty) without feeling we are off doing our own things in isolation; the healing energy of nonviolence would unite us.

Television is said to be a form of "communication," but the communication is pretty one-way. In fact, television watching as we know it does nothing but isolate us. Each of us in our "techno-cocoon," we commune with the unreal. By form and content it is, at least as we use it now, the very technology of alienation. Even the fact that forty million Americans watch the same "news" at the same time has an isolating effect, for this is a good example not of *unity* but *uniformity* —a paradox we'll be revisiting in chapter 9. The thrust of our constructive program, like its great predecessor, has to be overcoming that isolation, getting back together.

In 1936 a delegation of African Americans headed by Dr. Howard Thurman made a pilgrimage to Gandhi in India. We can imagine the sense of hope with which African Americans had been following the rise of the great Indian leader. Bear in mind that Martin Luther King Jr. was seven years old back home in Atlanta at the time of this conversation. Many years later, as a student at Morehouse College, he would sit front and center listening to Dr. Thurman give a rousing address on the significance of Gandhi.

> Mrs. Thurman: We want you to come to America . . . we need you badly.
> MKG: How I wish I could, but I would have nothing to give you unless I had given an ocular demonstration here of all that I have been saying. I must make good the message here, before I bring it to you.[19]

Gandhi had long ago learned the lesson of *swadeshi,* a prominent guiding principle in both the constructive and obstructive modes of nonviolence. It states that by working in your own sphere of influence you create a resonance in widening circles, but if you overextend yourself, if you try to do everything too soon, you lose power there and here.

And in that very connection, Gandhi added a prophetic remark:

> Well . . . it may be through the Negroes that the unadulterated message of non-violence is delivered to the world.[20]

Twenty-some years later, Rosa Parks refused to yield her seat to a white man on a Montgomery bus, setting off a chain of events that punctured the legitimacy of institutional racism in the United States.

We know now, thanks mainly to Sudarshan Kapur, that the "ocular demonstration" of India shaking off her colonial shackles through nonviolence came to the United States as a force embodied in quite a few flesh-and-blood *satyagrahis*, who came to the South to advise and support the movement of the fifties and sixties.

We also know that for both countries the movement that collected around these great leaders is unfinished business. We teach it in schools, but we don't carry it forward in our lives. Of late, we've actually been losing, not gaining, ground to prejudice.

I had been in denial about this for some time until I gave a talk at Berkeley in the seventies, to a group of alumni who wanted to hear about my nonviolence course. I spoke enthusiastically, as I recall, about what we can do with this great force and how much it had done for us in the civil rights struggle. But this was Berkeley. One of those alums had been in the thick of that movement. She came up after the talk and tried to say something to the effect of, how could it be? How could we possibly be going back to race hatred after all they had suffered and achieved? She tried, but she could hardly speak through her tears. That broke the spell for me and I had to admit—first of all to myself—that even though the conscience of the nation had been roused by purely nonviolent principles for that brief, shining era, we were actually now going back into the stupidest and most destructive hatreds.

I needed an explanation. And after reflecting over what she'd said for some weeks, it did come: Martin Luther King delegitimated racism, but he did not delegitimate *violence*. He wanted to, but he never had the chance. Before he could get that far, someone or someones killed him. Violence stayed in the warp and woof of our culture, and along with it the energy of hate that it bears; and so racism, a form of hate and violence, was bound to return. You cannot expect steam not to leak out through the most convenient crack in the boiler: you have to seal all the cracks—or get even smarter and turn down the heat.

What the Weissers Did

It is not possible—at least it doesn't seem possible right now—to reignite the civil rights movement, nor would Martin Luther King necessarily want us to. I am quite sure he *would* want us to continue his legacy in the form of constructive action; in fact, that was the direction he himself was taking before reaction cut him off. And this would not have to start, necessarily, as a great movement. Let me share with you one of the most gripping news stories of 1992, the healing conversion of a grand dragon of the Ku Klux Klan, Larry Trapp, by a Jewish couple, Michael and Julie Weisser.

Michael Weisser is the cantor of the South Street Temple in Lincoln, Nebraska, and a prominent supporter of democratic issues. In 1992 he and his wife started getting a series of threatening phone calls and hate mail. The police warned him that a prominent local Klansman, Larry Trapp, was behind most of those calls, and though they put a tap on Trapp's phone they could not quite prove he was the one harassing them. So Weisser was not able to do much to protect himself—by the usual methods. One day Trapp was yelling at him over the phone, and Weisser decided, with his wife's support, that he had to resolve this for himself. "I was real quiet and calm," Cantor Weisser recollects. "I knew he had a hard time getting around [Trapp, who has since passed on, was in a wheelchair] and offered him a ride to the grocery store. . . . He just got completely quiet, and all the anger went out of his voice, and he said, 'I've got that taken care of, but thanks for asking.'"[21]

The Weissers had much more in mind, however, than just stopping the harassment. They wanted, if possible, to relieve the hate this man was suffering, who (they later found out) had been disabled for life— by a beating he received from a group of blacks. They now took the initiative and called *him*. Not long after, they went to his apartment for a friendly visit, taking a dinner they had made. When he opened his door to meet the Weissers, Trapp pulled two rings off his fingers and handed them over to his still slightly apprehensive guests. They were Nazi rings. He was symbolically, and actually, renouncing the Klan forever.

Larry Trapp, by his own admission, had been one of the most hard-case white supremacists in the country, a man who "wanted to build up the State of Nebraska into a state as hateful as North Carolina and Florida." Perhaps it is for that very reason that his conversion, compared to some of the other card-carrying supremacists who have made the break, was so complete. "I denounce everything they stand for," he said of his former Klan associates.

> But it's not the people in the organizations that I hate. . . .
> If I were to say I hate all Klansmen because they're
> Klansmen . . . I would still be a racist.[22] (my emphasis)

This shows a sophisticated grasp of true, redemptive nonviolence —of heart unity. I would submit that this story takes us to the heart of loving community. The Weissers' brilliantly successful act is a model of how to apply courage and compassion to the curse of racism, which has responded to virtually nothing else.

At the same time, you cannot disestablish racism, or any such division, by waiting until a spiritually ready hater who is beginning to look for a way out meets a particularly courageous and nonviolence-aware couple like the Weissers. We need not just more individuals like them but programs such that, if there were enough of them, they would make emergency cures like the Weissers' unnecessary. That means we are talking about young people, and education.

Elias Jabbour is an Israeli Arab, and a Christian. He has lived in Israel his whole life and has yet to see the peace process work. One day in 1987, he decided to stop waiting for peace to come from policy makers and started to ask himself what he could do himself. His scheme was simple: turn his home into an "oasis of peace" (like the famous school of that name: Neve Shalom/Wahat al-Salam). The children spend their days "in a colorful, warm, nurturing environment where it doesn't occur to them to treat one another differently based on race or religion" —until, that is, they go on to public school, and are once again segregated.[23] Those who have the privilege of working with young people get to see how easily the conditioned responses of prejudice can sometimes be peeled away. In Los Angeles, when members of the Fourth Reich Skinheads were brought together with a group of blacks and Jews their own age, once again they quickly came to accept their new friends, leaving the "Reich" and "Skinheads" stuff in the dust.[24]

Jan Øberg, head of the conflict mitigation team of Sweden's Transnational Foundation for Peace and Future Research, returned from the foundation's thirtieth mission to former Yugoslavia, where he conducted a series of "reconciliation seminars" in eastern Slavonia with 120 Croat and Serb gymnasium students from Vukovar, Osijek, and Vinkovci. For most of them it was the first time they had met "the other side," even though many of them lived in the same town. Various techniques such as fishbowl, role play, group discussions, and brainstorming were used. The students got to know each other and exchanged views, made friends, and sang songs. They cried about the hurt and pain they had experienced during the war, but were careful not to say things like "you did this to us," just to give vent to their grief. They allowed themselves to brainstorm fascinating ideas and visions about a peaceful Croatia, eastern Slavonia, and Vukovar. And here is the payoff: Øberg found that "it took Croat and Serb students less than an hour to find out that they have a lot in common, in contrast to what they have been told by their government, the media and often their parents since 1991."[25]

Less than an hour. How many people or groups are willing to give that hour for the young people of the world, to heal the wounds that come from and perpetuate war?

There are not many so far, but I would like to show how much good they're doing—and how to build on it.

THE COFFEE EPIPHANY: TOWARD A THERMODYNAMIC MODEL OF COMMUNITY

This question of renewing a culture can sometimes be understood best by comparison with a familiar model, the second law of thermodynamics. This law states that a physical system spontaneously goes to a state of higher entropy over time, meaning that it seeks a kind of equilibrium where everything is mixed up uniformly. Its order, or from another viewpoint its "information," decreases, eventually to zero. Things degrade. "Isolated systems move spontaneously toward maximum entropy."[26] The most dramatic example is the living organism, which without exception degrades irreversibly to the state of death. The universe itself, it is thought, is eventually approaching a state of "heat death" to become an undifferentiated cosmic soup of mass-energy. Any smaller system, however (and most of them are!), can reverse that entropic drift by receiving energy from outside itself. One important example is our planet.

> The state of nonequilibrium of the Earth irradiated by the much hotter Sun provides an environment in which the cells of plants and animals may build order—i.e., lower their local entropy at the expense of their environment.[27]

This is how we stay alive, even though "there is no evidence point-ing to any ability on the part of living matter to run counter to the principle of increasing (overall) disorder as formulated in the second law of thermodynamics."[28] A biological community is not dissimilar. Inbreeding can cause a dangerous loss of diversity, meaning a loss of its resilience and vitality, unless new genetic information comes into the gene pool from another source.

Imagine now a society as a "black box," or isolated system. In such a closed system, be it a test tube or a galaxy, energy inevitably runs down over the course of time; disorder increases and meaningful "information" is steadily lost. Similarly, do not cultures lose their vital-ity over time, does their focus not blur or their priorities start to drift as people lose their sense of what it is they're supposed to do in life? One obvious sign of this declining vitality—one we're only too famil-iar with—is that decision makers keep coming up with the same unworkable solutions to problems that go on increasing. Is alienation eroding our security? Let's put more people in jail. Is there a rogue state in the international system? Hit them with more sanctions—and if they don't fall in line, more bombs. On one level, violence, as we've seen before, is a serious lack of imagination.

One of the most studied decision-making processes in modern governmental history is that by which a series of American presidents, particularly President Johnson, kept on deluding themselves that they were about to "win" the war in Vietnam. Psychologists invented a new concept, "crisis decision making," to explain this cramping of the imagination (not to mention, of compassion). One way that worked was as drastic as it was simple: President Johnson surrounded himself with a small clique of men, a black box within a black box, who would scornfully dismiss anything but the "more-war" mentality. Anyone who came up with another idea was out, and so we were all doomed to stay the course—until we sank.

It was extreme, but President Johnson's war cabinet was also symptomatic of the way our thinking about violence in general is lim-ited by narrow, self-defeating notions. We need new ideas and fresh energy to break out of the closed circle of discourse surrounding violence, as living things on earth need energy from beyond our planet, from the sun, to organize themselves biologically and overcome entropy. The prevailing culture is "running down" toward thermodynamic death for want of a new energy that can vitalize new patterns of order, which can help us respond to the crisis and opportunity facing us.

Nonviolence is that new kind of energy. It is not really new, of course, any more than sunlight is new, but we have so turned our back on this dimension of life that we find ourselves trying, absurdly, to solve problem after violent problem as though that resource, that energy, did not exist. One way of looking at Constructive Programme (and Gandhi certainly saw it this way) was as an attempt to introduce nonviolence energy into the social order on a grand scale. Through Constructive Programme, for example, Gandhi and his close disciple Vinoba Bhave birthed institutions of every description—hospitals, schools, rural institutes, spinning centers—no less than 1,200 of which are still going strong in India today. The innate power of nonviolence is so impressive, as all this institution building hints, that we might think of Constructive Programme as the Van Allen Belt, filtering the immense power of nonviolence and stepping it down to useable amounts and wavelengths so it could enter society with minimum disruption and maximum ordering potential, the way the Great God, Shiva, absorbed the immense power of the Ganges onto his divine head so he could meter it out to bring life and purification to the Gangetic Plain.

Where our thermodynamic analogy breaks down, however, is that in our case the "outside" of the social system is really an "inside." Nonviolence is first and foremost a kind of energy that resides within a human being. We do not need different individuals in power, so much as we need a different kind of power in individuals. Some of the key campaigns of the civil rights movement—the Montgomery bus strike and the Greensboro, North Carolina, lunch counter sit-ins come to mind—were not sparked by Martin Luther King, or Bayard Rustin or by "outsiders" coming from up north, but respectively by a black seamstress named Rosa Parks and by four local college students who got it in their heads to do the "disruptive" actions that would eventually culminate in a higher level of social order.

We tend to know more about how the leaders went through the profound inner changes that allowed them access to new faith and courage, simply because of their public exposure. We know that Martin Luther King, for example, was at first unprepared for the level of hatred that rose like an angry sea that threatened to take, and eventually would take, his life. He passed through a profound crisis, his "Pietermaritzburg" if you will, that almost broke him. It came to a head on Friday, January 27, 1955, the day after his first jail experience, when a series of obscene and hateful phone calls shook his confidence. At midnight that night, after a particularly ugly and threatening call that left him unable to get back to sleep, his anxiety mounted.

> And I got to the point that I couldn't take it any longer. I was weak. Something said to me, you can't call on Daddy now, he's up in Atlanta a hundred and seventy-five miles away. You can't even call on Mama now. You've got to call on that something in that person that your Daddy used to tell you about, that power that can make a way out of no way.
> . . . And I bowed down over that cup of coffee. I never will forget it. . . . And it seemed at that moment that I could hear an inner voice saying to me, "Martin Luther, stand up for righteousness. Stand up for justice. Stand up for truth. And lo, I will be with you, even until the end of the world."[29]

Whatever we believe this inner voice was, however we explain it, it had the immediate effect of lifting King to a higher level of functioning: "Almost at once my fears began to go, my uncertainty disappeared." Three days later it allowed him to accept calmly the news that his house, with wife and children inside, had just been bombed: "My religious experience a few nights before had given me the strength to face it." In fact, that experience came back to him repeatedly over the months and years of struggle. It was his enduring strength.[30]

We could not find a better example of what I was calling a different energy coming into "the system," in this case American society and all whom it influences, through the deep experience of an individual. We should not be surprised that King was looking much more toward constructive work when death overtook him.

What, though, does this mean for the rest of us? These rare experiences do happen to people—to a rare leader in a crisis, to a group kneeling on the Birmingham sidewalk, to a nation roused by a Gandhi, but we can't count on them. We can't plan them, but maybe we can institutionalize them. That is, maybe we can make institutional and cultural changes that will encourage such experiences and make longer-lasting use of their effects. There is at least some indirect evidence that this is possible.

According to an important anthropological theory of violence, human groups have a kind of mob instinct that has been carried along the course of evolution and has been observed very clearly, for example, among primates.[31] Because of this instinct (or whatever name we should use for such a pre-rational behavior), certain kinds of tension within a community can cause the community to expend its violence on available victims who may have little to do with the original problem. Such a response has been inscribed, as it were, in the cultural code of many societies, expressing itself in varied institutions that would fit the term *scapegoating*. The Holocaust was a huge example of this—note that the word *holocaust* itself is drawn from a context of ritual sacrifice, which was a major form of victimization in archaic cultures.

Without going further into this fascinating theory, which explains so well how violent impulse becomes violent institution, we can use it the way we have used other aspects of violence in this book—we can stand it on its head. If destructive energy can be encoded and institutionalized, surely so can creative energy. This is what Gandhi's ashrams were supposed to do: "The Ashram holds that . . . society can be built up on the foundations of ahimsa," he explained, and it "conducts experiments with this end in view."[32]

This is what I had in mind when I pointed out how Joan Black, when she was confronted with a deranged individual in her emergency room, responded with behavior that followed a pattern laid down by ancient rhetoricians for roughly that kind of emotional work. Apparently, the ancients, with their relatively slow pace of life and stable institutions, observed how some clever individuals had calmed someone down who was in a dangerous fury, or bucked up somebody mired in a depression, and they literally wrote the script for anyone who needs to do this. And this is what Gandhi, King, and others lived for: so that no matter how much they had to suffer to show the power of nonviolence, we could come along and understand what was involved and learn how to make it work more systematically, eventually to make it not the odd exception but the way conflict is resolved and life is lived. In this sense, culture, like science, works by serendipity, noting examples of successful living and passing them on. In this particular transmission, we cannot afford to fail.

For this reason we have, in the above discussions, peered into the abyss of crime and into the abyss of racism, to see how nonviolence can send a ray of light even into those dark areas. In a moment, we will do the same with war. We have already seen moments of great illumination happening in sudden emergencies, at the climaxes of movements, and most importantly in the defining moments of certain individuals. And we already know that if we don't want to go on lurching from one emergency to the next, we have to let ourselves down the chain of causality, from spectacular late interventions like the Weissers' to earlier and less hair-raising ones like the Oasis of Peace school, or Elias Jabbour's private version of the same, or numerous projects like those mounted by the Search for Common Ground. The one thing needed for such moments and such projects to thrive is cultural support—which is why reforming the media takes pride of place as the sun around which other healing projects of our constructive program can revolve.

Early intervention, and especially earliest intervention at the foundation of culture itself, is what constructive programs are about. I have little doubt, as I've mentioned, that had King lived, he too would have moved from protest marches and sit-ins toward "cooperating with good" once he got past the necessary first step of "noncooperating with evil." The instinct was already there, even in the first campaign, which was designed not to put the Montgomery bus company out of business, but to put justice *in* business, "to achieve justice for ourselves as well as for the white man."[34] The arc from integrating buses to securing voting rights to building economic opportunity was bending toward an American constructive program; how do we complete the circle?

I have stressed two ways, privileging the first: our own personal engagement. As King said, "Nonviolence in the truest sense is not a strategy that one uses simply because it is expedient at the moment; nonviolence is ultimately a way of life that men [and women] live by because of the sheer morality of its claim,"[33] or, as I've been putting it, because of the quality of its energy. The other way is institutional change, starting with those institutions that shape our basic values. Why are we never told in school that the human being has an innate need for integration with others and, "as far as in him or her lies," with all life? Why are we never told that no one can live fully without realizing that his or her life has an overriding purpose? Are we to turn our back on our deepest needs simply because advertisers have no way to exploit them?

A nonviolent moment can be regarded as a kind of epiphany, a sudden eruption of some new and unexpected energy. Whether it be an individual bent over a midnight cup of coffee or a crowd suddenly roused to a higher mode of activity, this energy can be captured and developed. As reform or resistance, it can raise the consciousness of many and leaven the mainstream to the great benefit of us all.

In these last two chapters we have been exploring how nonviolence

—in "the truest sense" as King put it, a nonviolence universal in scope and deeply founded in individual commitment—could be systematically applied to two huge social problems, crime and racism. Our theme was loving community; our preferred mode of action was constructive. And so they will remain, as we move on to grapple with "the scourge of war."

CHAPTER SEVEN

A CLEAR PICTURE OF PEACE

If passive resistance could conquer racial hatred . . . Gandhi and Negroes like King would have shown the world how to conquer war itself.

—W. E. B. DuBois

SOME SIX WEEKS after the bombing of Hiroshima and Nagasaki, a group of distinguished nuclear scientists met in Chicago. It was here that Enrico Fermi had carried out the first chain reaction; now the bomb had shown its awful power and humanity had to face the question of how to live with it. The scientists were acutely aware that history had opened a window of rare possibility for them. On the one hand, the world was shocked and sickened by the horrors of war, and on the other, they who had created the weapon that ended it were held in an almost priestly authority. No one else had quite the prestige they enjoyed to chart a course for humanity that would lead toward peace. "Yet," Glenn Seaborg sadly recalls,

> no clear picture emerged of how we could achieve the objective nearly all of us had in mind—a world without nuclear weapons. It was as though the seeds of a nuclear arms race were embedded in human nature and political institutions.[1]

The seeds of a nuclear arms race are indeed embedded in human nature and political institutions—and so are the seeds of stable peace. Human choices, individual and collective, determine which set of those seeds will flourish and predominate. As we have seen often, there is absolutely nothing in human nature, as far as human nature is known to scientists or sages, that predetermines which of these outcomes civilization will eventually reach. If by "nature" we mean the deepest aspirations discoverable in the human psyche and the evolutionary mechanisms designed to implement those aspirations, then the cards are, in fact, fairly obviously stacked toward peace. If we are heading right now in the other direction, that is not nature calling, but a kind of perverse conditioning that is diverting us from the course of our rightful destiny.

This was the picture the scientists did not see—understandably, because while they were brilliant men in their field, their expertise, no matter what the public might think, was more or less irrelevant. As Kenneth Boulding pointed out, the field of integrative power has been left fallow. No one—that is, no category of "experts" we currently recognize—makes it his or her special study to learn and teach how to fertilize the field of peace and reap its rich harvest. Scientists and well-meaning people that they were, the Chicago group were nonetheless caught in the same constricted vision as the rest of us; like us, they tended to see the world and its potential from within the shadow side—the sad, greed-driven, media-constricted image of what is possible.

I have a reason for stressing this point. For a period of time, I was part of a remarkable series of meetings with nuclear weapons scientists, theologians, and professors convened by the bishop of Oakland, California, when the American Catholic Bishops' pastoral of 1983 had expressed grave concern about the morality of the nuclear arms race. Our discussions in the privileged atmosphere of a Catholic retreat house in the hills above the Central Valley were remarkably frank and searching. It was one of the best opportunities I had ever had to present nonviolence to an influential audience. I noticed, however, that a physical science colleague from Stanford laid claim to—and was granted—special authority because he "was the guy who knew how to restart the Stanford Linear Accelerator." I was impressed, like everyone else; I can barely restart my computer when it crashes. But what, exactly, does that have to do with the nature of violence or the psychology of deterrence? Have we become so obsessed with machines and technology that we've forgotten that the most important things in life are neither?

I believe it was George Bernard Shaw who said that there are some subjects about which almost anyone you meet on the street could enlighten you more than the experts. Peace is one of them. In the search for peace, "experts," like the solemn "news" reports of the media or the pronouncements of the elite who make our foreign policies, often do little more than obscure the common-sense intuition that, after all, can light up the path.

The Nobel Prize for Peace in 1979 went to Mother Teresa of Calcutta. The world's reaction, basically a paean of joy, was one of those sparks of intuition. "Now the mother of Bengal is the mother of the entire world," said an ecstatic Bengali on the streets of Calcutta. Mother Teresa had been honored by Pope Paul eight years earlier with the first Pope John XXIII Peace Prize, and now she was awarded the Nobel, though she had never played a role in a negotiation, signed a treaty, or used her influence to prevent a large-scale conflict. Yet world opinion rapturously approved the award, unconsciously sharing in the logic it implied—that he or she who lifts the human image out of the gutter, as Mother Teresa had literally done in the streets of Calcutta and around the world, does more for peace than haggling statesmen or threatening armies.

And in fact, Mother Teresa demonstrated her peacemaking power dramatically in 1982 when, upon hearing that an orphanage for disabled children in Beirut had been abandoned to its fate during intense fighting, she announced her intention to enter the city and rescue the children. And so she did: for ten days the mere presence of the diminutive nun, who owned virtually nothing and had access to no state authority, brought the spasm of raging conflict that no UN-brokered force, no Syrian presence, no Israeli armies had been able to control to a strange peace.

So the Nobel award, and the world's rapturous approval, were rare threads of bright intuition in a fabric of confusion surrounding peace and war. In the Beirut rescue drama, there resided, however, one of the wilder ironies of modern times. Mother Teresa's antagonist in this struggle, the man who ordered the rain of bombs and rockets on south Lebanon, was the prime minister of Israel, Menachem Begin—who had been awarded a Nobel Peace Prize the year before! This award was not given in cynicism. Prime Minister Begin and Egypt's Anwar el-Sadat had jointly signed a "peace" agreement that put a temporary slowdown on hostilities between Israel and Egypt (the award had been given to Le Duc Tho and Henry Kissinger for a similar achievement in 1973). This is what is called "negative peace," arguably better than positive war, and in this sense the award to Begin and Sadat was not made in cynicism. But it was certainly done in confusion, the confusion between the two definitions of "peace" that are now "reigning," as Emerson said, "in the minds of many persons": the confusion between "negative peace" (à la Begin) and "positive peace" (à la Mother Teresa), between a standoff characterized by the absence of physical war and an island of loving community nourished by the presence of spontaneous mutual concern.

Incidentally, the attack Prime Minister Begin had launched on Lebanon in 1981 was code-named "Peace for Galilee." *That* was cynical.

None other than Robert McNamara said, "Mother Teresa deserves Nobel's Peace Prize because she promotes peace in the most fundamental manner, by her confirmation of . . . human dignity."[2] But in her own acceptance speech at Oslo, speaking in what she called "her own special brand of English," Mother Teresa defined even more simply the contrast between her kind of peace and that promoted by presidents and prime ministers: "I am called to help the individual." Violence is always against the individual; the human individual is always the source, and individuality the ultimate beneficiary, of nonviolence.

This makes all the more arresting the idea that nonviolence can be used in war, which is the largest-scale form of violence, in which the actors are the largest groups or states.

Can nonviolence be used to defend a whole state—can it be led to a replacement of the war system? Even in the largely unworked field of peace itself some scholars will declare that nonviolence is not relevant to the solution of international conflict; it just can't reach that far: "Nonviolent action has never been *and will never be* a replacement for warfare."³ (my emphasis) But that thread of intuition we picked up in Calcutta and traced through Beirut and Oslo seems to be leading to a yes. As W. E. B. DuBois said, it indicates that those who cultivate the "arts of love" like King and Gandhi and Mother Teresa are the ones who bring peace to the world, not those who hold others at bay in an uneasy equilibrium of naked power. DuBois was speaking incredulously, even sarcastically; but I will be confirming it in all seriousness. For Gandhi, it was very clear—*only* nonviolence can replace warfare: "I can say with confidence that if the world is to have peace, nonviolence is the means to that end, and [there is] no other."⁴

I. I. Rabi, who received the Nobel Prize for Physics in 1944, later said ruefully of the nuclear arms race, "It gets worse and worse. I don't know why we failed. It's a mystery. It's the great mystery of the postwar period. . . . Anything that reduces nuclear weapons, I'm for."⁵

But isn't it intuitive that we cannot get to peace through the torturous maze of war? The reason the way to peace is such a mystery is, most of us cannot get from the heart intuition that we share with Mother Teresa to a coherent idea how we ourselves, who don't share her vocation, can nonetheless follow her lead. Politicians give lip service to her kind of contribution, but who tries to move that acknowledgment from the lips to somewhere near the heart? Let's dare to be intuitive. I suggest that the way to see the "clear picture" sought by the nuclear scientists, so far in vain, is to step out of the shadows. That is, not to be always thinking how to stop war so much as how to start nonviolence.

Body, Mind, and Spirit I:
Thinking Peace

When Joan Baez led the first group of protesters into Sproul Hall on the Berkeley campus, launching what is now known as the free speech movement, she stopped at the head of the long, wide stairway for a moment, turned, and said with her famous smile to the huge crowd of students who were all but intoxicated by the historic significance of their entry into the forbidden building, to remember that we weren't going in anger but with love in our hearts. We were going to be non-violent in thought, word, and deed. She was echoing what Martin Luther King before her and many nonviolent activists before and after her have said. Real nonviolence comes from each of us, from within ourselves. We have to do something about our thoughts, our speech, *and* our outer behavior to have a nonviolent effect on the world.

The trouble is, or was, that in 1964 even those who were inclined to agree with Ms. Baez didn't have the faintest idea how to be nonviolent in thought. To get any sort of systematic handle on our thoughts was never discussed in education; indeed, it was scarcely dreamed of, anywhere. *Meditation* was still an empty or a badly misunderstood word, outside of the rarest circles. How quickly that all changed. By the time the free speech movement was over, in little less than a year, alongside the political style that could in a way go back to centuries of student rebellion now filtered through what we took to be Marxism (none of us ever *read* Marx or Lenin, to my knowledge) came the "new age" consciousness that was to create yet another subculture. In the same cafés where we had sat discussing Camus and Fanon over cups of plain coffee, some of us now talked excitedly about Vivekananda and Buddhism over lattes.

Time will sort out what is real in this new way of thinking and what is romantic wish fulfillment. The "new age" is a reaction against materialism, which richly deserves one, but many reactions somehow end up stuck in the outworn creed that they're rejecting. It is still difficult to talk about—even think about—the mind in this still very material age. In the seventies there was a *Reader's Digest* series on health called "I Am Joe's Foot" or "Heart" or some other organ. As Sri Easwaran began to collect enthusiastic meditators around him on the Berkeley campus in that era, one of his oft-expressed desires, not entirely tongue in cheek, was to write an article called "I Am Joe's Mind." He even had his opening sentence: "Joe thinks he's me." It would have made the *Reader's Digest* a journal for all time.

Peacemaking is nothing more nor less than the application of soul force to human violence at its greatest scale. Therefore, it must begin, somehow, with deep changes that take place within the person—where the soul is. It doesn't stop there, to be sure. The fact is, it's nearly impossible to keep soul force from having effects on the world, eventually quite visible ones on the material aspect of the world. To begin to show how soul force, somehow resident in or reachable through the human mind, could become a peace system in the world, I am going to envision three steps, or projects, that, in the spirit of Joan Baez's rallying cry, illustrate three stages of the great change that has to happen —three threads to weave into an eventual fabric of peace: thought, word, and deed.

Whatever else the "new age" paradigm may have accomplished, or failed to, it has made it easier to talk about the baffling problem of large conflicts by making it somewhat more natural to bear in mind their connection with consciousness. Consciousness is within, but not limited to, the individual. However vast, however complex and "out there" the war system may be when it finally plays itself out, "wars begin in the minds of men." Emerson had long ago foreshadowed this truism of the UNESCO Charter in his musing about the Concord armory that I've often quoted: "It is really a thought that built this portentous war establishment, and a thought shall also melt it away."[6] The nonviolence that can overcome war must also begin in the minds of men and women. Any and all of us. During the Cold War that followed hard upon that resounding, but ignored, first clause of the UNESCO Charter, British historian E. P. Thompson was dismayed by the dangerous fixation on nuclear weapons as things—prophetically, because this trivialization of war was to reach a climax in the Gulf conflict some years later. He remarked then, rather chillingly, "The deformed human mind is the ultimate doomsday weapon."[7] Emerson said, "Timber, brick, lime and stone have flown into convenient shape, obedient to the master idea reigning in the minds of many persons";[8] now steel, silicon, glass, and radioactive isotopes have obediently flown into shapes far more destructive. Our thinking has not improved, and so the "improvements" in our technology take us backward into grave danger.

I would, however, propose a more compassionate, and in the end a more practical, handle on Thompson's grim observation: the *undisciplined* human mind is the ultimate doomsday weapon. Minds become deformed by lack of discipline, and formed by discipline. As the Buddha said, "More than those who hate you, more than all your enemies, an undisciplined mind does greater harm. More than your mother, more than your father, more than all your family, a well-disciplined mind does greater good."[9] An undisciplined mind is the most dangerous kind of loose cannon. Whoever owns such a mind will feel insecure no matter what situation you put him or her in and will spread insecurity to all those around, which in course of time can become the mass insecurity known as war.

The most powerful, direct, and immediate way to discipline the mind—to get our hands on the "master idea" reigning over it—is the method I extolled in chapter 3: meditation. Meditation—again, as I understand it—is "choosing responsiveness over violence" over and over again, systematically and doggedly putting the mind back in a positive channel (in my case, the inspirational passage) every time it starts wandering, as it will, to hell and gone. The relevance for nonviolence of such a struggle is that distractions are not as random as we think. Scratch any thought that's trying to distract you from something you are trying to think about, and you'll find that even the most innocent-seeming, the most pious train of associations is leading you into an ambush only two or three associations off the trail.

"Ah, that's a great verse."

"Wonder why more people don't realize that."

"I'm so smart!"

"Why on earth doesn't Genevieve appreciate me. Like the other day . . ."

Whoops, there we go again. When our thoughts are slow and positive (and slow and positive tend to come together, just as fast and negative do), it is relatively easy to keep them off that most boring of subjects—ourself. Our mind quickly regains its native responsiveness, i.e., to the needs of others. The fact is, when we speak of an uncontrolled mind, we are being a bit inaccurate. A mind that our better judgment does not direct is not really uncontrolled; it is controlled by forces of which we would not approve. Meditation is thus an ever-deepening tug-of-war between our better judgment and forces like anger, fear, and greed, which are in turn driven by the ultimate, chaotic principle within us; call it the ego or something more colorful—it is the "doomsday machine" in our own mind. We dismantle that machine definitively on the gala day when our better judgment gains spontaneous, unbroken control over the thoughts, images, and feelings produced, now more slowly and less seemingly randomly, in the factory of the mind.

In the centuries after Jesus's passing, tens of thousands of men and women took to the deserts of Egypt or the hills of Syria to practice what they called the "secret regimen." Later they would call it "the prayer of quiet" and practice it in monastic enclaves all across Europe, or at enclaved moments during otherwise normal lives. Today, relearning from the East what we have forgotten from our own traditions, we call it meditation—and the name matters little. If we look into our own pasts, millions of our fellow human beings have recognized that the mind as we know it is a problem that has to be solved for our own fulfillment and the world's peace.

Today, of course, the mass media have, seemingly by their very nature, made it more difficult than ever to recognize this problem. D.W. Griffith, the famous film pioneer, made some innovations in the early days of the silent movie that illustrate this all too well. He drastically accelerated scene changes in the typical one-reeler of the day from about a dozen separate shots to as many as sixty-eight.[10] This is the same man who, you may remember, produced one of the most pro-violent films of all time, the notorious *Birth of a Nation* (1915), a film that glorified the Ku Klux Klan and, as the title implies, what Griffith saw as the "nation building" significance for the United States of vigilante racism. To watch MTV today is to see the mind being made jerky and uncoordinated—and, once you understand the connection, wide open for violence.

In meditation you are dealing directly with that mysterious connection between speed, fragmentation, and violence. Key to the practice of meditation is not only the positive content of the passage you're meditating on, but your efforts at slowing down the rate at which you're going through it. I sometimes feel like a cowpoke, grabbing the mind by the horns (the words it's thinking) and wrestling it down, causing it to go through the passage as slowly as I can, until the blessed day when compulsive thinking does actually stop.

And along with it all its violence. This is the ultimate in making —and experiencing—peace. Then we will know for ourselves why Emperor Ashoka declared that there is nothing like meditation for making progress in the law of life.

BODY, MIND, AND SPIRIT II:
TALKING OUR WALK

To the extent that we can make peace rule our thoughts, to that extent, our speech and actions will be pure peace. When Gandhi said, "I have not the shadow of a doubt that any man or woman can achieve what I have achieved,"[11] he was not talking about founding spinning centers or leading salt marches. He was talking about the inner peace that, as he said, others often envied. The perfecting of this long, long process, however, is a long way off (judging by myself), and people are causing each other death and suffering all over the world even as we speak. What can we do *now*, while trying to work these deep changes on the mind and lay the secure foundations of peace from below?

There is—and we are leading up to it—a form of direct action ordinary people can take part in that, in my opinion, will help to roll back the monstrous momentum of the war system more effectively than urging our representatives to sign treaties or withhold some monies here or there from the military budget. But there is also an important middle ground between thought and action.

What causes, or allows, a human being to do inhuman actions? Here are the statements of two such people who found themselves swept up in World War II. Former soldier Shiro Azuma participated in the massacre of civilians in Nanking. Sixty-one years later, stricken with remorse, he explained quite simply, "We were able to kill them because we despised them."[12]

Once, after I had given a talk in Pasadena for the American Friends Service Committee, a man came up to me and told me that he and his wife had grown up in a small suburb of Berlin, where her father was the rabbi and was much respected in the whole community. As persecution intensified in the late thirties, orders came from Berlin to inflict greater and greater indignities on the Jews. But in this community, people found themselves unable to carry out those orders, at least when it came to the man's father-in-law. They were not particularly opposed to the Nazis, he told me, and certainly not openly trying to resist the government; they simply could not overcome their innate respect for the rabbi. A respect that nonviolence itself had roused, it occurred to me, in the case of the Birmingham marchers.

Respect, then, is a powerful antidote to violence. But it is the testimony of a second witness that I want to focus on: Adolf Eichmann, who was hunted down and brought to Israel to stand trial for his crimes against humanity. Eichmann reportedly said that it hadn't been hard for Nazi leaders to commit such acts, thanks to their language. Hannah Arendt explains that the Gestapo leaders were ordered to communicate, and therefore ended up thinking, in a bizarre code of euphemisms. No one spoke of killing, but of "final solution," "evacuation," "special treatment."

> The net effect of this language system was not to keep these people ignorant of what they were doing, but to prevent them from equating it with their old, "normal" knowledge of murder and lies. . . . Eichmann's great susceptibility to catch words and stock phrases, combined with his incapacity for ordinary speech, made him, of course, an ideal subject for [these] "language rules."[13]

We may be getting somewhere. If we look back on the Cold War era, it can give us a weird feeling of disorientation to see ordinary people like you and me blithely contemplating the extermination of the planet Earth, and to remember how we thought and spoke about it. It was not a time of democracy (times of tension and hysteria never are) but one in which a small elite had a handle on our way of thinking, which they seemed bent on cranking in the direction of more and more anxiety and war. A number of us scholars who were looking for a way out of this freakish condition hit on the idea of studying the language of the Cold War discourse going on among these "experts." Perhaps we could understand something of how we had gotten into that crazy way of looking at things and help them, the "defense intellectuals," understand it, too.

The approach had attractive features. We know how maddeningly difficult it can be to get someone who's opposed to us to change his or her thinking. A nonviolent moment can turn that trick, but we know how rare *that* is. So it occurred to our group of scholars that we could look at the imagery, metaphors, nuances, and suggestions in which these people speak and write and, by putting that aspect of their language under scrutiny of reason, help to show them—and the general public—how they were deceiving themselves. Wording began to look like the place to stir up the dovecote (or should we say hawkcote). It was anyway more constructive than simply despising those who went in for endless discussions of megatonnages and "throw —weights" or trying to talk to them about "the morality of the arms race," which would evoke nothing but a cold shoulder, which we perhaps deserved. To make others feel bad about what they're doing rarely works. Usually it just guarantees that they will stop listening, to protect their smarting conscience.

When the Peace and Conflict Studies program was just underway at Berkeley, I used to invite a captain from the Army ROTC (now called Military Science at Berkeley) to talk in the introductory course. He usually stood up to my students' impatient criticism very well, but on one occasion he casually mentioned, as people do, that of course "there have been wars throughout history." Fresh from reading Marija Gimbutas, I piped up, "Do you realize that that's not actually true? First of all there's the whole 'Old European' civilization, then there are scores of societies, for example a broad swath of Native American cultures who did not . . ." It was too late. He had changed the subject already. Wherever people are faced with the fact that their behavior doesn't accord with what they say, "the theory of cognitive dissonance suggests that [they] change their beliefs to be consistent with their behavior," not the other way around.[14]

So our group began exploring the world of language and metaphor, where we could hope to engage the defense community in constructive dialogue—and where, I now want to add, we can all do some constructive work today. People are not going to take charge of their thinking process in great numbers any time soon, for this involves the hardest disciplines in the world and the farthest removed from the mainstream culture's field of vision, but language is the key to thoughts, and language can be worked on independently. Whether or not we are systematically trying to control the *process* of our thinking, i.e., through meditation, we can pay some careful attention to its *content*. So what did that content look like in the Cold War era?

In an influential article called "Sex and Death in the Rational World of Defense Intellectuals," psychologist Carol Cohn led the way. Spending two weeks in a seminar with civilian "defense intellectuals" ("a feminist spy in the house of death," she fancied herself), Cohn shed some rather frightening light on the way this elite community was shaping the most fateful decisions of our time—indeed, if they had their way, perhaps of time itself. These men (and an occasional woman) thought of their mission as "formulat[ing] 'rational' systems for dealing with . . . nuclear weapons,"[15] but what Cohn picked up, listening in as a woman and a political outsider, was an odd language shot through with interlocking metaphors of eroticism and violence. Weapons "marry up"; some are called "slick-ems"; they try to achieve "deep penetration." One stereotype of these men was that they were if anything *too* rational, with their cold calculations of "megadeaths" and innumerable chilling euphemisms like "surgically clean strikes" and "countervalue attacks," but in an important way they were far from rational. With the lives of every one of us in the balance, they were psyching themselves up on the sex-and-violence appeal of Armageddon!

Cohn's important study focused on the key issue of gender and the rather bruising concept of maleness that's served up in our modern culture, but her work has even broader implications. Language—all levels of language, from the individual word to the complex argument—is a powerful handle on the mind. Within the interstices of our own language we can often encode—and thus to a degree conceal—arguments we do not want to spell out. Modern language is so pervaded by aggression now that we no longer notice we're using the language of conflict, even when we're doing peace.

> UNESCO distributes rucksacks to institutions which are part of its Network of some 4600 associated schools in 147 countries. Teachers and educators can add material *targeting* the specific needs of the region or community . . .[16] (my emphasis)

Oh dear. "Targeting" peace materials at schools! But we all do this —when we say, "This project is *targeted at* inner-city youth," instead of "designed for" them, or we say we are going to "impact" something instead of have an effect on it (making a verb out of a noun, to boot), or when we say something is "competitive" when we mean it's good. Noticed or not, these locutions—and the implications behind them— register in our consciousness. If they did not, there would be no such thing as poetry. Or advertising.

You might think with some justice that the words and imagery we're discussing here are too subtle to be called violent. But the effects of such speech are not so subtle. Some time in the seventies, I recall, an Irish revolutionist was taken into custody in this country, and the British wanted to get their hands on him. Should we extradite? The life or death outcome of this question, at least as far as the press was concerned, hinged on whether this person was a "freedom fighter" or a "terrorist." These are extremely polarizing words. In reality, of course, he was neither. In reality he was a person, one who had used violence to get what he wanted. We could certainly have talked about what to do with such a person—but the possibility for such discussion disappeared behind a debate over which stereotype defined him. This is dehumanization.

It is when we go from labels like these to the imagery and metaphors in ordinary language, however, that we really see the power of words to construct and at the same time conceal. Consider this remarkable passage from an interview with General Oscar Humberto Mejía, the military dictator (or was he chief of state?) of Guatemala, who described his campaign against the nation's guerilla army in the eighties:

> It's a curious thing, but sometimes the population supports the guerilla more than they support their own army. I don't know why. We were just doing our duty. We didn't *start* the war. But the population was the water and the guerillas were the fish. We realized that to kill the fish we had to drain out the water. We had to pull the indigenous population over to one side, and this is why we created the civil patrol system."[17]

The guerillas were the fish. That's a long way down the food chain from human beings!

But the indigenous people fared even worse in this conceptual fantasy; they were water, i.e., not even animals. They were inert and passive (like the army, which "had to" expel them), hardly relevant except as a hindrance to killing the "fish." And so one of the cruelest campaigns of the cruel twentieth century, in which an entire people was reduced to living in terror, became easy, the same way it became easy for Adolf Eichmann to mastermind the slaughter of tens of thousands of human beings. It became easy when the perpetrators imagined they were not killing and destroying, they were just "pulling the indigenous population to one side." I can almost hear the words of Mike McCullough, research director for the National Institute for Health Care Research: "Imagery is a major vehicle for increasing anger."[18]

We could try to make people stop using images and metaphors altogether—except that we would soon find ourselves unable to speak, or even think very much. Language is entirely based on metaphor; even the word *metaphor* is a metaphor, being a Greek expression meaning "carry across" (i.e., from one frame of reference, one meaning, to another). Rather, what I'm exposing here tells us to be careful how we metaphorize and create images, especially for people. Just as we have sensitized ourselves to the need to watch our traditional language around issues of race, gender, etc., we can sensitize ourselves to the power of language to disguise and promote violence toward all of us in general.[19]

Carolyn Merchant showed in her eye-opening book *The Death of Nature* that the guiding myth of our culture profoundly determines how we see everything around us. By changing the traditional underlying image of the earth as Mother to that of an inert thing, a process Merchant correctly calls "desacralization," our immediate ancestors destroyed a safeguard against the despoiling of their own environment, opening a way to the near destruction of the planet that is now facing us. I said "by changing," but who actually carried out that change? In the case of a huge cultural shift like this, a shift that goes on under the surface of our awareness, it is hard to identify who changes the surrounding language that makes such a shift possible. Do we all do it together; do we follow certain leaders, who may themselves be scarcely conscious of what they are doing? The images just seem to shift by themselves—but of course this is impossible. Rather, the elusiveness of this controlling process should make us aware of the potential importance of each speaker, of you and me.

Relearning to talk—this is about as much fun as relearning to walk or eat. That is why James O'Connor opened the Cuss Control Academy in Chicago and wrote *Cuss Control: The Complete Book on How to Curb Your Cursing:* because if people can learn to communicate better, he rightly says, they will also learn to cope more easily with life's inconveniences, thus leading straight to less violence.[20] The rise of cursing is keyed to the decline of idealism and compassion, but it's only part of the story. We have to painstakingly revisit old habits and make ourselves conscious of many things that are automatic: are we using euphemisms as an anaesthetic, are we indulging in the "techno-trivialization" that now takes the place of our thinking about war, have we succumbed to the "pseudospeciation" that turns people first into guerillas and then into fish—drops people out of sight by reducing them to labels and finally to objects?

Cultivating "right speech" is annoying, vexatious, socially awkward—and definitely worth it. There is a famous verse in the Bhagavad Gita describing the highest kind of happiness, which applies here: "What is poison at first but turns to nectar at the end."[21] Well, "nectar" may be a bit of an exaggeration, but if my own experience is in any way typical, we do enjoy a sense of realness, of solidity, when we begin to drop misleading euphemisms, evasive technicalities, and dehumanizing stereotypes—a sense of relief.

One kind of wrong speech in particular repays close attention. Euphemisms, as we've seen, can be as dangerous as stereotypes. Scrupulously calling things *what they are* is a form of Satyagraha—clinging to truth. Underneath all its conditioning, the human mind still inherently rejects violence; we have seen evidence for this in the etymology of the word *violence* itself, in behavioral science (when it looks for such evidence), and in numerous historical examples. There is enough innate rejection of violence inside a person that Satyagraha can often work just by making the violence in a situation unmistakably visible.

Euphemism has another side, which became all too manifest in the horrors of the Cold War rhetoric Carol Cohn analyzed. Remember that the all-important issue in violence is dehumanization, so graphically accomplished by the language of General Mejía. It is in this sense that "truth is the first victim in war," that the truth of the others' humanity is denied in all violence. In a way, this is understandable: before you can bring yourself to kill others or injure them, you have to reduce people to "enemies" or animals or, even better, to objects. But during the Cold War, the sword that violence wielded against truth in speech cut two ways. In this discourse, the living were dehumanized (cities became "targets," disasters became statistics) *and* nonliving objects were artificially invested with a borrowed life. Think of what it means to say a "rich harvest" of nuclear "kills" when you're talking about destroying enemy missiles (housed in "silos"), or what it means when "friendly" missiles colliding is called "fratricide." Think about the implication of "smart" bombs. This is the language of life— only what it's actually describing is certain death.

As Martin Luther King said, "We have guided missiles and misguided men."[22] The choice between God and Mammon is in a fundamental way a choice between honoring life where it is, in living beings, or transferring that reverence to things. Materialism, in other words, is fundamentally linked to violence. In an age of materialism we slide all too easily into the mental violence of calling cities "targets" and then turning around and naming missiles as though they had personalities (the two atomic bombs actually used in war were dubbed "Little Boy" and "Fat Man"). We have to worship *something*, as Dostoevsky reminded us—that is one of the redeeming features of the human being. But under the spell of violence we can end up putting that worship where it does not belong. In order to carry on war we have drawn a cloak of denial over the sanctity, or, if you prefer, the supreme value, of life, and then we find that some of us have turned around and vainly imagined life in inert machines—in the machines, in fact, of death. We denied life and worshipped death. Would the word *blasphemy* be too strong for this mistake?

One more example before we get from peace in thought and word to peace in deed.

Bill Kennedy is a financial guru (think about *that* metaphor for a minute!) who gives highly successful seminars for the rich on how to get very rich. Kennedy is a forthright sort of man. He likes to refer to his program with a rather unusual, attention-grabbing moniker.

> I came to the decision that "war college" was an appropriate name. . . . What better metaphor than war for the battle of accomplishment every person must wage to survive . . . amidst the financial firefights that are sure to follow the inevitable crashes of the 1990s.[23]

Social Darwinism can go no further—all life is a fight, in fact a war. Human accomplishment, nay, human survival, is about making more money than other people. "Investing is not a win/win proposition," Mr. Kennedy blandly tells us, so come to study with this "truly illustrious faculty . . . famous military leaders, acclaimed scientists, economists, journalists, historians and foreign dignitaries, . . . Defense Department, and CIA."[24] And by the way, only people with half a million in assets can apply to the Kennedy War College, so don't be too hasty to get out your uniform. I wonder what a mother on welfare or an indigenous farmer in Chiapas would say about this definition of "survival."

There is another element in this bizarre construction of the world, which I can only touch on, not so much because of limited space but because of my personal inability to deal with it. As a teacher, I have found the dedication of education to moneymaking, which is now the norm, so personally painful that it's one of the few issues I don't trust myself to talk about. This use of the words *college* and *faculty* —this idea that "education" is to help individuals fight each other for money—this is grim news for the culture of human beings at the beginning of the third Christian millennium. Recently, I was put on hold while waiting to talk to the produce clerk of a nearby food market that was, it happened, trolling for new employees. Naturally, I was not paying too much attention to the announcements, until I heard them say, "After all, working for us will give you more experience than any other educational institution." Any *other* educational institution? This is Safeway State? I can only say that the steady, unremarked shrinking of "education" to fiscal prowess that has overtaken our whole society over the last twenty or so years is profoundly relevant to the rise of violence. For if the purpose of education, which prepares us for life, is to make money, what does that say about the purpose of life?

The main point this description of the Kennedy War College raises for our concern with nonviolence and speech could be put as a question: what do war, sexual aggression, business, sports, politics, and criminal justice have in common? As activities, next to nothing; as expressions of the urge to compete, however, practically everything. If this is how you think about life, they can all be reduced to forms of competition, all played out in a paradigm of scarcity and separateness, as a zero-sum, win/lose proposition. But why stop there? After you've done this to everything that can reasonably be construed as a fight, everything that has at least an element of give-and-take, go on to make *everything* a fight, even relationships between doctor and patient, student and teacher, and—of course—husband and wife. I remember a divorce being covered by the papers some years back in which the husband explained that he was fighting his ex for custody of the children because "I have to get *something* out of this relationship."

This is another way that a certain amount of control over our speech can be effective. Because we nowadays tend to think of every sporting event, every business decision, every diplomatic exchange, and more and more every personal relationship in terms of "winning," we have become incapable of seeing that they could be, instead, links in the net of loving community and peace. During the 1994 gubernatorial race in California, senator Tom Hayden was asked what he thought of his opponent, Kathleen Brown. He startled the journalist by saying something to the effect of, "She's not my opponent; she's my friend. We're running for governor. It isn't a sport." A few more remarks like that and we could put an end to politics as we know it and start returning to politics as it was meant to be—the decision-making process of a democracy, not the power struggle of the arena.

While most of us are not "defense intellectuals" or senators, we all constantly participate in a mental environment with various subtexts of love and hate over which we have a certain measure of control. This world of thought and speech is a quiet but very real place in which to build a peace culture, and it's open to everyone. Personally, I try never to say something is "competitive" anymore when I mean that it's good, never "target" anyone when I mean I'm doing something for them, never say "impact" instead of "have an effect on" (or use "impact" as a verb, for that matter). I don't use euphemisms like "three strikes, you're out" when I'm talking about putting people in prison for the rest of their lives, and for some reason I don't even say that a particular restaurant has pasta "to die for." When unsuspecting people say to me that "this will help the economy grow," I calmly reply, "You mean 'expand,' don't you? Only living things grow, right?" I make myself thoroughly obnoxious, but I do this because the thoughts and images and feelings that go on in my own mind create the intimate environment that I live in, *and* they determine my contribution to the mental climate of the world around me. It's worth it. Even when I think, much less speak, I try to be as careful about dehumanization and shoot-'em-up images as I am about sexist bias.

Feminists have made some progress in getting us to change gender-biased language. We should take that lead and go on, go deeper, to the issue that concerns every one of us as human beings. The other day I was in a big hardware store, standing behind a customer who apparently was looking for a certain kind of hinge. When the clerk behind the counter told him they didn't have it in stock, he said, in the casual violence of the day, "Oooh, I hate you!" I happened to be looking at the man behind the counter, and I saw him flinch. These things matter. In the long run, they matter much more than hinges. Whatever we are talking about, under the surface we are carrying on a constant dialogue with one another, *about* one another, about our relationships. When we say "I hate you" instead of "rats," we are sending a damaging message when we could easily have sent a neutral, maybe even a healing, one.

A friend of mine was told by the same store a few weeks later that they had in stock a certain item that she needed. When she got there, it turned out that they do usually stock the item, but didn't have it there that day. Up came the usual words in her mind, "Why on earth did you . . ." Never mind. She silently repeated her mantram and decided to smile, stay calm, and say something soothing. It probably helped that clerk a lot. It *definitely* helped my friend, who felt good about it for days after. Instead of spreading "road rage," "air rage," "workplace rage," why don't we try to spread non-rage, i.e., love? Then one day we might wake up and find that instead of war we finally have peace.

The effect of each individual thought or word is very small, yes, but taken together, the effect of our thoughts and images is not at all small. When certain kinds of thought and image become a habit, they can become a worldview. What can we do about all this, when it is so pervasive and so automatic? No matter how sweeping the changes that have to be made, or how beyond our reach an Eichmann or a General Mejía may be, we can begin with what *appears* to be the smallest and most remote point of leverage—you and me. This no one can ever take away from us. It matters what we say and in what terms we think. As far as the issue of violence/nonviolence goes, it matters crucially. Whether we refer to a city as a "target" or a bustling community of human beings matters as much as whether we call a thirty-year-old woman a "girl" or a black adult "boy." The only difference is, in the latter case we know whom we're hurting, so we've tried to stop.

Yet if hurting somebody is bad, surely hurting everybody is worse. When violence "escapes the barrier of our teeth," as the poet Homer used to say, it hurts everybody at once on some level. And so, just as surely, the opposite is true: taking some care to use nonviolent, accurate words and imagery becomes second nature in course of time and creates an incalculable influence toward peace. The habit of truth also is formed by small, repeated, doable efforts—only in this case they have to be *conscious* efforts for longer than usual, because the whole speech environment we live in is tilted the wrong way. I don't hesitate to call such humble efforts "constructive program." They constitute, each of them, a truth act, available every moment, to everyone. They are nonconfrontational, even unpolitical, if you will, and yet so powerful. To speak and eventually to think as though life were sacred and human relationships mattered—that would be so powerful. Because, after all, it is so true.

CHAPTER EIGHT

FIGHTING FIRE WITH WATER

Perhaps the careful study of man's past will explain to me much that seems inexplicable in his disconcerting present. Perhaps the means of salvation are already there, implicit in history, unadvertised, carefully concealed by the war-mongers, only awaiting rediscovery to be acknowledged with enthusiasm by all thinking men and women.

—Vera Brittain

BY LIBERATING OUR own minds from the culture of violence (I keep coming back to the mass media here), and by consciously making our own thoughts and speech peaceworthy, we are preparing ourselves to act effectively for peace. It is now time to consider what that action might look like.

BODY, MIND, AND SPIRIT III: ARMIES OF PEACE

I want to focus on a dramatic way that peace activists are confronting violence, and I choose this way not only because of its high drama but because, while it has been done by a rather special set of people so far, there is room for everyone to take part and help them. Bear in mind that while the work done on our thoughts and speech is "proventive," and therefore indispensable, we will now be talking about much later-stage interventions, not so much about what to do before conflicts get out of hand as what we can still do after they have.

I met Ernesto Cardenal at Berkeley during the early eighties when he was minister of defense in the Sandinista government in Nicaragua—and by no means an advocate of nonviolence. I was eager to ask him whether the Witness for Peace groups in his country had helped any to deter Contra attacks. These are the groups, you remember, in which volunteers like my friend Sue Severin stumbled upon the protective effect of an unarmed presence. But at the same time I was a little apprehensive, because I knew nonviolence was not his thing. I need not have been. "We need more of these groups and need them quickly," he told me with great feeling. "Wherever they have been there has been no violence!"

A little later, when he was speaking through a translator to the small group who had gathered to hear him at the faculty club, he repeated what he had just told me privately: wherever these little groups of internationals went there were no attacks, no violence. At this point his translator unconsciously made a slight "correction." Evidently unable to quite believe what he was hearing, the translator said, ". . . there has been *nearly* no violence." Cardenal caught that at once and slammed his fist on the table: "I said, *absolutely* no violence!" I beamed. Cardenal was not a believer in principled nonviolence. But he was man enough to believe what he saw and not to "normalize" it away. This is all we need to see the antidote to war that intuition tells us must be contained in the repertoire of nonviolence.

What Cardenal did not know—even I was not quite aware of it at the time—is that the idea of "armies of peace," volunteers trained in nonviolence instead of threat power who could intervene in large-scale conflict situations, was about fifty years old when my friend Sue Severin and others left their safe homes and careers in the United States to stand with villagers in the "low-intensity" hell of Nicaragua. Gandhi, who seems to have wrestled with every problem in the modern world, did take on the big question of whether, and if so how, nonviolence could put an end to war. As soon as he began to see the power of the "new" method he was using in South Africa, he began to realize that it could be used not only in the social struggle of the disenfranchised Indians there, or any downtrodden groups like them, but against the "principalities and powers" that had led humankind into recurrent wars since the dawn of recorded history. Satyagraha was the opposite of war; it could be the cure for war. But how could a method, albeit highly successful, that was devised to resist injustice *within* a country be applied *between* countries?

He must have sensed, probably from the earliest days when he realized that "passive resistance" was the wrong word for the Indians' struggle, that the seed they were planting in Africa would one day give rise to a plant strong enough to break its way through the centuries-old concrete of the war system, to bloom into a world order that was truly, not cynically, new. This conviction never wavered: even at the very end of his life, when the newly separated India and Pakistan went to war over Kashmir, he held out the claim that the Kashmiris, whose cause was just, could have protected themselves through nonviolence.

At the same time, Gandhi knew perfectly well that a nonviolent construction of peace lay, as he put it, "in the womb of the future." It would fall to others to see this particular promise of nonviolence through to fruition; his job was to rebuild India, to midwife her out of the British grip and, by so doing, expose the illegitimacy and fragility of colonialism—enough work for a single lifetime, even by Gandhian standards! There could be no doubt, however, that the "ocular demonstration" of Satyagraha's power being staged in India was meant for the whole world. Gandhi stressed repeatedly that what may appear to be India's problem—exploitation, greed, violence, race hatred— is the world's problem,[1] and stressed even more explicitly that the technique used against communal strife in India, "though apparently conceived to apply to a corner of this world, is really intended to cover the whole world."[2]

Similarly, once we understand the power of nonviolence, we will see that it applies, mutatis mutandis, to all forms of violence, not excluding the biggest. Nonviolence does not stop at national boundaries any more than, as I've mentioned, the law of gravity applies only to apples. On this point Gandhi was not inclined to mince words: "It is blasphemy to say that non-violence can only be practised by individuals and never by nations which are composed of individuals."[3] In his own imagery for the South African struggle, the words "army" and "soldier" occurred frequently—even more often than "pilgrim."

By the year 1913, around the time Gandhi felt destiny was calling him home to confront the British Raj in its lair, he was talking openly about *Shanti Sena,* or "armies of peace," bands of trained volunteers whose nonviolent presence and nonviolent skills would make the police and national guard unnecessary.[4] They would be locally based, thus ending the reliance on outside power—a society that cannot manage its own disorder can never be free—and even more important, they would be completely nonviolent, thus ending the age-old reliance on threat power that perennially bedevils our hopes for a better future.

> The Congress should be able to put forth a nonviolent army of volunteers numbering not a few thousands but lakhs [tens of thousands] who would be equal to every occasion where the police and the military are required. . . . They would be constantly engaged in constructive activities that make riots impossible. . . . Such an army should be ready to cope with any emergency, and in order to still the frenzy of mobs should risk their lives in numbers sufficient for the purpose. . . . Surely a few hundred young men and women giving themselves deliberately to mob fury will be any day a cheaper and braver method of dealing with such madness than the display and use of the police and the military.[5]

Gandhi is here talking about a nonviolent equivalent to the police, and the military used as police; it's only a short step to replacing the military where they are normally used, in war. In 1942, when India and the Raj were cowering before the prospect of a Japanese invasion, he took that step. While the British rattled their sabers (for show, it turns out—they had no intention of defending India) and many Indians themselves rushed to enlist, Gandhi startled everyone by proposing that India could defend herself with nonviolent "armies."[6] Ironically, in view of popular concepts of "strength," while Churchill was trying to prepare Roosevelt for a British collapse, Gandhi was "preparing his unarmed countrymen to resist to the last man rather than submit, if the Japanese landed on Indian soil."[7]

He was never given a chance to put this bold vision to the test. The British put him in prison for most of the war years, and even most of his own Congress party members found they were not ready to follow him that far. Historically, wars always thin the ranks of pacifists. When danger stares one in the face, it is difficult to keep faith with an untested future.

One man, however, had already taken Gandhi at his word. By far the most dramatic *shanti sena* the world has ever seen was organized in what was then the North-West Frontier Province by the Mahatma's close disciple, Khan Abdul Ghaffar Khan; and Khan did this not among gentle Hindus but the notoriously warlike Pathans.[8] These are the same people who, along with other Afghans, would stand up to the overwhelmingly superior military force of the Soviet Union half a century later—and then, tragically, tear themselves to pieces in armed factions. But that was later, when they went back to more traditional methods of fighting. Our story concerns the days, under Khan's inspiring leadership, when nearly 100,000 Pathan fighters—all devout Muslims—vowed to resist the British without weapons in their hands or violence in their hearts, and kept that vow under unbelievable provocation, adding immeasurably to the unstoppable drive toward freedom.

Abdul Ghaffar Khan first heard Gandhi as a young man at the All India Congress party meeting at Calcutta in December of 1928. He had heard *of* Gandhi, of course, and must have been intrigued that the Mahatma was doing in grand style what he had been doing for his own people through village uplift, education, empowerment of the women, and a weaning away from violence, but he had not come to Calcutta to hear Gandhi. At that time the honeymoon between Muslims and Hindus that warmed the first part of the decade was largely history. There was not much love lost between the two communities, and Khan had come to Calcutta only to attend a meeting of the Muslim League.

It was, however, an unruly and distasteful meeting of the League that year; in fact, it soon broke up when one irate delegate pulled out a knife. So, more or less at a loss what to do with himself so far from home, Khan dropped around to the Congress pavilion. There, as it happens, Gandhiji was speaking to the accompaniment of a relentless heckler. Strangely, rather than being rattled, Gandhi seemed to get no end of amusement from his unruly "friend" and went right on speaking through his chuckles. Khan was deeply impressed. A leader himself, and gifted with an eye for the outwardly small things that reveal nonviolent power, he at once understood what he was seeing in the Mahatma's unflappable control of the situation. He went back to one of the Muslim leaders and suggested, rather naively, that they might get further with a little of that forbearance themselves. "So," the irate leader cut him off, "the wild Pathans have come to teach us about tolerance!"[9] This is exactly what Khan would do.

We must tarry here a moment because Khan's story explodes no less than four serious myths about nonviolence, and the Muslim leader's curt rebuff illustrates one of them, namely that *nonviolence is only for gentlefolk,* i.e., the weapon of the weak. Gandhi would explain that one had to be capable of violence before one could renounce it. It was precisely the Pathans, whose frontier-style traditions of revenge and violence went back uncounted centuries, who would most readily follow their *badshah,* their leader, when he created a new kind of army without weapons. These were the famous Khudai Khidmatgars, or "Servants of God." Years later, when Khan himself was at a loss to explain how his Pathans were still nonviolent when most of the Hindus had bolted, Gandhi explained to him, "Nonviolence is not for cowards. It is for the brave, the courageous. And the Pathans are more

An army without arms. Abdul Ghaffar Khan at the first meeting of the Khudai
Khidmatgars, April 1930 (Gandhi Peace Foundation)

courageous than the Hindus. That is why the Pathans were able to
remain nonviolent."[10]

A second widely accepted myth, as we've encountered often, is
that since nonviolence is weak it *can only work against weak opposition*. It
only worked in India, we are repeatedly told, because the British are
so fair-minded; (brace yourself now) "it would never have worked
against the Nazis." The British, however, were not so fair-minded with
the Servants of God. They dubbed them "Red Shirts" and used their
control of the press at home to play on age-old fears of Communism
and invoke the mystique of the "Great Game" Britain had played for
over a century against Russian influence in the Hindu Kush—quite
an irony, considering that it would later be the Pathans who would
thwart Soviet power in Afghanistan and thus be instrumental in

bringing down the Soviet regime. When the "Red Shirts" refused to knuckle under to ordinary methods, the British sealed off the North-West Frontier Province and set to work humbling the proud Pathans in the way of imperialism everywhere, as though they had not heard that they themselves were supposed to be a civilized people. Homes and crops were razed; people were beaten, stripped, and dragged through cesspools—civilians were bombed from the air for the first time in human history (ten years *before* Fascist planes bombed Guernica, which is usually cited as the breakthrough in this form of barbarism). They regarded the Pathans as "leopards" and treated them accordingly.

The following is an eyewitness description of the attack on a crowd of nonviolent demonstrators protesting Khan's arrest at the Kissa Kahani Bazaar in Peshawar on April 23, 1930. It does not give the impression of a people whose fair-mindedness made them a pushover for nonviolence.

> All of a sudden two or three armored cars came at great speed from behind without giving warning of their approach and drove into the crowd. Several people were run over, of whom some were injured and a few killed on the spot. The people . . . behaved with great restraint, collecting the wounded and dead.

Despite this, the Congress Inquiry Committee report noted that:

> . . . the troops were ordered to fire. Several people were killed and wounded and the crowd was pushed back some distance. At about half past eleven, endeavors were made by one or two outsiders to persuade the crowd to disperse and the authorities to remove the troops and the armored cars. The crowd was willing to disperse if they were allowed to remove the dead and the injured and if the armored

cars were removed. The authorities, on the other hand, expressed their determination not to remove the armored cars and the troops. The result was that the people did not disperse and were prepared to lay down their lives. The second firing then began and, off and on, lasted for more than three hours . . .

Gene Sharp continues:

When those in front fell down wounded by the shots, those behind came forward with their breasts bared and exposed themselves to the fire, so much so that some people got as many as 21 bullet wounds in their bodies, and all the people stood their ground without getting into a panic. A young Sikh boy came and stood in front of a soldier and asked him to fire at him, which the soldier unhesitatingly did, killing him. . . . This state of things continued from 11 till 5 o'clock in the evening.[11]

Enough said. The fierce repression gained the imperial power, in the end, a Pyrrhic victory. The Khudai Khidmatgars' leader was jailed over and over again, and his organization was disbanded and passed from the scene. The Raj itself soon followed. The Khudai Khidmatgars had played a signal role in the liberation struggle by which force would no longer intimidate India, and their efforts worked where they may have seemed not to "work," showing again that nonviolence can prevail, in its own way, against cruel and determined opposition.

Myth number three, and perhaps most crucial for today: *nonviolence is OK for Hindus and Buddhists; it is not for Muslims.* Whatever may be our stereotypes of "Islamic terrorists," the *jihad* and so forth, the Religion of the Prophet was not based on violence. No religion is. Like all other major world religions, Islam has a core devotion to positive, inward peace, however unevenly this commitment has been carried out in practice.[12] Of course, the Prophet and his followers fought for their place in history. Of course, many Muslims today believe, as many Christians and Jews believe, that they must fight their way to peace through the sword. But those who pray "in the Name of God, all Mercy, all Compassion" cannot believe that their Prophet was primarily a bringer of the sword, their Prophet who said, "Those who commit violence—God has given them respite only until the day their eyes become glazed."[13] There is another important *hadith,* or traditional saying, to the effect that the Prophet one day told his followers, "Help your brother, whether he is an aggressor or a victim of aggression." When one of them asked, "How are we supposed to help the aggressor?," he replied, "By doing your best to stop him from aggression."[14] The Religion of the Prophet, in other words, entails not just a sentiment but a sophisticated comprehension of nonviolence.

And Badshah Khan was quite aware of this:

> There is nothing surprising in a Muslim or a Pathan like me subscribing to the creed of nonviolence. It is not a new creed. It was followed fourteen hundred years ago by the Prophet all the time he was in Mecca. . . . But we had so far forgotten it that when Gandhi placed it before us, we thought he was sponsoring a novel creed.[15]

Myth number four, which is the "blasphemy" that we're primarily concerned with here: *nonviolence can't be used in, or instead of, war.* At its height, during the repression of 1930, the Khudai Khidmatgars numbered more than 80,000. They were trained, drilled, uniformed, and organized. They were committed to their leader and followed his orders even when they did not understand him—even unto death, as they demonstrated at the Kissa Khani Bazaar. That is, they were an army in every sense of the word, except that they were not armed with the physical instruments of death but rather, as far as they understood it, with the inner powers of life. The Servants showed that just as people can be trained and organized and steeled for war, they can be trained and organized and steeled for peace.

A Vision Is Born

When the British invited Gandhi to the Round Table Conference in 1931, they also invited his subversive ideas on peace. During his visit to Romain Rolland in Switzerland on his way home, Gandhi had a chance to air those ideas when a skeptic questioned the applicability of nonviolence to national defense:

> By enacting a Thermopylæ in Switzerland, you would have presented a living wall of men and women and children, inviting invaders to walk over your corpses. You may say that such a thing is beyond human experience and endurance. I say that it is not so. It was quite possible. Last year in Gujarat, women stood *lathi* charges unflinchingly, and in Peshawar, thousands stood hails of bullets without resorting to violence. . . . The army would be brutal enough to walk over them, you might say. I would then say . . . an army that dares to pass over the corpses of innocent men and women would not be able to repeat that experiment.[16]

In our time, we have seen so many "killing fields" that the Mahatma's faith may seem naive. In reality, though, those massacres are not the kind of suffering he is talking about. He is talking not about people herded unwillingly to their death but people going out willingly, when all else fails, to meet their death. This is not passivity, but endurance, the capacity of suffering voluntarily borne to awaken conscience. There is some evidence that he was not so naive, after all. In Rwanda a tribal militia, bent on genocide, herded children out of their school and ordered them to separate themselves into Hutus and Tutsis. The children knew what it meant. They refused. The soldiers yelled at them, but the children were undaunted. The soldiers gave up and went away. Amid all that slaughter, when the value of life had all but disappeared, the mere willingness of some schoolchildren to suffer for justice made a blood-crazed band of soldiers "not able to repeat the experiment"; in fact, not even carry it out.

Some ten years after the "Thermopylae" speech, back home in an India panicked by the prospect of a Japanese invasion, Gandhi would elaborate how this strange, new kind of defense would work. One of his talks is worth quoting at some length, because it shows that he not only had perdurable faith in the possibility of a nonviolent defense but had worked out its main principles in some detail.

> Japan is knocking at our gates. What are we to do in a non-violent way? If we were a free country, things could be done non-violently to prevent the Japanese from entering the country. As it is, non-violent resistance could commence the moment the Japanese effect a landing. Thus, non-violent resisters would refuse them any help, even water. For it is no part of their duty to help anyone to steal their country. But if a Japanese had missed his way and was dying of thirst and sought help as a human being, a non-violent resister, who may not regard anyone as his enemy, would give water to the thirsty one. Suppose the Japanese compel resisters to give them water, the resisters must die in the act of resistance. It is conceivable that they will exterminate all resisters. The underlying belief in such non-violent resistance is that the aggressor will in time be mentally and even physically tired of killing non-violent resisters. He will begin to search what this new (for him) force is which refuses co-operation without seeking to hurt,

and will probably desist from further slaughter. But the resisters may find that the Japanese are utterly heartless and that they do not care how many they kill. The non-violent resisters will have won the day, inasmuch as they will have preferred extermination to submission.[17]

Bear in mind that we're talking about the most difficult possible situation, way up on the high end of the escalation curve when all dice are loaded against you. This is outright invasion by a determined enemy with overwhelming military force; in other words, conflict at the most advanced stage and the biggest scale. If we look closely at Gandhi's plan for such an extremity, however, we see nothing that is not familiar from the principles of classic nonviolence. It may call for greater sacrifice because the conflict is already so far advanced, but the dynamics are the same: the consciousness-raising impact of the "new" force, the way nonviolent resisters mobilize that force by refusing to identify the humanity of the individual aggressor with his intention (the sin is not the sinner), and finally the dramatic declaration that success is primarily spiritual and long-term rather than visible and immediate. These are all familiar landmarks of nonviolence, and each of these principles has been known to work. That much is history. So is, as Gandhi pointed out in the "Thermopylae" speech ten years earlier, the possibility of self-sacrificing courage on a big scale. The only thing different is the boldness of imagination, Gandhi's signature, the audacity to make such a scheme public in all seriousness, as though every one of us were capable of so much more than we realize. And who knows . . .

"If we were a free country, things could be done non-violently to prevent the Japanese from entering." This again is a very important point. If the government had not tied their hands, the Indians could have begun nonviolent preparations much earlier. If they had, Gandhi claims, they may well have put their bodies on the line to prevent the invaders from entering the country in the first place. Would that have "worked"? Absent those preparations, would the kind of defense Gandhi outlined have actually thwarted a Japanese occupation? Unfortunately, we will never know. It's always easy to say "nonviolence wouldn't have worked" if we don't give it a chance.[18]

Gandhi's way was to extrapolate from the known successes of nonviolence to the cases where it had not yet been tried. Nothing said to him that armies of ordinary citizens steeled for nonviolent resistance would not work, or even "work." He called for organized nonviolence when fighting broke out over Kashmir right after independence, as I've said; he called a major meeting of the Shanti Sena for the beginning of February 1948. Only death called off that meeting, for the assassin's bullets struck Gandhi's chest the evening before he was to go.

The dream of nonviolent substitutes for war, however, did not die on the path to the prayer meeting at Birla House on January 30, 1948.

A Vision Lives: Civilian-Based Defense

While the Mahatma had been making his great plans, other people began to notice how spontaneous, unarmed crowds here and there were getting in and plugging up the war machine—something that had probably been going on, all unnoticed, forever. Excited peace activists have recently been documenting them:

- Fighting broke out in Algeria in 1962 between the regular army in exile and rebel forces in control of the country. There were over a hundred deaths, whereupon workers, women, seniors, and children got in between the two groups and stopped them, leading to an agreement.[19]

- Philippine citizens, with the full blessing of Cardinal Jaime Sin, protected heavily outnumbered troops of General Fidel Ramos from government forces still loyal to dictator Marcos. Peace observers

were not blind to the irony that there were unarmed civilians protecting a segment of the armed forces rather than the other way
around. "Both [General Enrile] and Ramos no doubt . . . realized
that they and the rebel forces were being protected far more by
unarmed supporters than they could be by the equivalent number
of armed supporters."[20]

- In 1968 in Beijing, when the "cultural revolution" raged, two Maoist
student groups, each claiming to have the "right line," opened fire
on each other from different corners of the university. About
50,000 people moved peacefully and spontaneously into the university; they got between the two groups and shouted slogans like,
"Use your sense: nonviolence." One group stopped firing at once;
the other went on, wounding over 700 people, but laid down their
weapons the following day—"unable to repeat the experiment."[21]

- The Tienanmen Square demonstrations ended in slaughter, but the
debacle "should not make us forget that, at least twice, the military
command to retake Tienanmen Square could not be carried out
because thousands of Beijing citizens had placed themselves between
the army and the students."[22] (My own campus was witness to a
miniversion of this when members of a small group called Berkeley
Students for Peace positioned themselves between Callahan Hall,
then home of the ROTC, and a large group of angry protestors
descending on the place with rocks and bricks. Crisis averted.)

- As we've seen, thousands of unarmed citizens stopped bloody confrontation between coup and government forces in Moscow, 1991.

All these cases involved rival factions within the same country, and
the third parties were the citizenry of that country. But we have
already looked at a case that was much more like a war: the Prague
Spring resistance to the Soviet invasion of 1968–69. I mentioned at
the time that this resistance held out for eight months even though

there were no nonviolent leaders to inspire or advise the people on how to proceed with their chosen strategy, if they even knew what to call it.

What we call it today is Civilian-Based Defense (CBD). We know of cases involving external invasion, as in Prague Spring, and internal takeovers, like the miserably failed Kapp Putch in Weimar Germany in 1920, when ultranationalist Wolfgang Kapp's attempt to overthrow the fledgling Weimar Republic was aborted by workers' strikes. Ideally, "classic" CBD could be said to operate on three principles:

(1) The resisters do not physically prevent invading troops from entering their territory, which is often a costly symbolic barrier; they are more concerned with the integrity of their institutions.[23]

(2) Everyone participates in the resistance—men, women, and children. This is not merely a matter of numbers, of course, and goes beyond the solidarity function we touched on when we were considering *charkha*; it has to do with taking responsibility for your own defense, rather than fobbing it off on an elite. In military defense you cannot avoid creating an elite, and that will seriously compromise the democracy you're trying to defend.

(3) Ideally (again), the resisters are scrupulously careful not to reject their opponents as people, while firmly noncooperating with them as invaders. When your intended victims stop relating to you as "Captain" or "Sergeant"—not to mention "fascist" or whatever—but as a person, that tends to remind you that under all the trappings that is, after all, what you *are*—human like them.

Prague Spring undoubtedly owed something to the fact that the Czechs had a long history of honoring nonviolence. The first stirrings of Protestantism in what was then Bohemia had a strongly nonviolent trend that went back to the late fourteenth century, and which we associate with names like Jan Hus and Peter Chelický (ca. 1380–1460). Chelický's classic, *The Net of Faith,* was first published in 1521. Its persuasive arguments that Jesus meant what he said, that Christians should not swear oaths, that they should definitely not live by the sword, led to the founding of the Czech Brethren, an important example of the periodic rediscovery that Jesus was nonviolent; this classic work would later provide strong support for Tolstoy when it came his turn to make the same discovery. It is perhaps because of this background that the Czech people were able to respond to their dire situation with a superb mix of humor and courage—an ideal recipe for nonviolence.

There are times on this planet of ours, however, when the people, trained or untrained, cannot by themselves act in time to protect themselves from violence. The conflict may be so unequal that resistance is crushed before it begins—think of some of the regimes of Central and South America, or Burma, or Cambodia. Merely to make your presence known sometimes in such regimes is to be "disappeared" by shadowy para-militaries, accountable to none or—as in Kosovo for one long decade—by heavily armed Serbian police ordered by Belgrade to terrorize the Albanian majority. There are times when conflict reaches such a pitch of madness that even if there is no clear victim and victimizer, mutual slaughter erupts before anyone can, or will, intervene: Somalia, Rwanda, Croatia. Sometimes the chaos is so extreme there are not even "sides," properly speaking, as in Madrid during the Spanish Civil War or more recently, again, in the Balkans. It is here that we need a somewhat different mechanism than CBD, and to create it, contemporary visionaries have carried the Mahatma's scheme a step further.

What if there were a network, they have dared to imagine, of "rapid response teams," which instead of belonging to the government of one nation or another were composed of international volunteers, and instead of being armed were recruited and trained to carry out nonviolent intervention? They would be courageous, these volunteers, peace-oriented, and knowledgeable about the region they were going to and about nonviolence—possibly they would somehow have developed a knack for it. The raw material is not lacking. People, mostly but not only young people, are volunteering as we speak to go to dangerous places and try to interpose an element of peace in intense conflicts. If they were better trained, better supported, acknowledged, and funded, could they not, when the "international community" is paralyzed between passivity and brutality, supply that "third way" by going and standing in the way of war?

It's easy to imagine that they'd simply be crushed, swept aside but as we've so often seen in this conflict business, it is easy to imagine many things that are not true. The women at the Rosenstraße prison were not swept aside—they saved their men. Karen Ridd was not swept aside—she went in to handcuffs and a blindfold and came out alive and well, with her friend Marcela to boot. In the three cases I mentioned—in the Philippines, Beijing, and Moscow—the people who stood between hostile armies or between a hostile army and its intended victims were not swept aside, and these are only a few of the cases on record.

Building on the salutary shock of their voluntary presence, these groups would do a variety of things, depending on the situation. They would curb rumors (as Shanti Sena members often did in India), offer themselves as go-betweens for the hostile factions, stand in solidarity with the threatened, aid and comfort the injured, and—in the worst case—interpose themselves in the line of fire, making their bodies speak where no one would listen to anything else.

Maybe they are killed, in the worst case, and then maybe another group comes, the way wave after wave came on at Dharasana. The way, we hear, when the shah's soldiers killed a mullah who had stood up to address a crowd, another mullah stepped forward to replace him, and then another, until one soldier couldn't stand it anymore and turned his rifle on his own commander—and then on himself. Maybe. And if so, then the world will see that there is something other than conquering others that's worth dying for. *Martyr* means "witness." In the worst case, they will have borne witness to the world that there is another kind of power, there is another meaning and definition of human relationships. And in course of time and suffering, the shooters will strangely find that they cannot repeat their experiment.

But that is the worst case, and even *it* is far better than the apparently bottomless pit the world is enduring right now: in Kosovo, East

Timor and Aceh, the Moluccas, Chiapas, Tibet, the Sudan, Colombia, Algeria, Afghanistan, Ethiopia/Eritrea, Rwanda, Israel/Palestine, Armenia, Iraq. . . . As Hans Scholl, the young leader of the "White Rose" conspiracy, said before his execution, "Better an end in terror than a terror without end."[24]

You have to start small. Absent a Gandhi to inspire and organize such a worldwide "army," a number of international groups (about twenty, as I write this) have taken on specific, doable, small-scale peacemaking tasks that can become the "points of light" in this brand new picture. One kind of work that can be done by very small groups indeed is to accompany human rights workers and others whose lives are in danger. It has been remarkably effective. When faced with the systematic assassination of their leadership in 1985, a daring human rights organization in Guatemala, Grupo de Apoyo Mutuo (GAM), asked members of Peace Brigades International (PBI) to accompany them. When team members moved into the apartments and offices of remaining directorate members, Liam Mahoney reported, the assassinations stopped.[25] This had the effect of opening up space for political dialogue in Guatemala. PBI members think they played a key role in moving Guatemala from armed chaos into a peace process, and so do I. This activity is what brought Karen Ridd to El Salvador, as we've seen. It's called protective accompaniment, and it is here, one-on-one, that we can often best understand the dynamic of nonviolent rehumanization. Karen was, if you will, a peace team of one when she voluntarily interposed herself as a third party between the Salvadoran soldiers and her *compañera* Marcela Rodriguez. The protective power of her interposition was not physical, of course, but moral, or, if you will, psychological. As Patty Motchnick, the PBI volunteer who had the honor of accompanying Rigoberta Menchú and her associates through a particularly harrowing period, testified:

> The actual physical protection I offered her was absurd, and to myself in that moment, laughable. I was absolutely vulnerable, and so were they.[26]

But they all survived. And turned the wheel of peace a bit more forward. Military force works by amplifying the weak physical power of the individual, and thereby forfeits his or her immeasurable spiritual power. Unarmed accompaniment renounces the negligible physical power to produce an effect that is not only protective in the short term but peacemaking on into the future. Large or small scale, the principle on which this works is the same, and it has been well expressed by another of these groups, Quaker Peace and Service (QPS), which was operating in Sri Lanka:

> While demonstrating a willingness to see the human-
> ity of everyone in the conflict, QPS could also help to
> break down misconceptions the various groups had of
> their alleged "enemies." This aspect of the work was
> fundamental to QPS's belief in the power of reconcil-
> iation.[27]

Incidentally, when PBI began that fateful accompaniment of the otherwise-doomed women of GAM, the PBI "team" was one person, Alain Richard, who had to leave the country just then to renew his visa.[28]

The dream now is to put third-party capabilities at the disposal of the world. At the Hague Peace Conference in the summer of 1999, two North American peace activists, Mel Duncan and David Hartsough, discovered each other. They had been working full time on this vision of a standing nonviolent "army" without knowing about each other for years. At the time of this writing, only a few years since that historic meeting, the "Nonviolent Peaceforce" has garnered a worldwide tide of enthusiasm. Nobel Prize winners, the UN Millennium Forum, organization-savvy businesspeople, an occasional head of state, and hundreds of volunteers have signed on as the over-worked visionaries scramble to make it happen.

This has created three levels of opportunity for you who see the power of this vision and want to put a hand to an oar: (1) Support any organization involved in third-party nonviolent intervention with time, money, or both (details at the end of this book). (2) Support a volunteer financially, logistically, or emotionally—remember, peace-team work requires as much or more courage, training, and support from the home front as war fighting does. (3) If you're over twenty-five and think you have a taste for it, go ahead and sign up for a dangerous, thankless mission that will probably be the most reward-ing experience of your life.

It may not be out of place to reiterate how nonviolent interven-tion works and often "works." War polarizes; our then-secretary of state John Foster Dulles defined the mental framework of the Cold War perfectly when he declared that it was "immoral" to be neutral. A third party stands outside the "with us or against us" mentality; he or she dissolves that all-too-simple polarity, embodying a universal longing for peace that is above all labels and all hatreds. A French peace-team coordinator put it this way:

> Even as a foreigner from far away, each of us can act
> so as to bring to bear a little of our own humanity and
> solidarity. Even if the volunteers do not interpose
> themselves between the belligerents their action con-
> tributes to . . . rein in the logic of war and the hate in
> people's hearts. Inasmuch as it does that, it is nonvio-
> lent action.[29] (my translation)

A Vision at Work

The worst had happened. The Contra soldier was leading away a Nicaraguan villager at gunpoint, his thumbs wired behind his back, when suddenly an American journalist ran up, camera clicking, and shouted, "International incident!" That villager lived. A group of plain-clothes policemen in Sri Lanka, waving their clubs, bore down on women protestors when a foreigner stepped in front of them and raised his camera. The police lowered their clubs and went away.[30] A group of angry Israeli Defense Force soldiers was threatening a small band of Palestinians in Hebron, but between them stood a Christian Peacemaker Team (CPT) of three people, one of whom, Marge Argelyan from Chicago, stepped in front of a soldier and told him, "Every time you point your rifle I'm going to point my camera." As she would do this, "the soldier's grip would loosen and the fury would dissipate."[31]

The previous incidents are a mere sample of what happens to come across my desk in the form of newsletters or e-mail. As Gandhi gave voice to the "dumb millions" of colonized India, international volunteers are shining friendly light on those who suffer in darkness. They are giving eyes to a world that did not know, or perhaps very much care, about their suffering.

Of course, there is another kind of example, too. In one particularly telling exchange, also in Hebron, CPT member Cliff Kindy was roughed up by a very angry settler while trying to protect a Palestinian being beaten by soldiers. "I don't think we've ever met. What is your name?" he asked the settler, holding his hand out. "My name is Hate and I hate you!" the settler said, and pushed Cliff off the sidewalk. The CPT team has been in Hebron for a relatively long time and the salutary shock value of their third-party witness has worn thin with these ideologically blinded settlers. The death threats against the team have been so serious that the FBI visited them in their Chicago office. Yet even in this case (and it's a relatively infrequent type, even in Hebron) the mirror did some good. It forced the settler to confront, or at least name, his own evil. No one can do that indefinitely without eventually rendering oneself, as Gandhi said, unable to repeat that experiment. However enraged, however blinded the hater is, the nonviolent mirror will pick up the glint of an underlying humanity and reflect it back to the hater. You can't count on such a person to snap out of it then and there, as "Mr. Hate's" example shows. The committed nonviolent actor is willing to take that chance. She or he is willing to wait for the inevitable good her or his witness evoked.

As any schoolyard monitor can tell you, stopping fights must have been a part of life since before history was recorded. Nonviolent intervention, sans the name, must have helped keep societies from destroying themselves with their own violence long before we became human—the evidence of de Waal and others makes this conclusion inescapable. The Buddha is said to have prevented a war between rival kingdoms in this way, and in the Chou dynasty, four centuries before Christ, the philosopher Mo Tsu made it his habit to travel to distant kingdoms whenever war threatened to break out between them, putting his philosophy of "universal love and mutual benefit" to the test. So there is nothing new about individuals and groups trying to stop wars by getting between the conflicting parties (one of the small peace-movement groups that arose during the antinuclear days called itself the "Mo Tsu Project"). What is new today is the conscious attempt to do it systematically, on a global scale. The goal here is not only to stop this or that war, but eventually to stop war itself—by providing a nonviolent alternative to the whole system.

More Non-bang for the Buck

As we start to think about nonviolent intervention, its vast advantages over the known, conventional methods really start to shine. For what are those conventional methods? They are two: fight or flight, threaten or ignore. Don't be fooled by the debate between sanctions and bombs, as so many were in the case of Iraq in 1990; from the nonviolence point of view it's a "choice" between threat power and threat power. The sanctions imposed on Iraq have killed more than 1.2 million human beings, the majority of them children, the majority of these not even born when their president made his fatal move. It is not a humane alternative. As Gandhi often said, "I care little whether you shoot a man or starve him to death by inches." In a way, shooting is better: it makes more noise.

The alternative of not getting involved may keep our hands clean, but it has dire consequences on the human level, even for ourselves. As Bishop Tutu said in connection with Bosnia, "Our own humanity is affected very deeply" when we ignore such suffering:

> You can't watch people behaving in a debased and dehumanized way and not, in fact, be affected. If we don't recognize that we have a common humanity, we are all going to be losers. . . . We are affected very profoundly, even when we don't at the time note that this is actually happening to us.[32]

What's actually happening to us is, we are living a lie. When we ignore the suffering of others, the message is, "Tough, but we're not you." This is simply not true. Every wisdom teacher who deserves the name has stressed the precise opposite, that we are all co-involved in each other's happiness. This is why, although it sometimes seems a harsh judgment, Gandhi classified passivity (and cowardice) in such cases as a form of violence. They are, if you will, an existential untruth.

So to be torn between doing nothing and dropping bombs, between invasion or crushing sanctions, is, again, to face a "choice" between violence and violence. In terms of the real forces that move human destiny, this is no choice at all.

From this nonviolent viewpoint, armed peacekeeping is only an apparent exception that proves the rule, even if we mean the work of the "blue helmets"—UN peacekeeping, as mandated by Section VII of the UN Charter—and not the more dangerous precedent of militarily strong states bombing select dictators into grudging submission. (A young friend I worked with, a Kosovar Albanian, was tortured in a Serbian prison *after,* and no doubt partially as revenge for, the "liberation" of Kosovo by NATO bombing. Thus, I may be forgiven a trace of bitterness about this kind of operation.) While motivated by the best possible impulses, UN peacekeeping is nonetheless, again from the point of view of nonviolence, a badly mixed bag. It is an attempt to get to positive ends through hurtful means—to make peace with weapons of war. Having weapons and not using them (UN contingents are generally supposed to return fire only when attacked) is the violent person's idea of nonviolence. Real nonviolence, remember, is not abjuring the instruments of threat power but relying on the appeal of integration—not pulling punches but extending a hand.

There may be a place for armed peacekeeping in certain cases, but because its means and ends are so fundamentally at odds, we can never expect it to be more than a patchwork solution—a case of "work" without work. It is because of this inherent contradiction, certainly not because of any lack of courage or will in the men and states involved, that the history of UN peacekeeping shows a few modestly successful operations but nothing like enough peace power to meet the demand for interventions that suddenly increased in the flare-ups of ethnic conflict after the Cold War. The record boasts a few operations like the Cyprus Resettlement Project, which has apparently put that island on a road toward peace, but when UN peacekeeping was called on as *the* way to move forward with peace as a whole, projects began to meet with ignominious collapse.

A friend of mine was in Somalia, trying to maintain a badly needed orphanage during the chaos of that region's competing warlords. (One morning, symbolically, the UN compound was attacked by machine-gun fire, and Jim, who had been meditating, went out and shook his fist: "How the hell's a guy supposed to meditate with all this going on!") In those days, Jim confided, convoys of food guarded by UN contingents would head out toward the refugee camps, only to meet up with a ragged band of fighters off in the desert. The bandits would fire a few shots in the air, and the UN escort would immediately surrender its weapons. The fighters—often seventeen-year-old boys —would jump into the trucks and giddily drive them off—weapons, food, and all. The UN soldiers were plenty brave; they were well trained and had the latest equipment. What went wrong? Where we usually go wrong in the modern world: in the big picture—the basic understanding of the dynamics of violence and its opposite, the awareness that opposites are after all opposites and weapons don't create peace. It's not that the blue helmets lacked courage; it is that, like Shakespeare's Edward, they could not be valiant where they were not honest. Peacekeeping with weapons is doomed to fail, in the long run. It cannot call up the special power that comes from matching right means with consistent ends. Another example:

> Khalil Atout of Pharmacists Without Borders was assessing medical needs of refugees at St. André School in Kigali, Rwanda, accompanied by a French photographer. Hutu militia surrounded the school and began shooting through the windows and walls, seriously wounding adults and children in the school, and also the photographer. Some were killed. UN observers were in vehicles outside the school, either unarmed or armed only with pistols, and were unable to help.[33]

Who *could* have helped? A peace team that was *heavily* armed—with soul force. They could have stood in front of the militia and taken the suffering on themselves; there's a good chance the militia could not have gone on with the experiment very long.

I have said that the volunteers who tried to be of some help in Bosnia in 1992 were hastily recruited and virtually without training. That doesn't mean they didn't have good instincts. A group of them managed to reach the outskirts of besieged Sarajevo in a few beat-up old buses. Before them lay "sniper's alley," which meant death for anyone the hidden Serb riflemen felt like shooting. The UN peace force for the region, UNPROFOR, offered them protection: UNPROFOR could put an armored vehicle or a tank before and after their column and guide them into town. After a brief consultation the volunteers politely declined; that kind of "protection," they explained, would vitiate everything they were there for. And they went down to Sarajevo on their own. And no one shot at them. When ends and means meet, something happens that is more than the sum of those parts.

When they do not, we are in the world of incessant contradictions, and that applies not only in the international arena but closer to home.

Joe Loya is a good writer who served time in Southern California for bank robbery. (Hopefully, not all of us writers end up that way.) After his release, when two New York City policemen were charged with torturing a Haitian prisoner, Abner Louima, Loya was able to shed some light on this act of violence that shocked the city and the nation with its brutality. Don't pick on these two policemen as though they were solely to blame, Loya urged, or on New York in particular. It's the prison system itself that turns responsible, feeling people into cynical, sometimes even sadistic, tough guys. "I saw a lot of new corrections officers come into the prison, fresh-faced, young, eager and sometimes a bit idealistic," he wrote. But in course of time "they all began to resemble us . . . using gutter-level profanity, swaggering like hoodlums and ironically. . . [they all] adopted our contemptuous attitude toward the 'good guys.'"

Alas, Loya observed, "It never worked the other way around. Inmates didn't begin to look like the fresh-faced boys who first came to law enforcement."[34]

Loya was catching sight of the important principle that when a system is based on threat power, it cannot but reduce the human beings who move within its circle to creatures of threat power. Reading his comment, I was struck by the parallel to the perceptive observation of Dr. Aziz in E. M. Forster's novel of the Raj, *A Passage to India:* "They have no chance here. . . . They come out intending to be gentlemen, and are told it will not do. . . . I give any Englishman two years."[35]

The prison system, the imperial system, and the war system—all are based on threat power. The answer is not to just get rid of those systems, much as we may like to, because to some degree the first and third at least serve necessary functions that no contemporary society can do entirely without, nor is likely to for some time to come. But as we know these systems today, they are pure conduits for threat power—they were set up at a time when that was the only kind of power generally understood. The answer is to reorganize these systems and let them act as channels for another kind of power. Nonviolent intervention in severe conflicts is the perfect example.

In *Gandhi's Peace Army: The Shanti Sena and Unarmed Peacekeeping,* one of the earliest books written about peace teams, Thomas Weber quotes from an Indian Shanti Sainik, or peace army volunteer, who served in Cyprus: "Whereas intimacy was a hindrance for a violent army, it was an essential for an effective nonviolent army."[36] This is the exact converse of what Joe Loya and E. M. Forster observed. In a threat system, intimacy is a disaster. World War I almost came apart on the first Christmas, when "enemy" soldiers who had been pinned down in trenches within hailing distance of one another declared their own truce and milled around in no-man's-land, swapping stories and sharing photos of their loved ones back home. Panicky officers on both sides had to threaten the men with draconian punishments to restart the war. In other words, war engages the wrong energies and cannot but lead to the wrong results; to quote journalist Chris Hedges, who has seen more wars than he cares to think about, "The very employment of violence corrupts those who carry it out."[37] When Lieutenant Max Plowman was court-martialed for resigning his commission in WWI, he explained to the judges that "disorder cannot breed order. Doing evil that good may come is apparent folly."[38]

There are, it could be argued, two legitimate functions of the present war system: intervention, when that is necessitated by severe conflict, and defense. What we have seen now is that both can be addressed by peace teams. That would put us on an entirely different road. "Nonviolent action implants, by anticipation within the very process of change itself, the values to which it will ultimately lead. Hence it does not sow peace by means of war. It does not attempt to build up by tearing down."[39] Perceiving this, Johan Galtung has actually defined nonviolence as "peacemaking by peaceful means."

Because it treats people with concern and respect, never dehumanizing them, nonviolent peacemaking succeeds even when it "fails," while "peacemaking as usual" fails to bring us closer to a more peaceful world, even when it "succeeds." Think of the old Roman paradox, "If you want peace, prepare for war." In the ever-spiraling dynamic of the Cold War, as in all arms races before or since, we experienced the folly of trying to live by such a paradox, yet what's a threatened country to do? Well, a population that would ready itself for the response of disobedience-cum-fraternization that Gandhi envisioned for India, and Czech citizens partly carried out in Prague, offers no threat whatever to the safety of other societies. It would be able to prepare a strong defense without in the least provoking an attacker. Nonviolence threatens no one except dictators, and then only if they understand what it can do.

In chapter 3 we talked about the testimony of Sue Severin who, with other volunteers from Witness for Peace, stumbled onto the power of protective accompaniment in 1982—how she found the psychological reward of it "addictive." She was not alone. Randy Bond went to Hebron with a small band organized by Michigan Peace Teams and wrote, "We were a small group of ordinary people doing some rather extraordinary things in a hurting part of our world. We had to stretch ourselves and our capabilities to do these things. That's the only way we grow."[40] The Vietnam War, by contrast, went on killing Americans long after the last helicopter left Saigon. It killed by the anguishing psychological pressure of having to do horrible things to people for no good reason, as became increasingly clear. One veteran friend of mine came back unhurt in body but for years afterward went into cold sweats and panic every time he heard a helicopter; it took about a year to cure himself after he'd learned to use a mantram, and many were not that lucky. The post-traumatic stress has been so ubiquitous that it was once believed that the number of Vietnam veterans who committed suicide after getting "safely" home to the States was more than those killed in action in Vietnam itself. Yet a marine who, by contrast, served in Somalia to do the famine relief in 1992 told the press, "This was the most satisfying work I've ever done," echoing what nonviolent actors often say, such as Marge Argelyan, whom we've just heard from in Hebron: "This experience had the most integrity of any work I've done." People are people; the kind of action you put them into, the kind of energy you expose them to, very largely determines what they will become.

MAKE LOVE *REPLACE* WAR: THE VISION GETS REAL

The point of this discussion has not been that peace teams can end war. It has been that nonviolence can end war. We have now thought some about the three levels of change that have to happen—changes in thought, speech, and action—for the creative influence of soul force to be applied by ordinary people toward creating a regime of peace. For this is what we want: a robust system of conflict absorption able to deal with war in such a creative way that it resonates with other changes leading to meaningful and lasting peace. Like all dynamics of major change, whether it be the "catastrophe theory" that tries to account for how an argument becomes a war or the "tipping point" that makes hush puppies a rage, there is a point at which the pressure toward peaceful change is enough to tilt the balance, where we could build what is now unthinkable to us—a world free from war.[41] No one knows exactly how much that amount is, or where the tipping points are, but there is clearly what Gandhi called a "law of progression" such that successes build on earlier successes. Clearly, the amount of energy needed to start the changes is very high when we begin the process, but later, when there is a discernible momentum, less can do more. All big changes are like that, and all real changes start out looking outlandish and at a certain point become the norm.

When I was first involved with meditation courses at Berkeley, in 1970, we had to explain to students (let alone to deans) what meditation was from the ground up. We often had to face raised parental eyebrows. Now I have to specify what *kind* of meditation I'm talking about, such is the smorgasbord available in most progressive college towns across the country ("passage meditation," we decided to call it). Fairly often, students tell me, "My parents got me into this—they've been meditating for years." Once it was a grandfather. The rhythm by which the world does finally phase from a war system to a regime of stable peace may be like that.

Peace teams will play a special role in realizing this vision, for several reasons. Peace teams, along with Civilian-Based Defense, are the kind of nonviolence that we could use to stop a war even after it starts. We could use them in the kind of extreme emergencies that are endemic in various parts of the globe, or slow-fuse emergencies like the "low-intensity" conflicts that were waged throughout Central America, where protective accompaniment was born. We could use them in inner-city conflicts throughout the industrial world, which would be more like what Gandhi had in mind for them. The biggest objection to the idea of using nonviolence in war is, of course, that "it would never work in a tough case." But these *are* tough cases. Often, in terms of dehumanization, the very toughest. If we can show that nonviolence can work here, we will be on our way to understanding that it can work anywhere.

Imagine a well-trained peace team defusing a war where the standard methods had failed—say in a far-gone situation like those that seemed to appear out of nowhere in Bosnia, Somalia, Rwanda, or Indonesia. International volunteers would show, first of all, that the world does indeed care what happens to other human beings, even when there is no strategic concern like oil or other "practical" interest they have to protect. Further, the successful nonviolent intervention would begin to change the "bottom line" in global security, showing that nonviolence, not violence, is the ultimate sanction we can rely on for international peace and defense. That would shake the war system as it has not been shaken during all these turbulent centuries. And that was just the hope of over a thousand volunteers who flocked to the makeshift offices of "Seeds of Peace" and "Balkan Peace Teams" in Italy, Germany, Holland, the United States, and elsewhere during the grim winter of 1991, when human beings in Bosnia forgot they were human beings.

The volunteers were not to meet with success that winter in Mostar, in Sarajevo, or in Tuzla—and I daresay that if they had, the world at large, given its priorities right now, would not have noticed. An "ocular demonstration" doesn't work if nobody's watching. This pretty clearly defines the two changes, in the movement and in the world, that we should work on to get peace teams off the drawing board and into the historic drama of leading us up the path to stable peace.

Remember: all the experiments so far have been carried on with a "chronic lack of resources . . . inadequate infrastructure, poor communications, and limited training opportunities," not to mention the near-total cold shoulder from the mass media and "little popular understanding of the dynamics and history of this manifestation of nonviolent action."[42] Just imagine what could be done with adequate resources, a good infrastructure, and communications, with public support, and with free, alert media. Imagine what the picture would be like if there were not a few thousand but "lakhs" of volunteers, well trained, decently supplied, and appropriately recognized. We could make "compassionate response teams" a fixture.

Nonviolence of any kind requires special preparation, much more when it's deployed in the crucible of an advanced conflict in a foreign country. The triumphs and tragedies of former Yugoslavia showed the peace-team movement that before volunteers go into situations of intense conflict they need to have careful training.

They also need support. And this is where we come in. For every soldier in the trenches during the Great War there were hundreds, no thousands, of supporters back home: the ladies who knitted socks, the kids who collected scrap metal, the speech makers, the decision makers, and at last the taxpayers. Likewise, the institutionalization of peace will open up needs for supporters with many different talents. *That* support will be more moral and less financial (far less financial), and it will have to include something that a conventional war does not: it will need what's called "interpretation." The world at large understands (or thinks it does) how violence works. It does not understand how nonviolence works. Even a dramatic success by a nonviolent peace team would likely be ignored or so mishandled by the press that it would not have its educational effect. We have seen so many examples of this, not only in individual cases (Joan Black) but others on a handsome scale (the *intifada,* Kosovo), so that we can't afford to hope that even a well-carried-off peacemaking operation using the kind of power appropriate to peace would make its mark. The logic of war may be deeply flawed, but it's dreadfully familiar and paralyzingly simple; it follows directly from what we like to think we know about human nature: that people are separate from each other and respond only to force. This is not the case with the logic of peace. Good writers, speakers, artists—every kind of culture maker and communicator, academics and ordinary folks talking to their neighbors—have a highly creative job cut out for them: to explain peace teams and the logic of peace itself. Today we tell each other the stories of war ad infinitum, ad nauseam: we shall have to learn to tell the stories of peace *and* spell out what they mean, at least at first.

Even protective accompaniment, the smallest, one-on-one kind of intervention, has already had wide repercussions, as we saw with the creation of "political space" in places like Guatemala, where it turned a process of pure terror into one of grudging dialogue. A Haitian team of only sixty-four people mounted by a PBI coalition defied the deadly FRAPH militia for six months, saving countless lives. At one scary moment in Guatemala, as we saw, the PBI presence was a "team" of one. Nonviolence can be done, if necessary, without large numbers. The thing is, it cannot be understood and institutionalized without large numbers.

The famed ethologist Konrad Lorenz—not a wild-eyed idealist but a distinguished scientist—decided after extensive scientific investigation that war is not programmed by nature. "Modern war has become an institution, and . . . being an institution, can be abolished."[43] What I am saying here is the converse, and the missing practical component to what Lorenz, like Margaret Mead and so many others, has discovered: *peace can be institutionalized.* When it is, then people will be willing to send war on its well-deserved way to the cabinet of bad memories.

LOOKING DOWN THE ROAD

Everything we know about paradigm shifts—for that is what we're talking about—tells us that this kind of enormous change is hard to create but definitely possible. It leaves us in the realm of the unpredictable with regard to when or exactly how such a shift could occur. We know only a little about how it can be guided and facilitated. But it seems certain that this particular shift will need more conscious direction than many that have taken place in times past. This is partly because the global situation we now face is so complex, and partly because the speed with which the conversion to truth has to occur is now so great. There won't be much left for humanity to rescue if we wait for this process to happen by itself.

To understand the needed change we should think about a slightly different kind of shift than the ones on which Thomas Kuhn based his *Structure of Scientific Revolutions,* the book that made "paradigm shift" a household expression. We should think about the incredible shift of consciousness awakened by the suffering of the first adherents, followed by the hard work of the Fathers (and Mothers) of the Church, who created a thought world with the sanctity of the individual and the One God at its center. That great shift, too, came from a deep groundswell of belief *and* needed a lot of careful thought to explain how the new system worked. Absent divine intervention, we have to work on this huge job in many ways.

So it is helpful to remember the two big things that make such an enormous change possible. The first is that peace is the deepest drive in our human being. Underneath all our conditioning—which admittedly can go pretty deep—"there is no human heart that does not crave for joy and peace." Appearances can be very dark. Right now they are very dark, indeed, but they still are only that, appearances.

> Think of men who are bent on war. What they want
> is to win, that is to say, their battles are but bridges to
> glory and peace. The whole point of victory is to bring
> opponents to their knees—this done, peace ensues.
> Peace, then, is the purpose of waging war . . . Notice
> that there can be life without pain, but no pain without some kind of life. In the same way, there can be
> peace without any kind of war, but no war that does
> not suppose some kind of peace.[44]

Even those who wage wars do so to reach some kind of "peace" within the limits of their understanding, as Augustine said—and these are limits that we can always push back by culture and education. "Peace is the quest, nay the hunger of every soul."[45] Through conditioning, we can come to think that threat force and destruction are unavoidable, but nonviolent logic rises to show up this superstition, and we quicken. Yes, it is a huge task to eliminate war, but it's the task we've all been called to, and we will not rest until it's done.

This is why, as Sherry Anderson and Paul Ray have recently shown, fifty million Americans are looking for a way out—which nothing points to on the standard political compass.[46]

The second encouraging truth is that, while many things have been tried in our sporadic approaches to this great task, one has not. Soul force has never been systematically put to work to create the conditions and institutions of sustained peace. So, as Norman Cousins used to say, "No one knows enough to be a pessimist." Before the twentieth century we never had the tool to apply nonviolence to world peace systematically—or did not know we had it. Gandhi lived and died to show us that we do; the women of Gujarat whom he me tions, the Pathans of the North-West Frontier—many groups and countless individuals have lived and died to show us the utility of this force. This is the time to learn their lesson. Let me restate what I think their work and suffering has taught us: the task is *not so much to stop war as to start nonviolence.*

The Chicago scientists had no way of knowing it, but the clear picture they sought that day in 1946 was already beginning to emerge.

CHAPTER NINE

TOWARD A METAPHYSICS OF COMPASSION

It is plain that the law against the slaughtering of animals is founded rather on vain superstition and womanish pity than on sound reason.

—Spinoza

Compassion is the radicalism of this age.

—His Holiness the Dalai Lama

BEFORE I TOOK to meditation, the two things that kept me in touch with reality were poetry and nature. There wasn't much "nature" in Brooklyn, to be sure, but my family would spend summers high in the Adirondacks, and the smell of deep pine woods on a hot summer afternoon has never quite left me, even when I hike through the tart smell of eucalyptus glades in California. As for poetry, I grew up in a warm household that was television free until just before I went to college, and that left me relatively able to preserve my sensitivity to the nuances of language—and the human comedy in general. For the first part of my academic career I spent many fruitful years studying the earliest and greatest poet in Western civilization, Homer, whose epics, the *Iliad* and the *Odyssey,* were to a large degree constitutive for the value system most of us grew up with. There were many things that kept my ear to his music, one of them being his profound understanding of war and what Wilfred Owen famously called "the pity of war" and what that kind of violence does to women and to the family and what kind of society you have if the only kind of "peace" you know is an uneasy respite in the shambles of intermittent conflict. One line of Homer in particular keeps coming to my mind to this day. It is spoken by the god Apollo in the final book of the *Iliad,* Book 24 (or as scholars say, Omega), line 54.

κωφὴν γὰρ δὴ γαῖαν ἀεικίζει μενεαίνων.
For look, he is outraging the mute earth in his fury.[1]

"He" is Achilles, the semidivine hero who represents war incarnate, and the offense he's committing is grave indeed. He's dragging the dead body of his enemy Hector 'round the camp from the back of his chariot. Apollo is trying to persuade the gods to intervene and stop the desecration, and this haunting hexameter concludes his exhortation. In life, Hector was a warrior who in the course of defending Troy, his homeland, slew Achilles' companion, but in death, the Greeks believed, he no longer belongs to his city *or* to Achilles, who slew him in turn. He belongs to the earth. Hector is no longer the individual person he was when alive; his human accounts are settled. Now he belongs to the cycle of nature itself. Achilles can take Hector's life—that is the warrior code—but not his *psyche,* his soul. What Achilles is trying to do now by refusing to relinquish Hector's body to the earth goes beyond that code. It is an outrage—in other words, violence (the same word in early Greek, *hybris,* means both).

Just prior to verse 54, Apollo has made a point about violence that is as sophisticated as this line is poignant: "For Achilles himself cannot but lose by doing this." By desecrating the body of his fallen enemy, and thus violating the prevailing war code, he will destroy the very value system on which he himself depends for the meaning of his own life and honor. Again, the innate contradictions of violence. Violence begets more violence, Apollo implies, and no one wins.

The "mute earth," however, is a striking image, one with as much resonance in the Vedic poetry of ancient India as in Homer's tradition (the two were distantly related), and it resonates to this day. The "mute earth" is Draupadi, whose humiliation at the court of the Kurus launches the gigantic Mahabharata war; she is Sita ("furrow") abducted by the archdemon of the Ramayana epic; she is the Trojan woman of Euripides' classic plays; she is whatever and whoever cannot make her voice heard in distress; she is all that is vulnerable. Achilles killed many, and the warrior code absorbed that; what Achilles is killing now is pity. No culture can absorb that and live. I would like in this chapter to talk about pity, to evoke it and connect with it a concept that may help us understand as well as feel it.

Who will hear the cry of the earth?[2] Apollo has been magically protecting Hector's body (and Achilles' reputation) from harm while the still-living hero vainly drags the body of his fallen enemy around his camp. Now he persuades the other gods to intervene, since nothing less than the whole value system, and by extension the world order, is at stake. Interestingly, there was a plan to steal Hector's body, but the gods did not go along with it. That would not work because what the system needs is the hero's change of heart. Although Homer doesn't explicitly talk about interior life as we do, he clearly tells us, when the gods refuse to steal Hector's body, that the change has to be inside Achilles; it has to come from his will.

Achilles' mother—Thetis, a goddess—soon comes to persuade him, with very maternal logic, to give Hector's body back to his family for proper treatment, but it's almost unnecessary; the hero has already changed. The great scene that follows, between Achilles and Hector's father, Priam, when the old man steels his courage to kiss the "man-slaughtering" hand that took his son's life, is a gripping climax of hard-won reconciliation; with it, the poem is ready to wind down.

Poetry is powerful where it speaks to all of us. We are all a little like Achilles. On our own scale, we too become blind to pity—and like him we can all open our eyes again. Absent Homer's genius and his tradition, perhaps the following thoughts and images can help:

Earlier this month [May 1998], several members of the Iraq Sanctions Challenge stood at the bedside of Mustafa, one of at least a dozen dying children in a crowded, wretched ward of the main hospital in Basra, Iraq's southern port city. His mother, tall, thin and quite beautiful, sat cross legged on the mattress beside him, waving away flies, as the doctor explained to us that the child, hospitalized for the past twenty days, now suffered from dehydration, diarrhea, acute renal failure and extensive brain atrophy. Lacking equipment and medicine to diagnose and treat Mustafa, the doctors could only stand by, helpless and frustrated, while the child's condition worsened over three weeks' time. If Mustafa survives, he will be severely crippled. Ima Nouri, his mother, is 35 years old. Her serious eyes, large and luminous, followed us as we paused before each bedside. She seemed surprised when we asked her to tell us a little about herself. We learned that she lives in a rural area north of Basra and has two children at home whom she misses very much. We asked the doctor to tell her that we are so very sorry, that we want to tell people in the US her story, that we will try hard to end the sanctions. She smiled slowly, nodded. Then we mentioned that people in the United States were celebrating Mother's Day on this day and asked if she had a message for mothers in our country. Ima suddenly became animated. "Yes," she said, "I have two messages. First, tell them, from Iraqi women, that these are our children and we love them so much." Stroking Mustafa's face, she continued, "Ask them to please try to help us protect them and take care of them. And, for American women,—I want them to feel what I am feeling."[3]

If we only could. In the valley of La Verna, as one tradition has it, Saint Francis asked Jesus to give him the uncompromising love he had felt for all that lives, *and* for the stigmata he had borne in his very flesh because of that love. The word *compassion* means literally "suffering with." Of course it hurts. But when we suffer with others we grow, and when we close our hearts against them we die within. In Hebrew, the word for compassion is *rehamim*. It is the plural of *rehem,* "womb." To have compassion is to be toward someone, in a little—or not so little—way, what every mother is to her own child.

This is an eternal issue, but it has a historical context. The painting that you see to the right was done by Joseph Wright of Derby in 1768, sixty-four years after Sir Isaac Newton taught that matter was built up of "solid, massy, hard impenetrable, moveable Particles,"[4] in other words, near the beginning of modern materialism and its decisive break with the ancient traditions that had pictured human beings as having an organic relationship with the living earth.

The adult facing us in the painting is a traveling science lecturer, if you will, a circuit rider of the new religion, demonstrating a vacuum pump to the rapt onlookers. He is pumping the air out of a glass cage, and to make that fact visible there is a bird inside the cage. By watching the bird gasp for breath, in other words, they can see that there's no more air in the cage, and be impressed with what technology can do. But what other impression are we to receive? The real dramatic interest in the painting, what grabs our eyes and holds them, is the children. For them this is not about the wonders of science. In their innocence they do not follow the explanation of the pump and the air; they just think a man is killing a little bird. The real story of the painting is in the contrast between the glazed lecturer holding the audience spellbound, a kind of high priest of technology, and the distress of the children—and the fact that they are children, and the adults just ignore them. When we hurt nature, it is not that we lack warnings. Not all of us lose our sensitivity at once. The real tragedy is to ignore those who are still aware of what we're doing—the way, in the *Iliad,* Hector and his wife, Andromache, laugh at their little son,

An Experiment on a Bird in the Air Pump, by Joseph Wright. (National Gallery, London.)

Astyanax, when he is frightened by his father's war helmet. Shortly after that laugh, however, Achilles kills Hector in that splendid helmet, and shortly after that the victorious Greeks throw Astyanax from the city walls so he can't grow up and avenge his father. Who is to be laughed at? Whose vision was more realistic?

Flaubert, who saw *An Experiment on a Bird in the Air Pump* in 1856, noted in his journal, *"Petite fille qui pleure. Charmant de naiveté et de profondeur."* That is, "A little girl crying. Charming in its naivete and profundity."[5] It is the naivete (if you want to call a child's unmediated awareness of life naive) that is the profundity.

Today we stand at the other end of the arc that began when Wright painted his enthusiast demonstrating the vacuum pump and the power of man over nature. Science and technology have taken over in a way that even the most enthusiastic rationalists in his eighteenth-century audience could hardly have imagined, and we now stand, or we should stand, aghast at the results. What we have done to the environment, and to the fabric of human life within it, could not have been imagined in 1768. Spinoza to the contrary notwithstanding, we must take "womanish" pity—and we must understand that it goes along with, rather than standing in conflict with, sound reasoning. We can no longer afford to set aside the simple, unmediated responses of the children.

Who even understands children today? The other day I went to my granddaughter's ballet recital—an art form millions have enjoyed since the seventeenth century. But in the twenty-first century I was appalled by the choices of the well-meaning directors, for none of the pieces they had choreographed was anything a child could relate to or enjoy. As the parents wildly applauded a particularly sexy number, the phrase "children without a childhood" came sadly to mind. I wondered how those parents would feel if their daughter came home pregnant, or worse.

The plight of children today makes Dickens's London seem like a paradise. In the decade 1985–95, two million children died in wars, and nearly half a million fought in them. Somewhere between four and five million were forced into refugee camps around the world, twelve million were left homeless, and some 200 million were engaged in child labor. In the United States, six million children under age six—that's one out of four American children from that age group—live below the poverty line. Juvenile crime increased 50 percent in the five years from 1989 to 1994 (though at the moment it's participating in the downturn of violent crime). Los Angeles Superior Court Justice Charles W. McCoy Jr. noted that "when a juvenile is tried in court, more than half the time no parent even shows up."[6] And economic sanctions imposed by the United Nations have killed a million children in Iraq.

By the time we see Achilles dragging Hector's body behind his chariot (the way American soldiers dragged the body of a Vietcong soldier behind their tank in an infamous photograph, the way three KKK members dragged a black youth to death in 1998), the hero had lost all sense of compassion in the madness of battle. He lost what the Greeks called *eleos* and *aidôs,* pity and respect, and became more like a lion than a man, capable of eating his enemies like a savage beast, but by the time his mother comes to him with the gods' message, he has already come back to his senses. If we tend to think of Homer as war poetry, it may be surprising to encounter such a change of heart—such a recovery of heart—serving as the climax of an epic that furnished war ideologies to two millennia of Western cultures, but it is not unrealistic; we've seen several such recoveries in the preceding pages. There is nothing unrealistic about the tension between compassion and savagery in the same person, because that is the condition in which we find ourselves.

"Dumb Earth," or Deaf Humanity?

Homer told his story in a traditional language that came embedded with ideas much older than himself. One of these, which comes to the surface in Omega 54, is the conception of Earth as a living, sentient being, a goddess. Fitting, that when Homer wanted to image humankind's crying need for compassion, he depicted a warrior outraging the "dumb" earth, oblivious to a pain that only the gods could hear. It makes me think of the stunning line that is said to be either a Russian proverb or a line of poetry: "Every bullet finds its target in a mother's heart."

Seeing connections like this is the basis of nonviolent consciousness. Recently, one of my students offered, as we were groping for a definition of violence, "If you damage anything you're damaging the big picture," for example, the earth. It should be so much easier to see this today, when fiendishly destructive bombs and rockets, not to mention chemicals and toxic organisms, are hurled at our enemies, and how prescient Homer appears, to have sensed this connection when warriors were fighting one-on-one with swords and spears. His was the poet's deep vision that sees that violence is violence, "damaging the whole picture," as only the gods knew. He was prescient, but he also had an advantage over us. He believed in the worldview—and sometimes I wish we still could—that Earth is alive.

The Greeks also had a myth that Agamemnon had to sacrifice his own daughter so he could get to Troy for the war of all wars. The myth's meaning is unmistakable: that war fighting and the family, the traditional preserves of men and of women, are in eternal opposition. It is either one or the other, because underneath all complexities they are based on fundamentally different values: destruction and preservation, triumphalism and nurturance. But in our age, when mothers appear in the news in their combat uniforms, leaving their children in America so they can go and bomb other mothers' children in Iraq, what will awaken us?

FROM PARADOX TO PARADIGM

In the summer of 1938, Niels Bohr, the "Grandfather of Quantum Theory" addressed an international gathering of physicists in Copenhagen. Bohr was best known to the general public for his famous theory of complementarity, describing the built-in limit to human understanding of the outside world, meaning that to completely describe anything "out there" we always need at least two mutually exclusive models, like a particle and a wave. The thing we want to know about—be it photon, electron, or any quantum entity, which ultimately means anything—is neither a particle nor a wave; it will appear as one or the other depending on how we observe it. On the occasion of this distinguished international gathering he applied his famous idea to things rather bigger than the electron:

> We may truly say that different human cultures are complementary to each other. Indeed, each such culture represents a harmonious balance of traditional conventions by means of which latent possibilities of human life can unfold themselves in a way which reveals to us new aspects of its unlimited richness and variety.[7]

At this shocking suggestion, Richard Rhodes laconically points out, "The German delegation walked out." As well they might. They were, after all, Nazis first, and scientists afterward. This was not just "Jewish physics" they were listening to (Bohr's mother was in fact Jewish), but a worldview utterly inimical to Nazi values, a challenge to their whole concept of human being and human value. "Totalitarianism," in Hannah Arendt's famous definition, "strives not toward despotic rule over men but toward a system in which men are superfluous."[8] Bohr's idea, that every race and community and even every individual has his or her role in the scheme of things, and that we need one another if any of us is to be fulfilled—this is gall and wormwood to Fascists. And therefore may well be the worldview to underpin a future of compassion.

Because Nazism represents the logic of violence carried to its ultimate and unsubtle conclusion, we can see in it several things that go along with the decision to use brute force to get what we want, though the connection may not be immediately obvious. The first of these—and probably the first thing to consider about any worldview—is its image of the human being. Hitler was kind of blunt about this. It's said that he once explained to an American journalist, "You know, every man has his price—and you'd be surprised how low that price is." Violence is keyed to the lowest image of the human being. Nonviolence is keyed to the most exalted. This is one of the reasons violence drives us apart, while nonviolence appeals directly to the mysterious unity among all of us, which is the hidden glory in each of us. It is one of the reasons that a nonviolent attitude leads to works that confer a sense of meaning, while a life of violence confers at best fleeting and shallow satisfactions. From today's Germany, where many youth have taken a lead in putting the Nazi legacy behind us, I recently received a handsome brochure blazoned with "Nonviolence" along one side and "Self-image" across the bottom[9]—an intuitively right connection.

Bohr's disruptive words were ahead of his time and we are still barely catching up to them. He saw that at the heart of the Fascist worldview was a concept of order utterly contrary to what we know to be true of biological life. Every biologist knows that the essence of life is diversity, but the Nazis held that life was two-dimensional and essentially uniform, with an extreme hierarchy such that only one race, one regime, ultimately only one person, was legitimate, clean, or whatever, while everyone and everything else was "with us or against us," destined to be assimilated or subordinated to the One Right Way. We might call this worldview "disunity through uniformity." The most direct antidote to Fascism on this level is the very different idea Hegel called *unity in diversity*. As a frame of reference, unity in diversity is a way to acknowledge the unique value of each life, through grasping its connection with all of life. Note Bohr's expression, "The latent possibilities of human life can unfold themselves."[10] This is exactly the definition of nonviolence that a young fellow Northman, Johan Galtung, would propose some years later: "the fulfillment of the individual." Conversely, Galtung would define violence as any "avoidable compromise of human needs"—anything that inhibits that fulfillment.[11] In this spirit the Dalai Lama, speaking from the margins of the UN NGO Human Rights Convention in 1993, said, "If we are prevented from using our creative potential, we are deprived of one of the basic characteristics of a human being." And he added, "It is very often the most gifted, dedicated, and creative members of our society who become victims of human rights abuses. Thus the political, social, cultural and economic developments of a society are obstructed by the violations of human rights."[12]

There is, therefore, a close connection between compassion—which is really more than a feeling but the force that holds family, society, and the planet together—and the concept, or vision, that all life is precious in its diversity and its unity. Bohr was apparently trying to trace the extension of biodiversity, which we understand relatively well, to cultural and individual diversity, which we do not. Unity in diversity goes hand-in-hand with nonviolence; unity in diversity is, if you will, the theology of compassion.

There are now more than six billion individuals in the human family, and growing. That does not matter. From the standpoint of unity in diversity each of them is invaluable. That foundational insight is growing dimmer instead of brighter at this time. The reinstatement of the death penalty, euthanasia, materialism, the countenancing of grotesque human rights violations, even the letting-slip of the family and the support systems that nurture a child—these are all ways we are compromising that insight because we see no other choice at present but to keep on using violence to control violence. But for every nonviolence advocate throughout time, it has been axiomatic that life is sacred, i.e., invaluable, that while the sum total of all life is in a way more precious than that of a given individual, in a way it is not. Infinity equals infinity.

In totalitarian logic, "one death is a tragedy, a million deaths is a statistic"[13] or "if you've seen one redwood tree, you've seen them all." Nonviolent logic does not work that way. Rather, "each is good, and taken all together very good, for 'our Lord made all things very good.'"[14] So to the nonviolent, one death is a tragedy and a million deaths is a million tragedies, even though our imaginations may not be able to grasp that enormity. In a way, a million deaths is not worse than the death of an individual: nothing is worse than the death of an individual. That's what the sanctity of life means.

Now, Gandhi, as a traditional Hindu, had a solid metaphysical basis for this principle, and he liked to quote a traditional wisdom proverb that articulates it: *"yatha pinde, tatha brahmande,"* "as with the fragment, so with the whole." Otherwise put, the macrocosm is in the microcosm. Everything that exists "out there" exists "in here," as philosophers say, *in potentia*. This is not the way we generally view things, but why should we think that when we're walking around in our normal buy-and-sell consciousness, we're seeing things as they really are? Quantum physicists, mystics, the world's faith traditions with their awkward belief in the sanctity of the individual—and a lurking suspicion in all of us in our more reflective moments—keep returning to this vision again and again. This vision prompted George Orwell, for example, to muse, as he watched the movements of a young Hindu over whose hanging he was about to preside, "One life less; one world less."[15] This is what drives good citizens to the picket lines when the state decides it has the right to snuff out a life, what makes them say the death penalty is "the supreme moral issue of our time," as a recent mailer from Death Penalty Focus said, because life is so precious that we dare not snuff it out under any circumstances, however impractical that may appear. The challenge instead is precisely the reverse: to make the supreme value of each life the basis of our practicality.

To do this, we turn to the positive corollary of the injunction against killing, namely, that in this microcosm that is each one of us are the seeds of the whole world order. We know the drop is in the ocean, but it's a mysterious truth that the ocean also is in the drop. This is why the Talmud, and the Koran, say in nearly identical language, "Whoever saves a single life, it is as though he saves the whole world."[16] In a very real sense, he (or she) does. It only took one individual, waking up and slowly unbending his back, to break up the colonial system and evaporate the myth that "it is natural for the weaker to lie down before the stronger." Physically, a ridiculously small fraction of our DNA is brought into play to manifest our bodies, while the rest lies latent and unused; analogously, in the depths of our consciousness, there is enough "information" in each of us to regenerate a world.

Nonviolence states, negatively, that life is sacred. Each life, regardless how humble it may seem to us, is too precious to be destroyed. And it states the positive corollary that the resources for creating the world order we want are born every minute, though they become fully realized only once in many centuries.

One fall day in 1943, 7,200 people, virtually the entire Jewish Danish population, were smuggled out under the noses of the occupation by the Danish underground. The motley flotilla, made up of fishing vessels and everything that would float, pitched and tossed in the rough sea but made Sweden with its huddled, seasick cargo by morning. Then, just when everyone thought they were finally safe, word came that the king of Sweden was afraid to give them asylum—

frightened of the Nazi presence. Perhaps he feared it would even jeopardize Sweden's neutrality.

As it happened, though, a famous Danish physicist was hiding out in Uppsala. When he heard about the dilemma, he calmly sent word to the king that if the refugees were not taken in he would turn himself over to the Nazis. The king immediately relented and accepted the refugees. Moved by political expediency or awakened compassion, he responded perfectly to Niels Bohr's Satyagraha of one.

HEART UNITY: DIVERSITY *AS* COMMUNITY

Every spring I show my class a stirring film about the civil rights movement that features a snatch of a sermon by Martin Luther King Jr. delivered in Montgomery. I can hear these words (and the audience chiming in) as I type them:

> And we're not wrong in what we're doing. *(No!)*
> If we're wrong, the Supreme Court is wrong.
> *(Uh huh!)*
> If we're wrong, the Constitution of the United
> States is wrong. *(Yeah!)*
> If we're wrong, God Almighty is wrong . . .

I feel, in a small way, that I've just been paraphrasing him: "If nonviolence is wrong, then unity in diversity is wrong—then the sanctity of life is wrong, then the basis of civilization is wrong." If we give up on the sanctity of life, which we are doing right now, step-by-step—for the convenience of assisted suicides, for the convenience of abortions, for the convenient delusion that executing "criminals" makes the rest of society safe—we are giving up on the principle of our civilization.

Of course, the idea of unity in diversity seems a bit paradoxical: "The more clearly one studies the character of individual human souls," wrote Rabbi Abraham Isaac Kook, "the more baffled one becomes over the great differences between personalities. . . . It is, however, *precisely through their differentiations that they are all united* toward one objective, to contribute toward the perfection of the world, each person according to his special talent."[17] (my emphasis) A certain amount of paradox is OK, no doubt, especially when a worldview is just being shaped, but in fact nonviolence gives us a simple way to resolve this paradox. The "unity" we're talking about is "heart unity"; it's a unity *beneath* the surface while the diversity we're talking about is *on* the surface—a diversity of outward characteristics. Gandhi never wanted Muslims to give up their religion or Brahmins to stop teaching or performing rituals and depend on spinning *rhadi* to make their living; he wanted everyone to stop feeling superior, or inferior, to each other—in other words, to stop feeling alienated. Brahmins would stay Brahmins, Christians would become good Christians, but all in a context of identifying with one another's welfare. And, as we've seen, he invented the term *heart unity* to designate that.

Heart unity, the empathetic desire for the welfare of others, could also be called "rejoicing in diversity." We are one in our underlying consciousness, which has no divisions. In practice I get in touch with that unity when I want you to be fulfilled in the way you can be fulfilled—not necessarily the way I'd be fulfilled. That we can and should both be fulfilled is a cardinal principle of faith in the world of Satyagraha; that we have different ways of getting there is equally cardinal. Unity of aspiration, down there in the heart, goes with diversity of attributes, of individuality on the surface. You really can't have one without the other. And this is not unduly paradoxical; unity is the signature, the fulfillment of our inner life; diversity, the natural characteristic of our outer life. Now, Gandhi did want Hindus to wean their Muslim brethren from cow slaughter, by means of love; he wanted Brahmins to take some time off and do "bread labour," but voluntarily. Accepting everyone does not mean accepting everything. Similarly, as the world grows smaller, opportunities to learn from one another increase, but the value of imitating each other does not. Too much "unity" on the surface (where it's really more like uniformity) always turns out to involve some kind of domination and/or dependency: belief in that kind of "unity" drove the Fascists out when Bohr described the real thing.

Attempting to water down the Dalai Lama's appeal to the "international community" for help in securing the basic rights of his captive people, the Chinese regime cynically played a card that has often been played honestly and well, namely, that this kind of "interference" would be an imposition of Western values on a non-Western people. His Holiness showed the flaw in that argument, using good Buddhist principles:

> All human beings, whatever their cultural or histori-
> cal background, suffer when they are intimidated,
> imprisoned or tortured. . . . There should be no
> difference of views on this. We must therefore insist
> on a global consensus not only on the need to respect
> human rights world wide but more importantly on
> the definition of these rights. Recently some Asian
> governments have contended that the standards of
> human rights laid down in the Universal Declaration
> of Human Rights are those advocated by the West and
> cannot be applied to Asia and other parts of the
> Third World because of differences in culture and
> differences in social and economic development. I
> do not share this view and I am convinced that the
> majority of Asian people do not support this view
> either, for it is the inherent nature of all human beings
> to yearn for freedom, equality and dignity. . . . The
> rich diversity of cultures and religions should help
> to strengthen the fundamental human rights in all
> communities.[18]

Indeed, even the august concept of human rights may not be vibrant enough to make us hear the cry of these basic needs. Speaking in the context of the struggle for animal welfare, Mary Midgley wrote that the biosphere "is the whole of which we are parts, and its other parts concern us for that reason. But the language of rights is rather ill-suited for expressing this."[19] Let us say, rather, that the drive to find happiness is close to the core of our being, and that is why it's identical in each of us. On the "heart level" there are basic needs and aspirations every human being has in common. We all have a need to serve, and we have the need as Augustine pointed out, to be united with each other—both areas in which modern societies let us seriously down. We have an inalienable, universal need for respect, meaning both to get basic human dignity and (as Dostoevsky said) to have someone or something *to* respect. Nonviolence makes full use of both of these dimensions. In the famous "people power" revolution in the Philippines (1983–86), yet another term for nonviolence was coined, and maybe the best yet: *alaydangal*, to "offer dignity."

There are, and must be, minor differences playing across the surface of this unity of the needs we all share in common, which strangely complement it. There can only be one Michael Nagler (happily, some may think), and while there are certain things I think will make me happy as an individual (the opportunity to teach nonviolence, an occasional hike through unspoiled forests), my desire for happiness is the same as, and has the same validity as, that in every person, indeed in every blessed creature. Violence denies both this surface uniqueness and underlying identity. Nonviolence affirms both, at their respective levels. Active nonviolence—a calling for each and every one of us—uses both in its blueprint for loving community.

Today, as the world is convulsed by ethnic and pseudoethnic and still other hatreds, people caught up in such hatreds cannot remotely remember that they share an underlying unity with surface differences; they see only differences, which then take on monstrous proportions. They fall into a condition that ethologist Eibl-Eibesfeldt called "pseudospeciation": the illusion that others belong to another species—that they aren't human. Today it is "criminals" and of course "terrorists"; yesterday it was "Communists," and who knows who may be the next group to be thrust beyond the "discourse of reason"—unless, as Einstein said, we "remember our humanity and forget all the rest."

Nonviolence helps us remember it. As a young activist friend of mine recently said, nonviolence is when you "humanize your enemy and let your 'enemy' humanize you." When you respond with courage and respect under duress, it raises your image, humanizes you, in the opponent's eyes—and helps, in however small a way, to enhance the awareness of humanness in the global culture. This awareness, in turn, defuses some of the world's violence. Pick any conflict—in the Middle East, in the Balkans, in Africa, in America: we would never be seeing the kind of unreasoning hate that's erupting around the world if our general worldview were not so dehumanized. There would still be problems like water rights and social entitlements, but they would be just that—problems. You don't hate problems; you solve them.

And so the idea of the world as a machine, made up of separate, solid, Newtonian particles, "even so very hard, as never to wear or break in pieces,"[20] had bad consequences, as Joseph Wright foresaw. It was a new idea when he painted *An Experiment* and still is relatively new in the sense that it replaced a myth humanity had held for countless centuries. Realizing this, many have thought—and I may seem to have implied—that what we need to do is bring back that myth. It won't be easy. Having spent much of my early career studying myth, I know well that along with the changes Wright was illustrating, myth itself has been weakened as a way of modeling our understanding of the world. Science became and remains, as my late friend Willis Harman often said, "the main knowledge-validating system of our culture."

This is not a problem for nonviolence. Gandhi himself constantly, and appropriately, presented nonviolence as a science in both the practical and theoretical senses of that term—meaning that it could be practiced systematically and explained within the canons of human logic. From the science of nonviolence, as it develops and becomes widespread, will grow again the "myth," in the nonpejorative sense of the agreed-upon world model, that there is life and consciousness interweaving all creation. After all, as Carolyn Merchant's study so well documents, it was because our forebears, in their zeal to industrialize, no longer *wanted* to believe that Earth was alive that they stigmatized that concept as a primitive, animistic, superstitious belief. Today we desperately need to reawaken our innate awareness that life is sacred. Scientific people that we are, it we'll be better off if we understand that beneath all the diversity we see lies some kind of unity that we do not.

During a period of terrible riots some years ago in Gujarat (Gandhi's home state), a "Hindu" mob descended on a rural village, primed to kill. Almost all the village men were out in the fields. The women reacted quickly, however, and took in their Muslim neighbors to hide them from the mob. As they lived mostly in one-room cottages, it often meant "hiding" the Muslims in the *puja* corner, underneath their household altar. The mob stormed up to home after home screaming, "You are hiding Muslims in there!" "Yes," the women calmly replied. "We are coming in to get them!" Then the women, one after the other said, "First kill me, then only you may enter." Every Muslim in the village was saved that day.[21]

Who are these women? We need their courage, their instinct, their vision. We need their faith. Who are they? They are every one of us, brought to intense life by the intersection of a culture that still had remnants of humane vision and an extreme emergency. Broadly speaking, we are all in such an emergency today, and there is every possibility that we can rebuild our culture to support us when we face our own opportunities to mobilize that kind of faith and courage. If we succeed (and we can afford nothing less), we shall be proud of our contribution to an otherwise bleak epoch of the human spirit.

EPILOGUE

—∞∞∞—

If you are deemed worthy of peace, you will rejoice at all times.
Seek understanding, not gold. Gain peace, not a kingdom.

—Saint Isaac of Syria

"THESE ARE EXCITING times," wrote Vandana Shiva in her book
Stolen Harvest: The Hijacking of the Global Food Supply:

> It is not inevitable that corporations will control our
> lives and rule the world. We have a real possibility to
> shape our own futures. We have an ecological and
> social duty to ensure that the food that nourishes us is
> not a stolen harvest . . . .
> We have the opportunity to work for the freedom
> and liberation of all species and all people. Something
> as simple and basic as food has become the site for
> these manifold and diverse liberations in which every
> one of us has an opportunity to participate—no mat-
> ter who we are, no matter where we are.[1]

The examples that excite Dr. Shiva, who was one of India's
leading physicists before she became one of the world's leading environmental activists and thinkers, are cases of spirited resistance by
ordinary Indians—grassroots, usually village-based, often consciously
Gandhian—to the piracy of earth's food resources by major transnational corporations. Several things about this struggle justify her
enthusiasm.

For one thing, and it is not lost on her or many of the "uneduca-ted" villagers, this is a life-and-death matter, ripe for nonviolent atten-tion. Recall that two of Gandhi's key campaigns were about concrete, basic staples of life: cloth and salt. From the theft through privatiza-tion of salt, which is a basic enough staple of life, similar world forces have now moved on the earth's seeds. By marketing "terminator" seeds that will not reproduce and crafting international trade agreements that force farmers to buy them, and by other means, corporations like Monsanto hope to make world farmers as dependent on their corpo-rate systems as they ever were on colonial regimes of yore. Before, exploiters had to wait until crops grew, or salt washed up on shore, before confiscating them in the name of whatever structures of authority they concocted; now the same shortsighted greed, more globally organized and more technically sophisticated, has got its hands on the reproductive resources of Nature herself. Enter the "Seed Satyagraha."

One of the reasons violence can't win out in the long run is, quite simply, we don't really want it to. Violence gets vulnerable when it goes too far because eventually the violent themselves recoil. Then it's only a matter of, once again, "compelling reason to be free." And so we are witnessing setbacks to the seemingly inexorable multinational cor-porate advance called globalism, setbacks that are occurring as it crosses the line from exploiting people, which is bad enough, to exploiting the very nature from which people derive their lives. Even in this age of insensitivity, when machines and money seemed to have blinded nearly everyone to the sacred nature of life and the sacred life in nature, that awareness is coming back.

When, as it inevitably must, violence pushes people from poverty into destitution, when people see their last hope of fulfillment being robbed, or when, in his colossal arrogance, man lays claims to parts of nature on which others have lived for centuries, they fight back.

And they must. But *how* makes all the difference. Members of the Irish Republican Army (IRA) have killed six times more people in their struggle than the British army and various police forces put together. More than half of IRA deaths have been caused by their own members. This is not a fluke, as we should now realize; this tragic absurdity comes from following the law of violence, and that law, as Ireland's John Hume says, is "obsolete."[2]

The resistance to nature theft has also, like the resistance to political freedom, gone down different roads. The same ecological struggles have been both violent, as with the early efforts of Earth First!, or nonviolent, as with the famed Chipko movement in northern India. Another reason Dr. Shiva is enthusiastic about these resistance movements is that they are committed to nonviolence and—something new since Gandhi's time—are a grassroots phenomenon answered by a much more "top-down" awareness of nonviolence than was possible in his day. UNESCO graced the start of the millennium with an ambitious Culture of Peace program; the parent body has declared the first millennial decade to be a "Decade of Education for a Culture of Peace and Nonviolence"—exactly the right focus. There have always been good fights, but rarely were they fought in a commensurately good way. If these times are exciting, it is because the new way, the way consistent with the goal, is gaining ground.

My friend Lee, a highly skilled physician's assistant, recently moved out to join our community in California, bringing her delightful deep Baton Rouge accent and all her compassion and experience. Lee found herself a nice position in a small medical practice, but shortly after she joined the pleasant, semirural operation in Sonoma County, the practice was "acquired" by a health-care corporation. Not one of the most rapacious; in fact, it was the Seventh Day Adventists, who have fine hospitals dotted around the state. But Adventists or not, they thought like a corporation. Within weeks, all the nurses were fired. The staff were now "personnel," not doctors or nurses, and the new managers started ordering them around and issuing bureaucratic directives that dropped like a guillotine between them and their patients, mostly friends they had served for years, making their work tedious and demeaning. Lee is sticking it out, for now. She hopes the senior doctor will come back—when he recovers from his heart attack.

That's corporate medicine. Corporate journalism is no different. Neither is corporate coffee (though, at the time of this writing, one major chain has agreed to sell "fair trade" coffee, which greatly helps small growers, mostly in Central and South America). As I said earlier, I don't even want to talk about corporate education. Chain bookstores are a particularly nasty threat to diversity. As Ivan Illich pointed out some time ago in a stunning and oft-reprinted article, violence always compromises diversity. What are we doing to ourselves?[3]

We are automatically following a Western tendency to centralize, which first took the form of a one-city empire (Roman), then a world religion (Catholic), and now globalism—a world corporate network. This idea of order is destructive, however, for two reasons: (1) Because when they outgrow human scale, corporations lose sight— let's be precise: the people in them lose sight—of the larger picture and of humane values. They end up doing anything for profits (there are some exceptions to this, but not many) and are no longer even aware of what they're doing to the earth and the people in their way. (2) Because it just isn't right to corporatize people, not to mention nature; it leaves no room for our diversity. So the corporate world order will one day have to go the way of the world empire, the world church, and the yet-unrealized idea of a top-down world federation. Dr. Shiva's enthusiasm is that she may be seeing that day's dawn. As she often says, "I think the movement is stronger than it realizes and that corporate rule is more vulnerable than we imagine."

Shortly before he passed away, the much-missed E. F. Schumacher, author of *Small Is Beautiful*, came to Berkeley, and I had him in to talk to my students. His first remark as he gazed around the featureless, underground classroom was, "Look how much trouble we've taken to get away from light and air so we can spend so much money to pipe them in again." I remembered this a few years later when a Russian chess master was pitted against a computer. This computer had been dubbed "Hal," if I recall. I was not fooled. Along with practically everyone else, I rejoiced when the wretched machine went down in ignominious defeat. In high school my friends and I had often sung

"John Henry" to approximate guitar chords and more enthusiasm than musicianship. John Henry, the legendary "driver" of railroad ties, was pitted against the new steam drill everyone secretly hoped would not outdrive him.

> John Henry, he drove his fourteen foot.
> Steamdrill, it drove only nine,
> Lord God, steamdrill, it drove only nine!

But think about the absurdity of it all: who built the nasty steam drill/computer in the first place? Did it arrive from Mars, or slouch up on land from a Jurassic swamp? Why do we work so hard to do something we hope will fail? I have no answer to that question, but I do know one thing: it means that we are not as committed to bleaching the world of life and diversity as we think we are, and that gives us hope that the corporate Goliath has a soft forehead—I'm sorry, has a soft heart that can be won over by the modern David's nonviolent witness.

Native Wisdom

The Chipko movement began in the seventies when Sunderlal Bahuguna, a Gandhian coworker, helped mobilize the villagers of the Uttarkhand district of the lower Himalayas to resist the government-inspired deforestation that had left the forest bereft of its native trees, robbing the villagers of not only their livelihood but often their very lives when they stood helpless before each season's disastrous floods. To a significant extent, the villagers, mostly women, have recovered control of their lands and their message has spread far beyond the Garhwal slopes to be a hope to nonviolent environmental movements everywhere. I said the Chipko movement began in the seventies, but you could also say it goes back centuries. In truth, it was only brought back to life in the sixties by the Gandhian spark: women and men had sacrificed themselves en masse, and successfully, when the maharaja of

Jodhpur came for the trees in 1731. It was reborn on March 27, 1973, when someone at a village meeting, possibly an old man, remembered an important piece of folk wisdom: "When a leopard attacks a child the mother takes the onslaught on her own body."[4]

It is not a coincidence that the Chipko Andolan ("movement") has indigenous roots. We were less violent when we were closer to nature. Nor is it only environmental struggles that have mined this resource. In other domains as well, the search for a nonviolent future is being carried forward by thinkers and activists who are rediscovering, or daring to draw upon, wisdom that industrialism made us forget. This is conspicuously true in the domain called criminal justice. Many cultures had much more restorative concepts of reconciliation in place before dehumanizing modernity overtook them, and are seeking to reassert them against their industrial overlay. It is happening from Canada to New Zealand, from the Victim Offender Reconciliation Program (VORP) to the Family Group Conferencing (FRG) meetings that combine modern restorative approaches with Maori ones to bring about a marked reduction in recidivism among young people.[5] "I was reminded of my traditional way of dealing with crime, actually referred to as 'brokenness,'" wrote a Methodist theology student from Kenya. "The elders recognized that a punishment that led to bitterness was counterproductive for healing a 'broken' person. Justice was supposed to be for preservation of life, not its destruction . . . punishment was always imposed for the purpose of enhancing the life of the person in community."[6]

Closer to home, Hon. Robert Yazzie is the chief justice of the Navajo Nation. Like many of his community, he only discovered after graduating from Oberlin and the New Mexico School of Law that an alternative to the galling system of justice that relies on hierarchies and power and aims at punishment (and produces alienation) lay right at his doorstep. Much of what he says about Navajo concepts echoes what we have been seeing throughout this book:

> Navajo concepts of justice are related to healing
> because many of the principles are the same. . . .

Navajo healing works through two processes: first, it drives away or removes the cause of the illness; and second, it restores the person to good relations in solidarity with his or her surroundings and self.

Navajo justice . . . favors methods which use solidarity to restore good relations among people. Most importantly, it restores good relations with self.[7]

In the restored, and restorative, Navajo system there are third-party mediators chosen by the community to bring about reconciliation between the community and the offender. The mediators are called "peacemakers." They are chosen on the basis of their reverence for life, and, to make Pepinsky's and Quinney's dream of "criminology as peacemaking" complete, the new legal institution set up for them is called the Navajo Peacemaker Court.

It is unwise to romanticize about the unspoiled past. Many of the conflict-avoidance mechanisms developed in preindustrial societies are unworkable in our enormous, complex current societies, and some, which worked for countless centuries before, collapsed when they encountered modernity. But it would be even more unwise to ignore gems of traditional wisdom that glitter in societies across the world. We can use them to brighten our own approaches to conflict resolution, peace, criminal justice, sports (many cultures had non-competitive ones), the environment, and any part of life that has been damaged by alienation.

The effort to recover these useful culture ways will be—it already is to some extent—itself an act of healing, for it throws a bridge of mutual respect across a relationship that has massively ruptured from its absence, the relationship of vulnerable, simpler cultures and the industrialized world that is still, in some guises, trying to exploit them.

After all is said and done, we are all human whether we live in an urban or a natural jungle; and wherever we are, compassion works and hatred destroys. Somewhere in Georgia in the early part of the nineties two white youths killed a black youth, and the Southern

Poverty Law Center helped bring them to justice. The mother of the dead boy was there in the courtroom when they were tried and convicted. One of those young men broke down on the stand. He looked at her and said, sobbing, "I only hope that someday you'll be able to forgive me."

She said, "Son, I've already forgiven you."

"Lay hold of goodness, not justice," wrote Saint Isaac of Syria. "Have clemency, not zeal, with respect to evil."[8]

I would like to conclude with three principles that can help us systematically follow what that mother did, so that we can participate in the great project of liberating life from violence, as Vandana Shiva says, "no matter who we are, no matter where we are."

(1) When William James wrote his classic essay on the "moral equivalent of war" in 1911, he definitely had *part* of the right idea, that the only way to take the inevitability out of war was to give young people something else to do with their restless energy. But what?

> If now—and this is my idea—there were, instead of military conscription a conscription of the whole youthful population to form . . . a part of the army enlisted against Nature. . . . They would have paid their blood-tax, done their part in the immemorial human warfare against nature; they would tread the earth more proudly.[9]

It is sobering to realize how in half a century the "immemorial" struggle against nature turned out to be a shockingly wrong approach to life. What could have saved James from that error? If he had known that nonviolence is a law threading through *every* relationship. The nonviolent writ runs everywhere; we have to start it in the imagery of our minds and spread outward to include everything that lives. As an Indian sage said, "If we don't see God in all, we don't see God at all." No substituting a war on nature for a war on people, no substituting television violence for real violence—not if we want to know real peace. Among many groups and organizations that have picked up the echo of nonviolence today, there is at least one that aims specifically at this universality, calling itself the Seamless Garment Network. I do like that image. It reminds me of Pepinsky's idea of "weaving combatants, weakest victims first, back into a social fabric"[10] and Stuart Cowan's call to "the great work of reweaving the human economy, process by process, product by product, industry by industry, back into the Earth economy."[11]

First principle: *a seamless nonviolent ethic toward all life and a nonviolent praxis for every life-threatening problem.*

(2) Remember that means and ends are one and indivisible. Some still see no contradiction in using violence to protect the earth, the unborn, the lab animal in its cage. We can sympathize, but these reactions are self-defeating (as Earth First! discovered from experience). Spiking trees, bombing clinics, hurling insults at researchers, or parading around with gruesome photos of lab animals being tortured —those means spread the poison they are intended to defeat. Taken to extremes, this would be like Ted Kaczynski blowing up people with technology to defeat technologism. It was on this note that we began this book, was it not? *We have to be against not this kind or that kind of violence, but violence.*

It is a big demand, but remember that the time is ripe. After the terrorist attacks on the U.S. embassies in Africa in 1998, the knee-jerk reaction swiftly followed: bomb somebody. This time, though, the press here and there felt visibly uncomfortable. There was even a headline that read, as I recall, "Strikes: Futile but Essential." Are you OK with that logic? Neither is anyone else, really.

(3) And thirdly, *remember that nonviolence is a science.* We do need the naive profundity Flaubert appreciated in Wright's painting. We need to look at life with the sensitivity of children *and* to protect it with the sophistication of very well-informed adults—the innocence of doves and the cunning of serpents. In the modern age that, for better or worse, we inhabit, we will not succeed by doing nonviolence on a hunch (though we'll get further than being violent on a hunch). We

need a compelling logic that both lights up the path and reveals pitfalls. Imagine if we thought, for example, that the parable of that forgiving mother in Georgia meant we should let all those who offend against life walk free. Not at all. We forgive totally in our hearts (or strive for that ideal), but when others' violence is out of control they—and we—have to be kept out of their own harm's way. Yes, forgive, for your own sake if none other. Yes, use forgiveness to rehumanize and reconcile. But don't put people in harm's way before they've had a chance to regain their sanity. And above all, remember that our nonviolence will not be complete unless we follow through and ask ourselves, all right, what caused this problem? Where are the unseen connections here? What can we do to stop such horrors happening again?

Paul and Annie are as down-home as you can get. When I spent two days on their farm in central Michigan—two days without store-bought food or mass media—I learned a lot about community-supported agriculture, for the Community Farm they've run for a decade or more is no mere family operation, nor is it a for-profit business (though Paul and Annie are quite well off, within the range of their sensible needs). Both committed meditators, these founders of Community Farm (think *fœrm,* in the broad *a* of the northern Midwest) have given birth to an institution as important as it is unpretentious, for it represents a parallel economic universe that is happening in scattered pockets all over North America. On farms, in communities, in vegetarian co-ops, and sometimes enclaved in the wilds of a big city, people who are often barely twenty years old are walking away from the money economy and its values, not unlike the way we did in the sixties—only with a lot more practical know-how. Paul and Annie may look folksy, but they also travel the world lecturing on the new/old science of biodynamics.

The nonviolence of Community Farm goes deep, Annie explained. "There's the whole practice of replenishing the earth as you live off it, so that while you get your nutrition *it* too gets more nourishing, not less." It occurred to me that this goal goes even beyond "sustainable." And later, helping Paul and Annie feed, water, milk, and talk to their four cows (I did pretty well on the milking, for a Brooklyn boy), I was deeply impressed with their relationship with animals. "We have no idea how much we've lost," my friend Steve later reflected. "Apartheid wasn't just in South Africa, and it isn't just about people." By removing animals from our streets and from our sight, by relegating them to zoos and circuses, we lose, they lose, and even the economy loses. Violence gains. As the philosopher Porphyry, a student of the great mystic Plotinus and the first in the West to write extensively about vegetarianism, said, "For he who abstains from [harming] every thing animated . . . will be much more careful not to injure those of his own species. . . . But he who confines justice to man alone, is prepared, like one in a narrow space, to hurl from him the prohibition of injustice."[12]

What I visited those two days was nonviolent agriculture. As Annie put it, "We don't hate—not the aphids, the viruses, or even the rats." Which doesn't mean they tolerate the rats. It was one thing when the sleek rodents ate the cow's grain and their own vegetables, but when they started trotting out their families to meet the visiting children ("Oh look, Mommy, what an interesting woodchuck!"), Paul and Annie had to do something. They did something, but they didn't hate. They used poison—once, in an emergency (the children, after all), and then they tried an ancient, improbable remedy, throwing together ingredients, that sounded to me more like the witches of *Macbeth* at work than science (biodynamic farmers call it the "woo-woo factor"), and it worked. There's not a rat in sight. "Even if we had gophers," Annie predicted, "we wouldn't hate them."

These are exciting times.

Of Hope and Practice: Five Steps to Your Own Nonviolent Future

A friend of mine was in Washington not long ago to lobby for the proposed Department of Peace (HR 1673). One evening she stepped into a hotel elevator to find four men in military garb, obviously there on a similar but opposite mission. They fell to talking, and the men explained what *they* were lobbying for—a new weapons system; what was she there for? When she told them brightly it was for a Department of Peace, one of the men, who had been silently staring at the floor the whole time, looked up and said, with much emotion, "Please hurry."

The war system and the whole pyramid of violence on which it rests can seem unshakable, but it is weak from its own internal contradictions. Peace has friends everywhere; nobody really wants violence unless he or she has not heard or cannot grasp the power of the alternative. The war system—and the materialism on which it rests—could give way quickly before the felt presence of a better world. Nonetheless, we visionaries have much to do to make that alternative a felt reality.

I was, therefore, very pleased when, on the campuses, in the churches, bookstores, and other places I've spoken since the first edition of this book appeared, there was always someone, speaking for many perhaps, asking me, "Yes, but what can I *do* about this?" The unprecedented success of *MoveOn's 50 Ways to Love Your Country* shows the same thing on a wider scale: we Americans are ready to act to save our democracy and our destiny. Accordingly, I came up with five things every one of us can do to play our part in the search party for a nonviolent future. They all come directly from the principles we've discovered in the course of this book, especially the arch principle that nonviolence (like its opposite) begins within us and moves out from the personal to the political. In fact, to act on this realization itself begins to end the big lie of the violent world we live in, namely, that you and I are not important as individuals, that we achieve significance only as corporations, governments, or some group identity. Totalitarianism—which is violence in its political form—strives "not toward despotic rule over men," in Hannah Arendt's chilling words, "but toward a system in which men are superfluous." The first step into a nonviolent future is taken when we put women and men—the individual—back at the very source of all change and power. It would, of course, make the system a little less bad to pass better laws, and we should do that. But if what we want is a whole *new* system, we can only grow it from within, which we do when we embody, promote, and enjoy the life of nonviolence.

This is not to say that the suggestions that follow have to be taken up strictly in order. We can write letters to our congresspeople before we have totally given up television (yes, I'm leading up to that). We can work on these suggestions when and as opportunities arise. But it's good to remember that without a good *base* in step one we won't get very far with step two, etc. Think of them as being in order of priority, if not of time.

1. Truth in Thinking

My dad, God bless him, wanted us to be the last family in my neighborhood to buy a television set. At the time I resented this no end. But I now know that he was not only motivated by, shall we say, his fiscal conservancy. He also had an intuitive sense of values. When he did finally let us install the big box on the porch off our living room, he had me build in a toggle switch so we could cut out the sound during commercials. There's nothing like the sight of an actor soundlessly trying to wax ecstatic over chewing gum to give one an ironic distance from the world of advertising. It has lasted my whole life.

So perhaps it was, thanks to Dad, relatively easy for me to keep commercialism, and the values of materiality and competition that it leads to, at arm's length. Even so, it required a lot of effort and self-knowledge and alertness even for me. I heard recently that the average city dweller is exposed to 30,000 commercial messages a day. Remember, every one of those messages has a subtext that, in one way or another, resonates with the value system that belongs to a world of violence. Too many of us (I would say one is too many) live a virtual life instead of a real life, are driven by a lust for excitement instead of a search for fulfillment. Too many of us come to regard others and finally ourselves as objects. And I say, paraphrasing Attenborough's Gandhi, "It must be fought."

But how?

Individually, of course. Individual, family, circle of friends—tomorrow the world. And today it's much easier to disengage from the commercial mass media than it was when I soldered my toggle switch into the sound system of the family's primitive TV, even though the mass media are now more sophisticated and powerful and ubiquitous. Because today we have an alternative: the ever-expanding world of independent, alternative media.

Almost none of the key stories you have read in this book came my way through the mass media. How could they? They came partly from my personal contacts in the peace movement, partly from books, largely from local independent news sources like the *North Bay Progressive*—a high-quality paper with a circulation of about 1,000 folks in the Sonoma Coast region, and—for in-depth commentary by distinguished, in-the-field journalists—sources like the *New York Review of Books*. These, plus a steady flow of blogs and e-mails that have to be expertly skimmed, yield priceless information not available from mainstream sources. I do read, selectively, the local paper. And that's about it. That's about my only voluntary exposure to the commercial mass media. Yet I consider myself pretty well informed. When my students say, "Man, are you out of it," they are usually not thinking about current events but what seem to them my quaint moral attitudes about certain things.

Which leads me to the other function of the mass media: entertainment. We need it, but we're not getting it from the media. Agitation and the further fragmentation of our minds, already reeling from what Gandhi called the "multiplication of wants" in our current value system, are not entertainment. I have discovered a superb alternative that is real entertainment: *people.* Friends. Friends can be a pain in the neck at times, but they're real. They're people; they're what life is all about. I will come back to this in suggestion number three, but by spending time on relationships on the one hand and finding our personal repertoire of alternative media on the other, we can position ourselves to let the cord that binds us to the hollow ideas of commercial civilization gradually thin, and snap. Concretely, suggestion number one is, cultivate substitutes for and *then divest ourselves of exposure to the big mass media.* Don't watch TV. It's that simple, and that powerful.

2. Taking Care of Ourselves Spiritually

On September 20, 2001, the Peace Studies students put on a teach-in at Berkeley to discuss 9/11 and the impending disastrous response of our government. It was, as you might imagine, a hugely successful and emotionally charged meeting. The high point came when Rabbi Michael Lerner said what was in the back of many minds that evening: "This is a spiritual crisis." He got a standing ovation. When E. F. Schumacher said we need a "metaphysical reconstruction," when Martin Luther King said we need a "revolution of values," they were saying the same thing.

Spiritual crises call for spiritual remedies. That's why I spent some time describing meditation in chapter 3, and why I talk about it whenever I get the chance. As a friend of mine said at a conference recently, "Television is the perfect antidote to meditation." The reverse is just as true. Those 30,000 commercial messages I referred to agitate our minds whether we want them to or not; they infect us with a frenetic excitement about things that do not matter and, what may be worse, with an indifference toward people, who do. Even if we can take the cold-turkey remedy for TV and the movies, it will require a bit more for us to regain our balance and become aware of the hope that's hiding in the midst of all the turmoil. We need live contact with inner peace.

The good news about meditation is its incredible promise. The bad news is its fiendish difficulty. Helpfully, meditation is coming in for overdue attention in the mainstream today, not only as a way to health, which it is, but in a raft of scientific studies that show the evolutionary predisposition of the human being to selflessness.[1] Health, the successful coping with stress, is the first fruit of a spiritual practice. There are many others. But in the end, spirituality is a highly individual thing, and I should leave you with the encouragement to undertake your own exploration, and refer you again to the one resource I personally find most inspiring, my own Blue Mountain Center. However you choose to explore your path, and you should choose it with some care, I encourage you to search out some reliable discipline that enables you to find, and in the end reside in, that state of inner peace that wisdom assures us is our heritage.

3. Truth in Relating

The first step on the Buddha's eightfold path is "Right View." I have addressed this now with my first two suggestions. He also said, "Trust is the best of relationships." We go further from trust with every new "security" measure we employ. We go further from it every time we get cynical.

This is all a sad part of the dehumanization that I've frequently cited as a root cause of violence. The good news is that as individuals we can do a lot to repersonalize, which means to rehumanize, our lives. Often it only requires the conscious effort to go through the "convenient" barriers to communication in our lives. Call instead of write, meet and talk instead of calling, give people your complete attention when they talk to you, and consciously avoid what we euphemistically call "incivility"; more honestly, it's a form of that distancing, which is always a distant precursor to violence.

Let me share a small trick with you, because nothing you can do in the way of relating more deeply to others is really small. I meet many people, in widely different contexts—students, other peace activists, meditators, and fellow bus passengers. It's not easy to remember so many names! But I've noticed that there's a certain timing to forgetting someone's name: if you can fetch it back just as it's disappearing over the edge of memory, you can hold onto it much longer. Accordingly, after I've met someone I will often remind myself of who they are a few minutes after the conversation. That was Jack, right? Very helpful.

So along with those "random acts of kindness," practice revolutionary civility. Find creative ways to live in a human world instead of a world of objects, in a world of ever-expanding and yet deepening relationships.

This is an extremely rewarding challenge. We are rehumanizing the world with every conversation, every encounter. We are also enhancing our own health, as numerous studies show—but it's always the case that when we do the right thing its benefits spread out in all directions.

4. Nonviolence Literacy

Congratulations! You are (I like to think) well into point four already if you read this book. Seriously, however, in this day and age anyone who cannot perceive, understand, and evaluate a nonviolent event is not educated, whatever letters trail behind his or her name. Educational institutions are slowly beginning to recognize this need. We can applaud their efforts, but we cannot afford to wait for them to catch up, nor need we wait for them. *Learn and share the basics of nonviolence*—its history, its logic, and its promise.

We also learn by doing in this field, of course, but it will go far toward changing our culture if we can simply detect and understand what Gandhi called "the greatest force mankind has been endowed with."[2]

5. Action for Peace

The war system, seemingly ubiquitous in our culture, our budget, our circumscribed vision of the possible, is really nothing more than an endlessly propped-up house of cards. Every time we try to solve a problem militarily, its counterproductiveness becomes more obvious, and the alternative becomes more appealing. We who would help to make that alternative real should remember always that every human heart holds within it an unquenchable longing for peace, a longing that Saint Augustine hymned so beautifully in Book Nineteen of his *City of God* and that we still vaguely sense even over the din of war. The very uselessness of war in this age of terrorism helps bring that eternal longing closer to our grasp.

Yet the war system is everywhere, and we are few, and we must know how to direct our efforts for maximum effect. Fortunately, the perspective of nonviolence offers pretty clear guidelines for doing that.

- *Always look for articulate, positive alternatives.* Especially in writing or speaking, the temptation is to start by making our opponents feel guilty, but that kind of start is usually also the end of the conversation. Toynbee said that Gandhi "made it impossible for us to go on ruling India, but at the same time he made it possible for us to abdicate . . . without dishonour."[3] It is our job to point a way out. We are not in this to feel good (steps one through four address that), but to make the world better. Just as a constructive program has a natural priority over an obstructive program, though each has its place, so positive alternatives obviate much of the need to condemn or blame others. Always remember our silent friend in the elevator.

  It was also Toynbee to whom is attributed the oft-quoted observation that "apathy can only be overcome by enthusiasm, and enthusiasm can only be aroused by two things: first, an ideal which takes the imagination by storm, and second, a definite, intelligible plan for carrying that ideal into practice." Nonviolence definitely takes the imagination by storm, the moment we begin to grasp what it really is. Where we need more work is the "definite, intelligible plan," or plans, to show its applications to peace in all its aspects. One superb framework for doing this is the Five Hundred Year Plan for peace developed by the Sarvodaya organization of Sri Lanka (for impatient Westerners, a hundred-year plan may have to do). A more direct answer to the war system is, of course, the Nonviolent Peaceforce—see Resources and Opportunities for both, and www .transformingviolence.org for a database of peace organizations.

- *Don't place much emphasis on or hope in projects that are symbolic only.* This is especially true if the intensity of the problem has developed past phase one of the escalation curve that we described in chapter 4.

- *Don't put all your energy into a single-issue campaign that's not likely to resonate with our overall aim: to create a nonviolent culture.* Saving the turtles is worthwhile in itself, but won't help much if we're losing the oceans. Saving the turtles by a conspicuous use of creative, principled nonviolence will be more helpful, since those effects will resonate with the "revolution of values."

- *Never sacrifice the future for the present.* Violent solutions do that so characteristically; think of how we have laced Afghanistan and Iraq with depleted uranium (DU), in order to destroy a tank or break into a bunker during a given battle. DU poisons the ground and water for a quarter of a million years! A project informed by principled nonviolence will never do this; on the contrary, its good effects will go on multiplying. So wherever you choose to grapple with the juggernaut of war—be it the military budget, exposing war crimes that are often carried out in our name in some remote part of the world, counseling conscientious objectors, or refusing to pay taxes for war—try to find projects that carry forward into the future. As mentioned, to the extent that we engage principled nonviolence on anything, it will resonate with nonviolence generally, and so we will be able to, in Mathew Arnold's poignant phrase, "keep up our own communication with the future."[4] We are in it for the long haul.

- *Reach out.* Way out, if you're up for it. I went to the extent of letting myself be interviewed on two of the hate radio programs that are doing so much damage around the country. It was an exercise in masochism, if not futility. But if this is too much, find someone—the mail carrier, your brother-in-law, someone at work—and learn to reason with him or her, politely but confidently. America is breaking down into isolated groups, and it is up to us to build bridges across them, because those whom violence has in its grip will not. The logic of violence does not stand up to the light of reason. Patient and compassionate communication is bound to succeed on some level.

Here is a wallet-sized version of what we've just covered:

- Use alternative media (and commercial media only with extreme care)

- Take care of yourself spiritually

- Relate kindly and personally to others

- Learn nonviolence

- Build peace

Notes and References

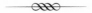

CWMG = *The Collected Works of Mahatma Gandhi*, CD-ROM (New Delhi: Government of India). (See Resources for more information.) Most quotations from Gandhi are drawn from this source. If they can also be found in readily available books, these sources are listed in addition.

Preface

1 The Talk of the Town, *New Yorker*, September 16, 2002, 32.
2 Krystal Kyer, 27, member of the Olympia Movement for Justice and Peace (OMJP), e-mail.
3 Jane Perlez, *New York Times*, September 11, 2002. Filing her report from Cairo, Perlez added, "The resolve of President Bush to use force against Iraq, they say, compounds the antagonism, which is expressed with particularly unvarnished dismay in Egypt and neighboring Jordan, Washington's crucial Arab allies."
4 Paul H. Ray and Sherry Ruth Anderson, *The Cultural Creatives: How 50 Million People Are Changing the World* (New York: Three Rivers, 2001).

Introduction

1 Alan Weisman, *Gaviotas: A Village to Reinvent the World* (White River Junction, Vermont: Chelsea Green, 1998), back cover.
2 Ibid., 14, 175–76.
3 Ibid., 33. For further information, see http://friendsofgaviotas.org/about.htm.

Chapter One

1 Hannah Arendt, *On Violence* (New York: Harcourt, Brace & World, 1969), 6.
2 *CWMG*, vol. 53, 354. Also in *Harijan* (April 14, 1946): 90.
3 Jacques Ellul, *Contre les Violents* (Vienna: Le Centurion, 1972), 7.
4 William Johnston, trans., *The Cloud of Unknowing* (New York: Doubleday, Image 1973), 129.
5 John W. Burton, *Violence Explained: The Sources of Conflict, Violence and Crime and Their Prevention* (Manchester: University of Manchester Press, 1997), 10.
6 Joel R. Davitz, "The Effects of Previous Training on Postfrustration Behavior," *Journal of Abnormal Social Psychology* 47 (1952): 309–15.
7 Ben Ngubane, Associated Press, July 27, 1998.
8 David Sobel and Robert Ornstein, "Bad News on TV Is Bad News All Around," *Mental Medicine Update* IV.1 (1995) 1.
9 Joel Goleman, "Today's Lesson: Curbing Kids' Violent Emotions," *San Francisco*

Chronicle, March 5, 1992, D3, D6.

10 Daniel Schorr, "TV Violence: What We Know but Ignore," *Christian Science Monitor*, September 7, 1993, 19.

11 Andre Brink, "*Time* Magazine's 100 Leaders and Revolutionaries of the 20th Century," *Time* 151, no. 14, 1998, 188–90.

12 Fatima Meer, *Higher than Hope: The Authorized Biography of Nelson Mandela* (New York: Harper & Row, 1990), 218–20.

13 John Daniszewski, Associated Press, "Mandela, de Klerk Debate," *Santa Rosa Press Democrat*, April 15, 1984, A5.

14 *CWMG*, vol. 75, 409.

15 David Remnick, "Dumb Luck: Bush's Cold War," *New Yorker*, January 25, 1993, 105.

16 E-mail to Peacemedia mailing list (peacemedia@gn.apc.org), Peacenet Conference, September 28, 1991 .

17 British independent TV journalist Gaby Rado quoted on location, *Washington Spectator,* February 1, 1994, 2.

18 This quote and the next from a Sonoma County school newsletter, *Kid Konnection*, July 1994, 21.

19 See Lt. Col. Dave Grossman and Gloria Degaetano, *Stop Teaching Our Kids to Kill: A Call to Action against TV, Movie and Video Game Violence* (New York: Random House, 1999), and Kara Platoni, "The Pentagon Goes to the Video Arcade," *The Progressive*, July 1999, 27.

20 Wendell Berry, *Standing by Words* (San Francisco: North Point, 1983), 65.

21 *Isha Upanishad*, verse 12 (my translation).

22 Rich'ard Magee, quoted in *Youth Outlook*, September 11–15, 1995, 6.

23 Heraclitus frag. B 45: "You will never reach the limits of the soul [or, life principle], travel as far as you will by any road: so deep is its meaning" (my translation).

24 Robert Sanders, "Berkeley, LBNL Scientists Snap First 3-D Pictures of the 'Heart' of the Genetic Transcription Machine," *Berkeleyan*, January 19–25, 2000, 3.

25 Quoted in Steven Glazer, *The Heart of Learning* (New York: Jeremy P. Tarcher/ Putnam, 1999), 218.

26 Fyodor Dostoevsky, *The Possessed* (New York: The Heritage Press, 1959), 571. Though this sentiment is put in the mouth of an unlikely character, there is no doubt Dostoevsky himself subscribed to it.

27 Dorothy Conniff, "Day Care: A Grand and Troubling Social Experiment," *Utne Reader* (reprinted from *The Progressive*), May/June 1993, 67.

Chapter Two

1 L. Mahoney and L. Eguren, *Unarmed Bodyguards: International Accompaniment for*

the Protection of Human Rights (West Hartford, CT: Kumarian, 1997), 176.

2   I am drawing in this section on verbal reports from several PBI workers (this story was well known in PBI circles before Mahoney's and Eguren's important book appeared).

3   Kenneth E. Boulding, *Three Faces of Power* (Newbury Park, CA: Sage, 1989).

4   Ibid., 10.

5   David V. Erdman, ed., *The Poetry and Prose of William Blake* (Garden City, NY: Doubleday, 1970), 36.

6   Saint Augustine, *The City of God* XIX:12 (my translation).

7   Charleton Lewis and Charles Short, *A Latin Dictionary* (Oxford: Oxford University Press, 1962), s.v. "Violare."

8   Jacques Lusseyran, *And There Was Light* (New York: Parabola, 1987), 178.

9   Mt. 5:21–22.

10 Johan Galtung, "Violence, Peace, and Peace Research," *Journal of Peace Research* 6, no. 3 (1969): 168–70. Galtung restated this definition several times elsewhere, with minor changes.

11 See Rachel M. Macnair, *Perpetration-Induced Traumatic Stress* (Westport, CT: Praeger, 2002). Also see her *The Psychology of Peace* (Westport, CT: Praeger, 2003).

12 Saint Augustine, *Confessions* I:xviii (my translation).

13 See Everett Worthington, ed., *Dimensions of Forgiveness: Psychological Research and Theological Perspectives* (Radnor, PA: Templeton Foundation Press, 1998); and Michael E. McCullough, Kenneth I. Pargament, and Carl E. Thoresen, eds., *Forgiveness: Theory, Research, and Practise* (New York: Guilford Press, 2000).

14 *San Francisco Chronicle*, July 8, 1997, A4, citing an article from the *Los Angeles Times*.

15 *Medical Abstracts Newsletter*, 1993.

16 Cf. Robert L. Ivie, "Metaphor and the Rhetorical Invention of Cold War 'Idealists,'" *Communication Monographs* 54 (1954): 165–81.

17 Associated Press, *Los Angeles Times*, August 11, 1993, B7.

18 Deborah Prothrow-Stith, *Harvard Alumni Gazette*, April 23, 1992, 23.

19 Ibid., 24.

20 Swami Ramdas, *Ramdas Speaks*, vol. III (Bombay: Bharatiya Vidya Bhavan, 1957), 149.

21 See Pam McAllister, *You Can't Kill the Spirit: Women and Nonviolent Action* (Philadelphia: New Society, 1988), 9. The reference here is to Western writers: the word appeared earlier, of course, in Gandhi's English writings or translations.

22 Cf. the following quote from Roshi Jiyu Kennet, "Buddhism states what the Eternal is not. (I use the term Eternal rather than God. God has the implication of being a deity with a beard and a long stick.) It does not state what it is because if it did we would be stuck with a concept. Buddhism states specifically what we know for certain. It will not state that which is taken on faith. We can

find this out for ourselves . . . but we cannot state what it is." Lenore Friedman, *Meetings with Remarkable Women* (Boston: Shambala, 1957), 168.

23 James D. Hunt, *Gandhi and the Nonconformists* (New Delhi: Promilla, 1986), 54–56.

24 *CWMG*, vol. 34, 94. Also see *Satyagraha in South Africa* (Ahmadabad: Navajiovan, 1928), 103.

25 Ibid.

26 Ibid.

27 Robert I. Friedman, "An Unholy Rage," *New Yorker*, May 7, 1994, 54. Friedman's claim is misleading in another respect as well: the settlers' actions he cites are only symbolic. As we'll see, this isn't Gandhian either.

28 Frans de Waal, *Peacemaking among Primates* (Cambridge: Harvard University Press, 1989), 1.

29 Bill Bailey, *America's Good News Almanac* (New York: Simon and Schuster, Pocket Books, 1996), 40–42.

30 *CWMG*, vol. 34, 267.

31 Pyarelal, *The Epic Fast* (Ahmadabad: Navajivan, 1932), 35.

32 Brandon Astor Jones, "Cell 38," *New Internationalist*, no. 294 (1997): 35.

33 Hannah Arendt, *On Violence* (New York: Harcourt, Brace & World, 1969), 80.

34 Marshall Frady, "The Outsider, II," *New Yorker*, March 10, 1992, 70.

35 *CWMG*, vol. 30, 66–67.

36 *CWMG*, vol. 9, 392.

37 See chapter 8 for more on this strange similarity between "new" physics and nonviolence.

38 Harold E. Pepinsky, *The Geometry of Violence and Democracy* (Bloomington: Indiana University Press, 1991), 44.

39 Ibid., 127.

40 M. K. Gandhi, *Hind Swaraj, or Indian Home Rule* (Ahmadabad: Navajivan, 1938), 70.

41 Frans de Waal, *Peacemaking among Primates*, 233.

42 John Dominic Crossan, *The Historical Jesus: The Life of a Mediterranean Jewish Peasant* (San Francisco: Harper Collins, 1991), 130–32.

43 Ibid., 136. See also Keith Akers, *The Lost Religion of Jesus: Simple Living and Nonviolence in Early Christianity* (New York: Lantern Books, 2000). Gandhi once observed that the only people who are not aware that Jesus was nonviolent are the Christians.

44 Louise B. Young, "Easter Island: Scary Parable," *World Monitor*, August 1991, 45.

Chapter Three

1 Staughton Lynd, *Nonviolence in America* (Indianapolis: Bobbs Merrill, 1966), 525–26. (See chapter 4, note 25, for the new edition of this valuable

resource.)

2 Yehudah Mirsky, "Jewish Perspectives," in *Perspectives on Pacifism*, David R. Smock, ed. (Washington, DC: U.S. Institute of Peace, 1995), 23. I cannot subscribe to Mirsky's commonplace interpretation of nonviolence as passive, but I otherwise recommend this perceptive article.

3 From the film *A Time for Justice* (Atlanta: Teaching Tolerance, 1992).

4 "I Refuse to Live in Fear," *San Francisco Examiner Parade*, October 23, 1994, 22–23.

5 Eva Fogelman, *Conscience and Courage* (New York: Anchor Doubleday, 1994), 6, 59.

6 Michael Henderson, *All Her Paths Are Peace: Women Pioneers in Peacemaking* (West Hartford, CT: Kumarian Press, 1994), 162.

7 *CWMG*, vol. 5, 335. Also in *Satyagraha in South Africa*, op. cit., 100.

8 Cf. Stephen Zunes, "The Origins of People Power in the Philippines," in *Nonviolent Social Movements: A Geographical Perspective*, Lester Kurtz, Stephen Zunes and Sarah Asher, eds. (Oxford: Blackwell, 2000), 151.

9 Louis Menand, "The War of All Against All," *New Yorker*, March 14, 1994, 74.

10 Eknath Easwaran, *Gandhi the Man* (Petaluma, CA: Nilgiri Press, 1978), 92. Also in *CWMG*, vol. 35, 365.

11 Eva Fogelman, *Conscience and Courage*, 228.

12 Personal communication with author. I was startled to find, after writing this section, that there is actually now "hard" evidence that altruistic behavior causes a "high" like that of taking drugs or doing something intensely pleasurable. Much of the evidence is summarized by Natalie Angier, "Why We're So Nice: We're Wired to Cooperate," *New York Times*, July 23, 2002.

13 "Walking the Talk of Nonviolent Intervention," *Signs of the Times* (Christian Peacemaker Teams newsletter) VI, no. 1, 1996, 2.

14 Solange Muller, talk given to ad hoc organizational meeting for peace teams, New York City, 1992.

15 Harold Flender, *Rescue in Denmark* (New York: Simon & Schuster, 1963), 144.

16 Ibid., 149.

17 Ibid., 148.

18 "An Irish Airman Foresees His Death," *The Collected Poems of W. B. Yeats* (New York: Macmillan, 1955), 133.

19 M. Scott Peck, *The Different Drum: Community Making and Peace* (New York: Simon and Schuster, Touchstone, 1987), 35. See the study by British psychologist Dr. John Drury, titled "Protesting Can Be Good for Your Health," released by Reuters at http://www.eurocbc.org/page582.html.

20 Jawaharlal Nehru, *An Autobiography*, C. D. Narasimhaiah, ed. (Delhi: Oxford, 1936), 91. Also available in paperback from Oxford, 1991.

21 Thich Nhat Hanh, *Love in Action: Writings on Nonviolent Social Change* (Berkeley: Parallax Press, 1973), 71.

22 Personal communication with author.

23 Kevin Weston, "Why I Don't Pack," *Youth Outlook*, Winter 1994, 4.

24 *Michigan Peace Team Bulletin*, Spring 1998, 2.

25 P. V. Narasimha Rao, quoted in *India News*, October 1, 1994.

26 N. Nikam and R. McKeon, trans., *Edicts of Ashoka* (Chicago: University of Chicago Press, 1959), 27–28.

27 Yoga Sutras I.2 (my translation).

28 Whitall N. Perry, *Treasury of Traditional Wisdom* (Cambridge, UK: Quinta Essentia, 1971), 533.

29 Robert Livingston, *Sensory Processing, Perception, and Behavior* (New York: Raven Press, 1978), 8.

30 Swami Ritajananda, *Swami Turiyananda* (Madras: Sri Ramakrishna Math, 1963), 172–73.

31 Lowell Cohn, "Montana Was Cool in the Eye of the Storm," *San Francisco Chronicle*, January 24, 1989, Special Souvenir Section, 2.

32 William James, *Principles of Psychology*, reprinted in *Great Books of the Western World* (Chicago: Encyclopedia Britannica, 1952), 274–75.

33 Marcus Borg, *Jesus: A New Vision* (New York: Harper & Row, 1987), 43–44.

34 Bhagavad Gita VI:vv, 34f (my translation).

35 Eva Fogelman, *Conscience and Courage*, 178.

36 M. K. Gandhi, *All Men Are Brothers* (Ahmadabad: Navajivan, 1960), 111–12. This quote seems not to be in *CWMG*.

Chapter Four

 1 *CWMG*, vol. 81, 358. The full statement is, "This non-violence is not the inanity for which we have mistaken it through all these long ages; it is the most potent force as yet known to mankind and on which its very existence is dependent."

 2 Robert Jewett and John S. Lawrence, *The American Monomyth* (Garden City, NY: Anchor Doubleday, 1977).

 3 A. L. Kellermann and others, "Gun Ownership as a Risk Factor for Homicide in the Home," *New England Journal of Medicine* 329, no. 15 (1993): 1084–91; also Janice Somerville, "Gun Control as Immunization," *American Medical News* (January 3, 1994): 7.

 4 This figure from the U.N. Compensation Commission can be found at www.onog.ch/uncc/claims/e_claims. The cost to the allies was $60 billion, not counting subsequent interventions on behalf of the Kurds *or* the continuing military costs.

 5 Vera Brittain, "Massacre by Bombing," *Fellowship*, March 1944, 50. Also note page 51: *"It is the infliction of suffering, far more than its endurance, which morally damages the soul of a nation."* (her emphasis) This article was reprinted by *Fellowship* in 1996 and may be obtained from the Fellowship of Reconciliation

(see Resources).

6   For studies done after the war, see Ernest R. May, *"Lessons" of the Past* (New York: New York University Press, 1973). See especially page 141f for striking cases of bombing having opposite results from those intended.

7   D. G. Tendulkar, *Mahatma: Life of Mohandas Karamchand Gandhi* (New Delhi: Government of India, 1951), 39.

8   Henri J. M. Nouwen, "Saying No to Death," in *Peace Is the Way,* Walter Wink, ed. (Maryknoll, New York: Orbis Books, 2000), 144.

9   Lt. Col. Dave Grossman, *On Killing: The Psychological Cost of Learning to Kill in War and Society* (New York: Little, Brown and Company, 1996); also see Grossman and DeGaetano, *Stop Teaching Our Kids to Kill.*

10 K. N. Waltz, *Man, the State, and War: A Theoretical Analysis* (New York: Columbia University Press, 1964), 231.

11 William J. Bowers and Glenn Pierce, "Deterrence or Brutalization: What Is the Effect of Executions?," *Crime and Delinquency* 26, no. 4 (1980): 453–84. Twenty years have not changed this. According to Steven Mesaner, criminologist at SUNY Albany, "It is difficult to make a case for any deterrent effect" from recent FBI statistics: see R. Bonner and F. Fessended, "Death Penalty Not Factor in Homicide Rates," *Santa Rosa Press Democrat*, September 22, 2000, A16.

12 Sister Helen Prejean, *Dead Man Walking: An Eyewitness Account of the Death Penalty in the United States* (New York: Random House, 1993), 232.

13 Kevin Weston, *Youth Outlook*, 4.

14 Though her organization was not doing a third-party accompaniment, I must report that, alas, Rachel Corrie, a volunteer with the International Solidarity Movement, was killed by an Israeli bulldozer on March 16, 2003, in the Gaza Strip while courageously trying to prevent the demolition of a Palestinian home. In the following month, Brian Avery, Tom Hurndall, and James Miller were shot, the latter two fatally, by Israeli soldiers while carrying out similar interventions.

15 Martin Luther King Jr. in James M. Washington, *A Testament of Hope* (San Francisco: Harper San Francisco, 1986), 56. On the preceding page, King points out that the sniper at the University of Texas at Austin killed more people in one day than all the people killed in race riots since the Harlem riot of 1964.

16 B. R. Nanda, *Mahatma Gandhi* (Delhi: Oxford University Press, 1958), 167. One other peculiarity deserves mention: the architect of the whole Salt Satyagraha, Gandhi, had sworn off salt at that period!

17 Gernot Jochheim, *Die Gewaltfreie Aktion: Idee und Methoden, Vorbilder und Wirkungen* (Hamburg-Zurich: Rasch und Röhring Verlag, 1984), 262.

18 Nathan Stoltzfus, *Resistance of the Heart: Intermarriage and the Rosenstrasse Protest in Nazi Germany* (New York: Norton, 1996), 215–57, etc.

19 Sergius C. Lorit, *The Last Days of Maximilian Kolbe* (New York: New City Press, 1988), 15–16.

20 Patricia Treece, *A Man for Others* (San Francisco: Harper and Row, 1982), 178.

21 Viktor E. Frankl, *Man's Search for Meaning: An Introduction to Logotherapy*, Ilse Lasch, trans. (Boston: Beacon Press, 1959), 102. My editor, Bernadette Smyth, has kindly brought to my attention that women generally fared better at the camps than the men, not because they were treated any more humanely by their captors but because they took better care of each other: picking lice from children's hair, talking to one another, touching, building community so as to give one another more will to live.

22 For other examples of nonviolence in World War II, see Roger S. Powers and William B. Vogele, eds., *Protest, Power, and Change: An Encyclopedia of Nonviolent Action from ACT-UP to Women's Suffrage* (New York: Garland, 1995), and Jean-Marie Muller, *Vous Avez Dîtes, "Pacifisme"?: De la Menace Nucleaire à la Defense Civile Non-violente* (Paris: Cerf, 1984), especially pages 251f, 265, and 279.

23 *CWMG*, vol. 54, 48. Also in *All Men Are Brothers*, 118.

24 Sudarshan Kapur, *Raising Up a Prophet: The African-American Encounter with Gandhi* (Boston: Beacon, 1992).

25 Staughton Lynd and Alice Lynd, *Nonviolence in America: A Documentary History* (Maryknoll, NY: Orbis, 1995), 2.

26 John B. B. Trussell, *William Penn, Architect of a Nation* (Pennsylvania Historical and Museum Commission, 1983), 37.

27 This fact and the next from Howard Haines Brinton, *Friends for 300 Years: The History and Beliefs of the Society of Friends Since George Fox Started the Quaker Movement* (Wallingford, PA: Pendle Hall Publications and the Philadelphia Yearly Meeting of the Religious Society of Friends, 1965), 151–52.

28 Ibid., 79.

29 *CWMG*, vol. 79, 199.

30 A. L. Basham, *The Wonder That Was India* (Calcutta: Rupa & Co, 1967), 53–55.

31 Alan Weisman, *Gaviotas! A Village to Reinvent the World*, 112–13. Paolo Lugari himself was once kidnapped by the M-19 guerilla faction, but after two days they released him, exhausted by his energy and enthusiasm (Ibid., 101).

32 Gene Sharp, *Making Europe Unconquerable* (Cambridge: Ballinger, 1985); also see *National Security through Civilian-Based Defense* (Omaha: Association for Transarmament Studies, 1985).

33 Petra Kelly, *Thinking Green!* (Berkeley, CA: Parallax Press, 1994), 57–58.

34 Philip Hallie, *Lest Innocent Blood Be Shed* (New York: Harper & Row, 1979), 275. It is interesting to note that Schindler was also from a strongly Catholic family.

35 Ibid., 245.

36 Ibid., 114.

37 Gandhi became a master of the theatrical: his goats in London, the pinch of salt put in his tea with the viceroy—note that both were quite concrete. A case

could be made that some of the protests against the prince of Wales's visit in 1919 were symbolic, but then the whole visit was. To my knowledge, no *proactive* measure of Gandhi's was an empty symbol at any time in his long career (and Arun Gandhi, the Mahatma's grandson, has confirmed this). It's interesting that many symbolic statements made in the peace movement are attempts to monumentalize acts of extreme evil: Hiroshima, Auschwitz, etc. One wonders whether this is consistent with the Gandhian spirit of constructivism and "seeing no evil."

38 See chapter 2, note 34.

39 Tom R. Tyler, *Why People Obey the Law* (New Haven: Yale University, 1990).

40 Albert Szent-Gyeorgyi, *The Crazy Ape* (New York: The Philosophical Library, 1970), 44.

41 M. Sherif, *In Common Predicament* (Washington, DC: Public Affairs Press, 1966).

42 Grossman and DeGaetano, *Stop Teaching Our Kids to Kill*, 127.

43 See note 1.

44 Gordon Fellman, *Rambo and the Dalai Lama* (Albany: State University of New York Press, 1998), 20.

45 Pyarelal and Sushila Nayar, *In Gandhiji's Mirror* (Delhi: Oxford University Press, 1991), 268.

Chapter Five

1 Frank Browning, "Drug Users Defy Stereotypes," *Pacific News Service Newswire* 4:6, 1992, 3.

2 This study was covered by, among others, William Raspberry in the *International Herald Tribune*, February 7, 1988. Similarly, young suicides among Australia's aboriginal communities are predominantly "those who feel and think"; see Michael Gordon, "A Journey into a World Apart," *World Press Review* (reprinted from *The Age*), September 2000, 16.

3 *Youth Outlook*, January/February 1997, 7.

4 *San Francisco Chronicle*, November 10, 1997. The "war" cost $60 million in 1968 before escalating to these levels, with no appreciable difference in result.

5 Cf. Steven R. Donziger, ed., *The Real War on Crime: The Report of the National Criminal Justice Commission* (New York: Harper Collins, 1996), xvii.

6 Harold E. Pepinsky and Richard Quinney, *Criminology as Peacemaking* (Bloomington: Indiana University Press, 1991), 3.

7 Ruth Morris, *Penal Abolition: The Practical Choice* (Toronto: Canadian Scholar's Press, 1995), 5.

8 James M. Washington, ed., *Testament of Hope* (San Francisco: Harper & Row, 1986), 243.

9 Vincent Schiraldi, quoted in *UC Focus* (University of California, Berkeley) 8, no. 6 (1994): 1.

10   Sharon Roberts, "Ex-Offenders Aid World of Disabled," *New York Times*, February 4, 1990, Y33.

11   Ibid.

12   See the *Buffalo Report for March 1, 2002*, at http://buffaloreport.com/020301abbott.html.

13   Ruth Morris, *Penal Abolition*, 33.

14   *CWMG*, vol. 19, 466.

15   Ibid.

16   Arnold Trebacher, interview in *Pacific News Service* editorial, June 24–28, 1991, 2.

17   Harold Pepinsky, "Alternative Social Control Systems" (course syllabus, CJUS P202, Spring 1996).

18   Lila Rucker, "Peacemaking in Prisons: A Process," in Pepinsky and Quinney, *Criminology as Peacemaking*, 174. Rucker is quoting various authorities.

19   Ibid., 177.

20   Ibid., 172. In fact, "correctional" would be a step forward, in some places. The purpose of the California penal system was explicitly changed in 1976 from correctional to punitive. According to a Sonoma County official I interviewed twenty years later, this "regressive" change had no visible impact on the state's crime rate. We now have a system that in fact frequently turns nonviolent offenders into violent ones.

21   Ruth Morris, *Penal Abolition*, 44.

22   Ibid., 46.

23   Richard Woodbury, "A Convict's View: 'People Don't Want Solutions,'" *Time*, August 23, 1993, 33.

24   Katherine Webster, "Verdict, Guilty; Sentence, Literature," *Santa Rosa Press Democrat*, May 31, 1994, A6.

25   Martin Luther King, "Why I Am Opposed to the War in Vietnam" (speech, Atlanta, 3rd Sunday in April, 1967).

26   Cf. the National School Boards report cited in the *Washington Spectator*, January 1, 1993, and Karen S. Peterson quoted in *USA Today*, June 19, 1998.

27   Meyer Friedman and Diane Ulmer, *Treating Type A Behavior—and Your Heart* (New York: Ballantine, Fawcett Crest, 1984), 196.

28   Deepak Chopra, quoted in *Noetic Sciences Review*, no. 28 (Winter, 1993): 19.

29   *Pacific News Service Newswire*, August 9, 1992, 6.

30   *San Francisco Chronicle*, March 18, 1997, A24.

31   Viktor E. Frankl, *Man's Search for Meaning: An Introduction to Logotherapy*, Ilse Lasch, trans. (Boston: Beacon Press, 1959), 101.

32   E. Midlarsky and E. Kahana, *Altruism in Later Life* (Thousand Oaks, CA: Sage Publications, 1994), 79.

33   Reprinted in the *New York Times*, March 29, 1972.

34 Oscar Romero, *The Violence of Love: The Pastoral Wisdom of Archbishop Oscar Romero*, James R. Brockman, trans. (San Francisco: Harper & Row, 1988), 81.

35 Becky Benenate and Joseph Durepos, eds., *No Greater Love* (Novato, CA: New World Library, 1997), 94–95.

Chapter Six

1 *CWMG*, vol. 79, 309.

2 Working Assets mailer, May 1998.

3 Johnson Foundation mailer reprinted from *Wingspread Journal*, Spring 1997.

4 *CWMG*, vol. 34, 42. Also in *Satyagraha in South Africa*, op. cit., 43.

5 *CWMG*, vol. 10, 283. Also in *Hind Swaraj, or Indian Home Rule*, op. cit., 60.

6 *CWMG*, vol. 24, 77.

7 Conversation with Tara Bhattacharjee, published in the East Bay newsletter *Gandhi Mela* VII, 1995, 19.

8 M. Sherif, *In Common Predicament* (Washington, DC: Public Affairs Press, 1966).

9 B. R. Nanda, *India News,* October 1, 1994, 11.

10 D. G. Tendulkar, *Mahatma*, vol. 3, 123.

11 Ibid., 115.

12 Those programs were: Women (9), Kisans [peasant farmers] (14), Labour (15), Adivasis [indigenous peoples—still a contentious issue in India] (16), Lepers (17), and in a sense Students (18). The pamphlet *Constructive Programme, Its Meaning and Place* was first published in 1941 and is still available from Navajivan Press in Ahmadabad as well as U.S. outlets (see Gandhi section of Resources).

13 Eknath Easwaran, trans., *The Dhammapada* (Petaluma, CA: Nilgiri Press, 1990).

14 Marie Winn, *The Plug-In Drug* (New York: Viking Press, 1980), 193.

15 Ibid., 197.

16 Urie Bronfenbrenner, "The Origins of Alienation," *Scientific American* 231, no. 2 (1974): 61.

17 Terry Orlick, *Winning through Cooperation: Competitive Insanity, Cooperative Alternatives* (Washington: Acropolis Books, 1978), 79.

18 This is a term used by *Adbusters* magazine; it is also found in a key article from the *Canadian Broadcast Review* magazine at www.broadcastdialogue.com/Magazine/fullstory_blue.asp?article=287.

19 D. G. Tendulkar, *Mahatma*, vol. 4, 50.

20 Ibid., 51.

21 Daniel Levy, "The Cantor and the Klansman," *Time*, February 14, 1992, 14–15. There is also a book on this dramatic episode: Kathryn Watterson, *Not by the Sword* (New York: Simon and Schuster, 1995).

22 Ibid., 14.

23 Patti Malin, Coordinator, Institute for Global Communication, e-mail to

author, December 8, 1997.

24 *350 Tested Strategies to Prevent Crime: A Resource for Municipal Agencies and Community Groups* (National Crime Prevention Council, 1995); available at http://www.ncpc.org/ncpc/ncpc/?pg=2088-9280.

25 Transnational Forum, April 30, 1998. This excellent resource can be communicated with and browsed at http://www.transnational.org.

26 Ian Marshall and Danah Zohar, *Who's Afraid of Schrödinger's Cat? All the New Science Ideas You Need to Keep Up with the New Thinking* (New York: Morrow, 1997), 139.

27 *Encyclopædia Britannica*, CD Deluxe Edition, s.v. "Chaos."

28 Ibid. The *Britannica* wryly adds, "The idea that a system cannot spontaneously become better ordered but can readily become more disordered, even if left to itself, appeals to one's experience of domestic economy."

29 David J. Garrow, *Bearing the Cross: Martin Luther King, Jr. and the Southern Christian Leadership Conference* (New York: Morrow, 1986), 58.

30 Ibid., 58, 60. I will note in passing that the threatening phone call had the exactly opposite effect that the callers intended, and that this was even more true of the bombing: in response, the Montgomery Improvement Association increased their demand from a polite form of "separate but equal" to outright desegregation of public buses, and generally steeled their resistance (Ibid., 61). That's how violence usually "works," when it's stood up to.

31 This theory of scapegoating and "mimetic violence" had its first major appearance in French in 1972, then was translated by Patrick Gregory in René Girard, *Violence and the Sacred* (Baltimore: Johns Hopkins University, 1978). See also Girard's *Job, the Victim of His People* (London: Athlone Press, 1987). The latter is highly recommended as an accessible introduction to the main points of Girard's important theory.

32 *CWMG*, vol. 56, 163.

33 Martin Luther King Jr., *Stride toward Freedom* (New York: Harper and Row, 1958), 111.

Chapter Seven

1 Glenn T. Seaborg, "Premonitions after the Bombs," *Bulletin of the Atomic Scientists* 41, no. 11 (1985): 33.

2 Ervin Lazlo and Jong Youl Yoo, *World Encyclopedia of Peace*, vol. 3 (Oxford: Pergamon Press, 1986), 350.

3 Steven Huxley in *Civilian-Based Defense* newsletter (Civilian-Based Defense Association, Omaha), August 1992, 4.

4 R. K. Prabhu and U. R. Rao, *The Mind of Mahatma Gandhi* (Ahmadabad: Navajivan, 1967), 458. Cf. *CWMG*, vol. 31, 482, uttered much earlier (1925): "The conviction is daily growing stronger that there is no peace for India, and

indeed for the world, save through non-violence."

5   Quoted in Nuclear Freeze mailer, 1982.

6   Ralph Waldo Emerson, "War," quoted in *Instead of Violence: Writings by the Great Advocates of Peace and Nonviolence Throughout History*, Arthur and Lila Weinberg, eds. (New York: Grossman Publishers, 1963), 379.

7   From the essay "Protest and Survive," in *Protest and Survive,* E. P. Thompson and Dan Smith, eds. (Harmondsworth, UK: Penguin, 1980), 52.

8   See note 5.

9   Eknath Easwaran, trans., *The Dhammapada* (Petaluma, CA: Nilgiri Press, 1990), 88.

10 Michael P. Rogin, *Reagan, the Movie and Other Episodes in Political Demonology* (Berkeley: University of California, 1987), 192.

11 Eknath Easwaran, *Gandhi the Man*, 145.

12 *San Francisco Chronicle,* August 18, 1998, A11.

13 Hannah Arendt, *Eichmann in Jerusalem: A Report on the Banality of Evil* (New York: Penguin Books, 1987), 85–86.

14 Cf. Mahoney and Eguren, *Unarmed Bodyguards*, 36.

15 Carol Cohn, "Sex and Death in the Rational World of Defense Intellectuals," *Signs* 12, no. 4 (1987): 687.

16 *UNESCO News* 5:2 (February 20, 1998): 8.

17 Mahoney and Eguren, *Unarmed Bodyguards*, 32. Ironically, I believe this image comes from Che Guevara, who in turn got it from Mao Tze-tung.

18 Review of Mike McCullough, et al., *To Forgive is Human* (Downers Grove, IL: InterVarsity Press, 1997) in *Utne Reader*, March/April 1997, 71. The full quote, incidentally, begins, "The old theory was that if you're angry, you need to express it. But expression actually makes it worse, and imagery . . ."

19 This field has gotten a good deal of well-deserved scholarly attention. See, for example, George Lakoff and Mark Johnson, *Metaphors We Live By* (Chicago: University of Chicago, 1980), and of particular interest, Lakoff's "Metaphor and War: The Metaphor System Used to Justify War in the Gulf," 1991; draft obtainable from lakoff@cogsci.berkeley.edu.

20 Ovetta Sampson, "Curse of the Word," *Santa Rosa Press Democrat,* May 16, 2000, D1–2.

21 Bhagavad Gita, 18.37.

22 James M. Washington, *Testament of Hope,* 211.

23 Advertisement for the U.S. Monetary War College in *Insight* (June 9, 1990): 27.

24 Ibid.

Chapter Eight

1   D. G. Tendulkar, *Mahatma: The Life of Mohandas Karamchand Gandhi*, vol. 2 (New Delhi: Government of India, Publications Division, 1951), 237; second quote

from *CWMG*, vol. 57, 107; also in Pyarelal, *The Epic Fast*, 133.

2   *CWMG*, vol.74, 194. Also in Prabhu and Rao, *The Mind of Mahatma Gandhi* (Ahmadabad: Navajivan, 1967), 128.

3   *CWMG*, vol. 73, 24–25.

4   Charles C. Walker, *A World Peace Guard: An Unarmed Agency for Peacekeeping* (Hyderabad: Academy of Gandhian Studies, 1981), 3. This little book was one of the first writings on the peace-team movement.

5   *CWMG*, vol. 73, 2425.

6   Pyarelal, *The Last Phase* (Ahmadabad: Navajivan, 1968), 709. Another irony: It seems that the army Britain had brought into existence in India was not only not capable of protecting the country (the cardinal justification for holding India at that time) but was attracting a Japanese attack (see Tendulkar, 1953, 75).

7   Ibid., 10.

8   *Pathan* is an anglicized spelling for *Pashtun*, now coming back in vogue. The tribal homeland of the Pathans spans modern Pakistan (the North-West Frontier Province of India) and Afghanistan.

9   Eknath Easwaran, *Nonviolent Soldier of Islam: Badshah Khan, a Man to Match His Mountains* (Petaluma, CA: Nilgiri Press, 1999), 107.

10   Ibid., 195. On the Khudai Khidmatgars see Mukulika Bannerjee, *The Pathan Unarmed: Opposition and Memory in the North West Frontier* (Karachi: Oxford University Press, 2000).

11   Ibid., 122–23.

12   Glenn Paige and others, *Islam and Nonviolence* (Honolulu: Matsunaga Institute for Peace, University of Hawai'i, 1993); see also Michael Nagler, "Is There a Tradition of Nonviolence in Islam?" in *War and Its Discontents: Pacifism and Quietism in the Abrahamic Traditions*, J. Patout Burns, ed. (Washington, DC: Georgetown University Press, 1996), 161–66. An excellent book is: Mohammed Abu-Nimer, *Nonviolence and Peace Building in Islam* (Gainseville: University Press of Florida, 2003).

13   *Complete Sahih Bukhari: A Collection of the Hadith in Sahih Bukhari*, vol. 3, book 43, no. 624, to be found at www.usc.edu/dept/MSA/fundamentals/hadithsunnah/bukhari/043.sbt.html.

14   Ibid.

15   Eknath Easwaran, *Nonviolent Soldier of Islam,* 183.

16   *CWMG*, vol. 54, 286. Also in Prabhu and Rao, *The Mind of Mahatma Gandhi*, 452–53. Thermopylae is the narrow mountain pass where, in 480 B.C.E., a small Spartan army under Leonidas died to the last man trying to hold off a vastly greater Persian force.

17   *CWMG*, vol. 82, 167. Also in Tendulkar, *Mahatma,* vol. 6, 69.

18   The absence of evidence does not seem to prevent skeptics from decrying the scheme now any more than it did at the time: "Gandhi held to his belief that nonviolence could defeat the Japanese, despite their lack of the inhibitions

derived from English-speaking public morality [sic]. This belief, *fortunately for the Indians*, was never tested in practice." D. C. Watt in *20th Century Culture,* Alan Bullock and R. B. Woodings, eds. (New York: Harper and Row, 1983), 256. Even most of Gandhi's congress believed the myth—and we now know that it was purely a myth—that British arms were the only thing standing between them and the Japanese.

19 Unless otherwise indicated, these references are from the article "Nonviolent Interventions" by Alberto L'Abate in *Peace Courier*, March 1994, 2.

20 Stephen Zunes, "Unarmed Insurrections against Authoritarian Governments in the Third World: A New Kind of Revolution," *Third World Quarterly* 15, no. 3 (1994): 417.

21 See note 19.

22 See note 19.

23 Cf. the Greek philosopher Heraclitus: "Citizens should be as zealous to defend their institutions as they are their walls" (Frag. B44 [my translation]).

24 Inge Scholl, *The White Rose: Munich 1942–1943* (Middlebury, CT: Wesleyan University, 1970), 95.

25 Yeshua Moser-Puangsuwan and Thomas Weber, *Nonviolent Intervention across Borders: A Recurrent Vision* (Honolulu: University of Hawai'i, 2000), 138. UN (armed) peacekeeping has been much more dangerous. By way of example, fourteen Indian troops with UNEF in the Sinai were killed and twenty wounded in a single engagement in 1967: "So far as [the Israelis] were concerned, anybody in uniform facing them was an enemy" (Indar Jit Rikhye and others, *The Thin Blue Line* [New Haven: Yale University, 1974], 61).

26 Moser-Puangsuwan and Weber, *Nonviolent Intervention*, 14.

27 Mahoney and Eguren, *Unarmed Bodyguards*, 216.

28 Moser-Puangsuwan and Weber, *Nonviolent Intervention*, 13.

29 Christian Le Meut, interview in *Non-Violence Actualité* (February 1994): 10.

30 Peace Brigades International Report, "Sri Lanka Seminar, 1992" (unpublished; available from Bob Siedle-Khan, PBI, 59 E. Van Buren St. #1400, Chicago, IL, 60605, 312-362-1732).

31 Marge Argelyan, "Walking the Talk of Nonviolent Intervention," *Signs of the Times* (CPT newsletter) VI, no. 1 (1996): 2.

32 Bishop Tutu (speech, National Public Radio, January 2, 1993); cf. Robert Siegel, ed., *The NPR Interviews* (Boston: Houghton Mifflin, 1994), 213.

33 From a letter by Elise Boulding to "Colleagues Concerned with International Nonviolent Peace Services," June 10, 1994.

34 Joe S. Loya, "How Cops Are Turned," *Cleveland Plain Dealer*, August 26, 1997.

35 E. M. Forster, *A Passage to India* (New York: Harcourt, Brace and Co., 1952), 11.

36 Thomas Weber, *Gandhi's Peace Army: The Shanti Sena and Unarmed Peacekeeping* (Syracuse: Syracuse University Press, 1996), 133.

37 Chris Hedges, "What I Read at War," *Harvard Magazine*, July/August, 2000, 61.

38 *Housman's Peace Diary* (Stony Creek, CT: New Society Publishers, 1998).

39 Adolfo Perez Esquivel, *Christ in a Poncho: Testimonials of the Nonviolent Struggles in Latin America* (New York: Orbis Books, 1984), 127.

40 *Michigan Peace Team Bulletin* 2 (1998): 8.

41 Cf. Malcolm Gladwell, *The Tipping Point* (New York: Little Brown, 2000).

42 Moser-Puangsuwan and Weber, *Nonviolent Intervention*, 320.

43 Konrad Lorenz, *On Aggression*, Marjorie Kerr Wilson, trans. (New York: Harcourt, Brace & World, Inc., 1966), 284. See also the famous essay of Margaret Mead, "Warfare Is Only an Invention—Not a Biological Necessity," *The Dolphin Reader*, 2nd edition, Douglas Hunt, ed. (Boston: Houghton Mifflin Company, 1990), 415–21.

44 Gerald G. Walsh and others, *St. Augustine, City of God* (New York: Image, 1958), 451, 457.

45 Swami Ramdas, *Ramdas Speaks*, 43.

46 Ray and Anderson, *The Cultural Creatives* (see Preface, note 4.).

Chapter Nine

1 At line 22 the poet himself told us that Achilles was "dishonoring brilliant Hector in his fury," thus putting the dead body and the earth, with their complementary sets of symbolic resonances, into close parallelism, and bringing his own voice into resonance with the gods'.

2 Subtitle to the German edition of Sri Eknath Easwaran's *The Compassionate Universe* (Berkeley, CA: Nilgiri Press, 1989).

3 E-mail to author, "To Feel What Ima Feels," Kathy Kelly of the Voices in the Wilderness, May 24, 1998 (reproduced with her permission).

4 Isaac Newton, *Opticks* (London: Smith and Walford, 1704), quoted by Richard Rhodes, *The Making of the Atomic Bomb* (New York: Simon & Schuster, Touchstone, 1988), 30. It is noteworthy that Newton began this oft-quoted sentence with the clause, "It seems probable to me." That probability became certainty in the minds of his followers, until it all fell apart in the early twentieth century.

5 Metropolitan Museum exhibit catalog, September 6–December 2, 1990, 58.

6 These statistics respectively from "Every Fifth Child," *Bread for the World* newsletter, 4:2 (March 1992), and *San Francisco Chronicle*, op-ed page, March 28, 1994.

7 Richard Rhodes, *The Making of the Atomic Bomb*, 243.

8 Hannah Arendt, *The Origins of Totalitarianism* (New York: Harcourt, Brace and Company, 1951), 428.

9 Respectively, *Gewaltfreiheit*, or "freedom from violence" (German is one of the few languages with a positive translation of *nonviolence*), and *Selbstdarstellung*. Brochure of a regional Educational Project for Peace Work (Fränkisches

Bildungswerk für Friedensarbeit e.V.), 1994.

10 See note 7.

11 Johan Galtung, "Violence, Peace, and Peace Research," *Journal of Peace Research*, no. 3 (1959): 167–91. Cf. Aldous Huxley, *Means and Ends* (New York: Harper and Brothers, 1937), 1: "The free development of each will lead to the free development of all."

12 Speech, Non-Governmental Organizations, United Nations World Conference on Human Rights, Vienna, Austria, June 15, 1993; available at www.tibet.com/DL/vienna.html.

13 This quote is variously attributed to Goebbels and Stalin; see Norman Soloman, "Wizards of Media Oz: Behind the Curtain of Mainstream News," www.labridge.com/change-links/GOODGRIEF.html.

14 Saint Augustine, *Confessions* vii:12 (my translation). The embedded quote is, of course, Genesis I:31.

15 George Orwell, "A Hanging," in *The Collected Essays, Journalism and Letters of George Orwell*, Ian Angus and Sonya Orwell, eds. (London: Secker and Warburg, 1968), 46.

16 Respectively, Mishnah Sanhedrin IV:5 and Koran 5:35.

17 Abraham Isaac Kook, *The Lights of Penitence: The Moral Principles, Lights of Holiness, Essays, Letters, Poems* (New York: Paulist Press, 1978), 6.

18 This comment of His Holiness's is also from 1993, and can be found at www.tibet.com/DL/vienna.html.

19 Mary Midgley, *Evolution as a Religion* (London: Methuen, 1985), 157; cf. 153: "Words like *rights* and *duties* are awkward because they do indeed have narrow senses approximating to the legal, but they also have much wider ones in which they cover the whole of the moral sphere. . . . 'Animal rights' may be hard to formulate, as indeed are the rights of man. But 'no rights' will not do. The word may need to be dropped entirely."

20 See note 4.

21 Eyewitness report of Nirmala Deshpande of the Association of People of Asia (speech, San Francisco, Spring 2003).

Epilogue

1 Vandana Shiva, *Stolen Harvest: The Hijacking of the Global Food Supply* (Cambridge: South End Press, 2000), 4.

2 John Hume, *A New Ireland: Politics, Peace and Reconciliation* (Boulder, CO: Roberts Rinehart, 1996), 113–14.

3 Ivan Illich, "The Delinking of Peace and Development," *Alternatives* VII: 4 (1981): 409–16.

4 Thomas Weber, *Hugging the Trees: The Story of the Chipko Movement* (New Delhi: Penguin, 1989), 92f; following quote from 40f.

5   For more on this and other "culturally appropriate" aspects of the new justice paradigm, consult www.restorativejustice.org.

6   L. Ringera Karembu, quoted in Progress Report of the African Great Lakes Initiative (*Friends Peace Teams*), Fall 2003, 1.

7   Hon. Robert Yazzie, "'Life Comes from It': Navajo Justice Concepts," *New Mexico Law Review* 24 (1994); this and following quote from 180–81, 186.

8   Saint Isaac, *The Ascetical Homilies of St. Isaac the Syrian* (Brookline, MA: Holy Transfiguration Monastery, 1984), 246.

9   William S. James, *Memories and Studies,* "The Moral Equivalent of War" (New York: Longmans, Green & Co, 1911), 290–91.

10   See chapter 5, note 17. The Seamless Garment Network, however, has become the Consistent Life Ethic.

11   Stuart Cowan, "A Design Revolution," *Yes!*, Summer 1998, 30.

12   Thomas Taylor, trans., *Porphyry on Abstinence from Animal Food* (New York: Barnes and Noble, 1965), 140.

Action Guide

1   For some of these studies, see M. Murphy, S. Donovan, and E. Taylor, *The Physical and Psychological Effects of Meditation: A Review of Contemporary Research with a Comprehensive Bibliography, 1931–1996*, 2nd edition (Sausalito, CA: Institute of Noetic Sciences, 1999). A more recent treatment is Teresa E. Seeman, Linda Fagan Dubin, and Melvin Seeman, "Religiosity/Spirituality and Health: A Critical Review of the Evidence for Biological Pathways," *American Psychologist* 58, no. 1 (January 2003): 53–63.

2   CWMG, vol. 81, 358.

3   See chapter 6, note 9.

4   Mathew Arnold, *Culture and Anarchy* (Cambridge: Cambridge University Press, 1993), 73.

Resources and Opportunities

———❧———

Happily, the world of nonviolence—the organizations that do it and the books and articles about it—is expanding so rapidly that a complete list of such resources would require a separate volume. I cannot close, however, without giving at least a sample of this richness. I trust that other worthy organizations, writers, and individuals will forgive me for omitting them.

(Quite a few groups have been using this book in study circles. Responding to this interest, the nonprofit that I work with, METTA, has created a chapter-by-chapter study guide that may be downloaded free of charge: www.mettacenter.org. Those happy few who are still without computers may contact us at our street address.)

Meditation

First things first. There are many methods of meditation abroad, but I can speak responsibly only of the one I know and practice, which is spelled out in *Meditation* by Sri Eknath Easwaran (Nilgiri Press, various editions). For more information about this highly popular book or other resources and projects of the Blue Mountain Center of Meditation, check our Web site, www.nilgiri.org, or call (800) 475-2369.

Alternative Media

It's in the nature of the rapidly expanding world of alternative media to be partly local, like the *North Bay Progressive,* which, circulates in my area with a little over 1,000 subscribers, or many a low-wattage radio station throughout the country. It is now possible to get eyewitness reports from personal friends in conflict zones, even in Iraq, which are much more reliable than the "embedded" professional media, and many of the peace groups listed below can help. However, this being the age of the Internet, many networks have a global reach as well. Here are some of the most active at the present time:

www.alternet.org
www.indymedia.org
www.truthout.org
www.nationinstitute.org/tomdispatch
www.cursor.org

The following will be glad to send you regular e-updates:

www.oriononline.org
ksvp@sinewave.com

Nonviolence

Hard to know where to begin. The venerable Fellowship of Reconciliation (FOR), based in Nyack, New York, but present most everywhere, has been publishing *Fellowship* and promoting the learning and the doing of nonviolence for decades. Through FOR, and their international arm (IFOR), one can contact denominational organizations like the Jewish or Buddhist Peace Fellowship around the world. More recent, but somehow at the center of things, is Nonviolence International, set up in Washington, D.C., by Mubarak Awad. Worthy of note for its "broad spectrum" rejection of violence is the Institute for Integrated Social Analysis (formerly the Seamless Garment Network). My own outfit is called METTA (an acronym, but also the Buddhist term for "loving kindness," or nonviolence), and we specialize in education on nonviolence in all its applications. A like-minded Franciscan-based organization is Pace e Bene. All the above-mentioned organizations accept tax-deductible donations.

Fellowship of Reconciliation
P.O. Box 271
Nyack, NY 10960-9988
www.forusa.org

Nonviolence International
4545 42nd Street N.W.
Washington, DC 20016
(202) 244-0951, or info@nonviolenceinternational.net
www.nonviolenceinternational.net

METTA Center for Nonviolence Education
P.O. Box 183
Tomales, CA 94971
www.mettacenter.org

Pace e Bene
1420 West Bartlett Avenue
Las Vegas, NV 89106
(702) 648-2281, or www.paceebene.org

A good hub for religious and secular nonviolence groups is:

The Other Side
300 W. Apsley
Philadelphia, PA 19144
(800) 700-9280, or
www.theotherside.org/resources/nv/index.html

For insightful commentary into European events from a nonviolent perspective, an excellent site is: www.transnational.org/new/index .html.

Some books on nonviolence (see also under Peace Armies) are:

Stephen Zunes, Lester R. Kurtz, and Sarah Beth Asher, eds., *Nonviolent Social Movements: A Geographical Perspective* (Oxford: Blackwell, 1999). See also Zunes, "Unarmed Insurrections against Authoritarian Governments in the Third World: A New Kind of Revolution," *Third World Quarterly* 15.3 (1994): 403–26.

A reference book for many historical events is: L. Kurtz and Jennifer Turpin, eds., *Encyclopedia of Violence, Peace and Conflict* (3 vols.) (San Diego: Academic Publishing, 1999). Another is Powers and Voegele, *Protest, Power and Change* cited in notes, chapter 4. Consult also Peter Ackerman and Jack DuVall, *A Force More Powerful,* and the PBS documentary of the same title, by Steve York, for documentation of civil uprisings of (hyphenated) non-violent character of the last century. A more selective, and dramatic, treatment is Zev Ilan, *Power of the People* (a.k.a. *Where There Is Hatred*).

There are a number of fine essays by various writers and activists in two recent collections: Walter Wink, ed., *Peace Is the Way* (Maryknoll, NY: Orbis Books, 2000), and G. Simon Harak, ed., *Nonviolence for the Third Millennium* (Macon, GA: Mercer University Press, 2000).

Any works by Elise Boulding, e.g., her recent *Culture of Peace* or *Nonviolence of the Brave*, come highly recommended.

There are two recent manuals of interest:

Ken Butigan and others, *From Violence to Wholeness* (available from Pace e Bene), for those wishing to experiment with a more nonviolent lifestyle, and Michael Nagler, *The Steps of Nonviolence* (available from FOR), for those who find themselves in a major dispute or conflict and wish to resolve it nonviolently.

Gandhi

As you've gathered from the references to this book, the *Collected Works of Mahatma Gandhi* is now on CD-ROM and is available from www.gandhiserve.com or, in the United States, from Arun Gandhi's institute, (901) 452-2824, Gandhi@cbu.edu. Prior to reading those ninety-plus volumes in any form, however, I recommend *Gandhi the Man* by Sri Eknath Easwaran, and his *Nonviolent Soldier of Islam*, as superb introductions (both are available from Nilgiri Press; see under Meditation). Contact METTA for other suggestions.

Books by and about Gandhi can be purchased directly from Greenleaf Books, Canton, ME, 04221, (207) 388-2860, or from South Asia Books in Columbia, MO, (573) 474-0116.

Berkeley Hills Books has brought out a series of books by Gandhi in convenient American editions. Fortunately, good books on Gandhi are appearing in increasing tempo.(510) 559-8650.

Restorative Justice

In addition to the books cited in chapter 5, the film *Doing Time, Doing Vipassana* documents a bold experiment to teach prisoners to meditate that began in one of India's largest penal institutions and has spread all over the world. It can be ordered from:

Vipassana Publications
P.O. Box 15926
Seattle, WA 98115
fax: (206) 522-8295
sales@vrpa.com

Yes! magazine, Fall 2000, is dedicated to restorative justice, or consult Howard Zehr, *Changing Lenses* (Scottdale, PA: Herald Press, 2000) for additional resources—or just search for "restorative justice" on the Internet for a trove of sites. Don't miss the Prison Ashram Project run by Bo and Sita Lozoff's superbly named:

Human Kindness Foundation
P.O. Box 61619
Durham, NC 27715
(919) 304-2220, or www.humankindness.org

Other sources include:

Alternatives to Violence Project (AVP)
Bill McMechan, International-Network Convenor
P.O. Box 157
Hastings, Ontario
K0L 1Y0 CANADA
(705) 696-2153, or mcmechan.avp@sympatico.ca

Victim-Offender Reconciliation Program (VORP)
19813 N.E. 13th Street
Camas, WA 98607
(360) 260-1551, fax: (360) 260-1563
e-mail: martyprice@vorp.com

Peace Armies

In addition to Peace Brigades International, Christian Peacemaker Teams and the other groups working in this field (see Moser-Puangsuwan and Weber's book), Nonviolent PeaceForce is a world-wide effort to develop nonviolent intervention, or "peace armies," on a large scale. The U.S. office is:

801 Front Avenue
St. Paul, MN 55103
(651) 487-0800 or www.nonviolentpeaceforce.org

The major books on this key development have been cited in the notes and are given again below:

Yeshua Moser-Puangsuwan and Thomas Weber, *Nonviolent Intervention across Borders: A Recurrent Vision* (Honolulu: University of Hawai'i, 2000)

L. Mahoney and L. Eguren, *Unarmed Bodyguards: International Accompaniment for the Protection of Human Rights* (West Hartford, CT: Kumarian, 1997)

Thomas Weber, *Gandhi's Peace Army: The Shanti Sena and Unarmed Peacekeeping* (Syracuse: Syracuse University Press, 1996).

New-Paradigm Thinking on the Environment, Economies of Justice, etc.

Two works that might help us understand paradigms themselves (aside from Kuhn's famous one, of course) are: Malcolm Gladwell, *The Tipping Point* (New York: Little Brown, 2000), and Paul H. Ray and Sherry R. Anderson, *The Cultural Creatives* (New York: Three Rivers Press, 2000).

The "classic" nonviolent environmental struggle is the Chipko movement, for which a place to start is Thomas Weber, *Hugging the Trees: The Story of the Chipko Movement* (New Delhi: Penguin, 1989).

The Positive Futures Network, based in Bainbridge, Washington, and their journal, *Yes!*, are good ways to stay in touch with new thinking on organization and the economy, lifestyle, etc.

Of many books that try to explain the new physics to laypersons, I personally get the most out of Nick Herbert, *Quantum Reality* (New York: Anchor Doubleday, 1985).

This is also a good place to mention the cooperative paradigm in biology, and for that I will cite F. B. M. de Waal, *Peacemaking among Primates* (Cambridge: Harvard University Press, 1989).

A representative writer on alternative economic models is Hazel Henderson; consult her *Paradigms in Progress: Life beyond Economics* (San Francisco: Berrett-Kohler, 1991–1995).

Finally, for a superb overview of the many hopeful experiments that are occurring across many domains the search for a nonviolent future, see Frances Moore Lappé and Anna Lappé, *Hope's Edge* (New York: Tarcher Putnam, 2002). Thank you, Frankie and Anna!

INDEX